IMAGES
of America

JURUPA

ON THE COVER: The cast of the 1933 pageant, "Coming of Louis Robidoux and Gen, John Fremont," is shown here on the grounds of the West Riverside School. The pageant was performed in association with the West Riverside Harvest Festival.

IMAGES
of America

JURUPA

Kim Jarrell Johnson

ARCADIA
PUBLISHING

ISBN 9780-0-7385-3082-6

Published by Arcadia Publishing
Charleston, South Carolina

Printed in Great Britain

Library of Congress Catalog Card Number: 2005932497

For all general information contact Arcadia Publishing at:
Telephone 843-853-2070
Fax 843-853-0044
E-mail sales@arcadiapublishing.com
For customer service and orders:
Toll-Free 1-888-313-2665

Visit us on the Internet at www.arcadiapublishing.com

Contents

ACKNOWLEDGMENTS

This book would not have been possible without the computer expertise of my husband, Mark. He spent many hours helping me and deserves the biggest thank you. I want to thank my daughters Corinne and Elyse for their help as I organized this book. Thank you to Steve Lech for his invaluable knowledge and postcard collection, both of which he generously shared with me. My thanks go out to four people who went out of their way to help me: Marjorie Paige, Gwynn Harrison, Grace Sollecito, and Dorothy Brown. I want to thank the 39 organizations, families, and individuals for sharing their photographs, time, and memories with me. I enjoyed my trip into the past with them more than I can ever say.

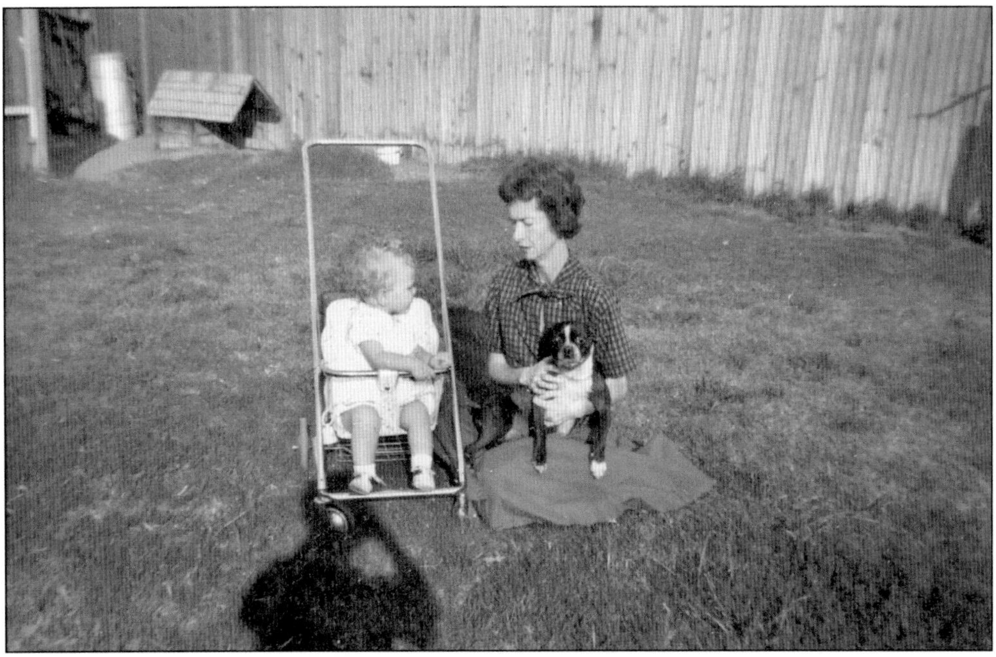

GLEN AVON FAMILY. In 1962, the author, her mother, Nell Jarrell, and the dog JoJo are in the backyard of their house on Gordon Way in Glen Avon. (Courtesy author.)

INTRODUCTION

The Jurupa area is located in the upper western corner of Riverside County, California, north and west of the Santa Ana River and south of the San Bernardino–Riverside County line. Before the cities of Riverside, Corona, or Norco were founded, there was the Rancho Jurupa. In the late 1800s, Jurupa began to live in the shadow of the more well-known and incorporated City of Riverside. Much of the Jurupa area has a Riverside mailing address. Yet settlement of the area in and around what is now Riverside actually began in Jurupa, many years before Riverside's founding.

The name Jurupa is derived from the languages of the first inhabitants of the area, the American Indians who called Jurupa home. The Jurupa area lies at the intersection of the territories of at least two different tribes. Research indicates that the root of the word is Gabrielino and the ending of the word that makes it a place name is Serrano. It is appropriate that the name Jurupa reflects that dual heritage. Over the years, three different meanings of Jurupa have been proposed. The most romantic but least likely is that Jurupa was a greeting made by a chief to the first padre that entered the area. This greeting was supposed to have meant "peace and friendship." A second theory was put forth by Fr. Juan Caballeria, who studied American Indian languages in the San Bernardino area. In 1902, he wrote that each of the mission rancherias had a name that suggested the place where is was located. "Jurumpa," as he spelled it, meant "water place." The third and most likely theory is that Jurupa originated from the term for an aromatic plant common to the area, now known as California Sagebrush.

Jurupa was always a more rural area. Scattered around were small communities such as West Riverside, Mira Loma, Glen Avon, Belltown, Crestmore Heights, Sunnyslope, and Pedley. Between these communities was open and agricultural land with scattered homes and farms. Through the years, as Jurupa was further developed, those open and agricultural lands have been subdivided, and the dividing lines between the communities have blurred. However, community distinctions still remain and newer areas such as Jurupa Hills, Indian Hills, Eastvale, and Sky Country have joined the older communities.

In spite of development, Jurupa still retains a rural atmosphere. Many areas have large lots that allow horses. Horse riders throughout Jurupa enjoy the close proximity of the trails in the Santa Ana River bottom. Animal keeping is still common in some areas. Efforts to incorporate in the past have failed due in no small part to peoples' desire to avoid what they felt would be the complexities of "city life."

Jurupa's importance in the early settlement of the inland region makes it vital to record its history. Since Jurupa never incorporated, it does not have the institutions that surrounding cities have to research, record, and report its history as it deserves. Without such an archive, I was forced to go out into the community, make countless phone calls, and draw photographs out of people and organizations—all of whom modestly assumed that they did not have anything I would be interested in. Most of the photographs in this book were literally taken out of drawers, boxes, cabinets, and closets where they had not seen the light of day in many years. Exploring what was available in the community, I determined that the 200 "historic" photographs needed for this book probably would not be available. I did, however, have the privilege of seeing many snapshots from people's lives that give a better understanding of not just Jurupa's history but Jurupa's families as well. I have included some of these snapshots in this book and hope the readers of Jurupa will enjoy these glimpses into people's lives as much as I have.

This book is divided into six categories. The "Early Days" presents the earliest history and images surrounding the settlement of Jurupa. "Events and Landmarks" has images of natural disasters, significant landmarks, and well-known events. "School Life" presents images from the early schools and school districts of Jurupa. "Community Life" has images of the groups and organizations, public and private, that people belonged to and benefited from. "Business Life" shows the streets and businesses that made up Jurupa. "Home Life" shows images from the private lives of Jurupa's citizens, including their homes and celebrations. I organized the book in this way so similar images could be kept together. For example, I prefer to see all the images of West Riverside School together instead of scattered throughout chapters based on decades. It is my personal preference and I hope that you, the reader, will not mind that I took this liberty.

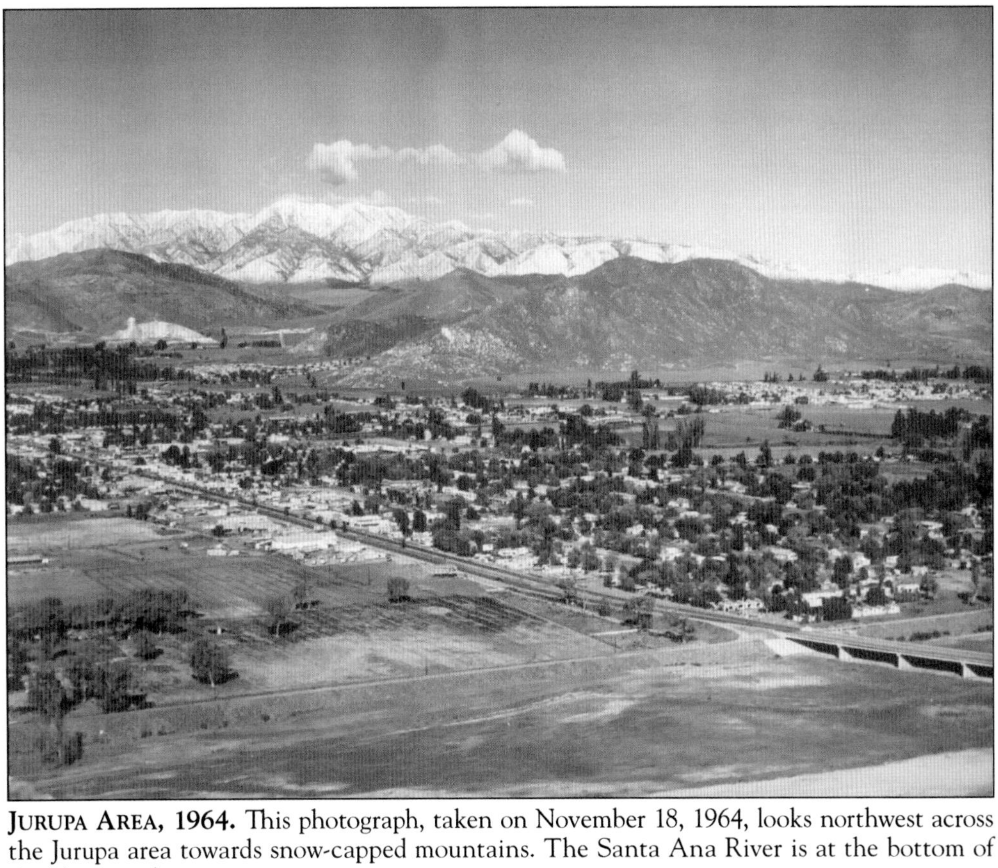

JURUPA AREA, 1964. This photograph, taken on November 18, 1964, looks northwest across the Jurupa area towards snow-capped mountains. The Santa Ana River is at the bottom of the photograph.

One

EARLY DAYS

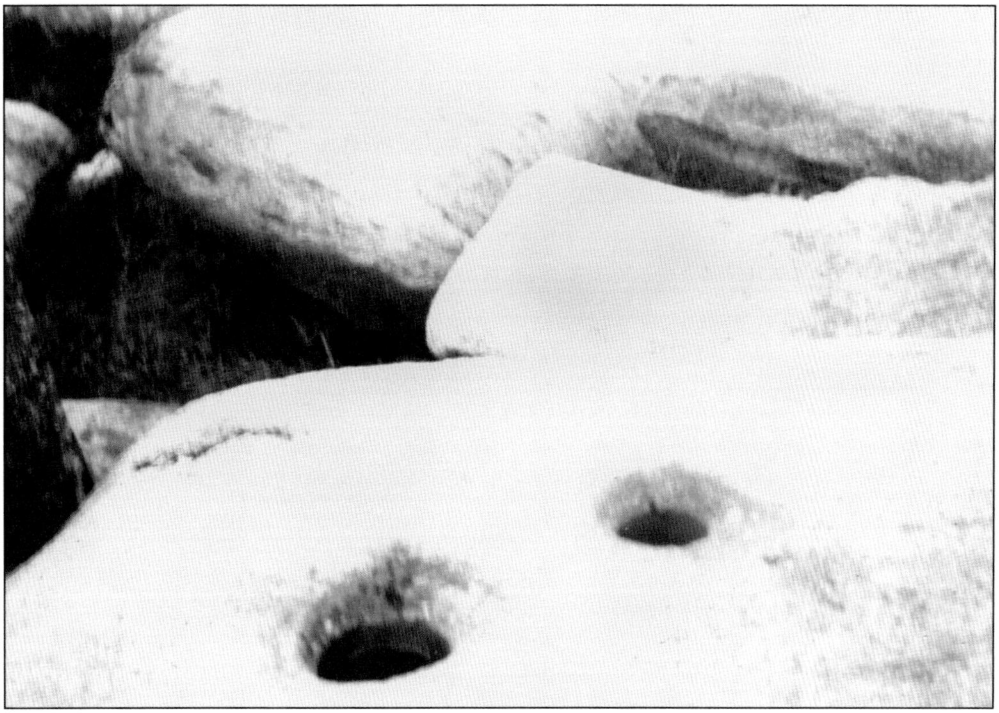

AMERICAN INDIAN GRINDING HOLES. This 1930s photograph shows evidence of Jurupa's earliest settlers. These boulders were located near the Union Pacific Bridge that crosses the Santa Ana River. The American Indians would have taken advantage of the Santa Ana River and its surroundings. (Courtesy Jensen family.)

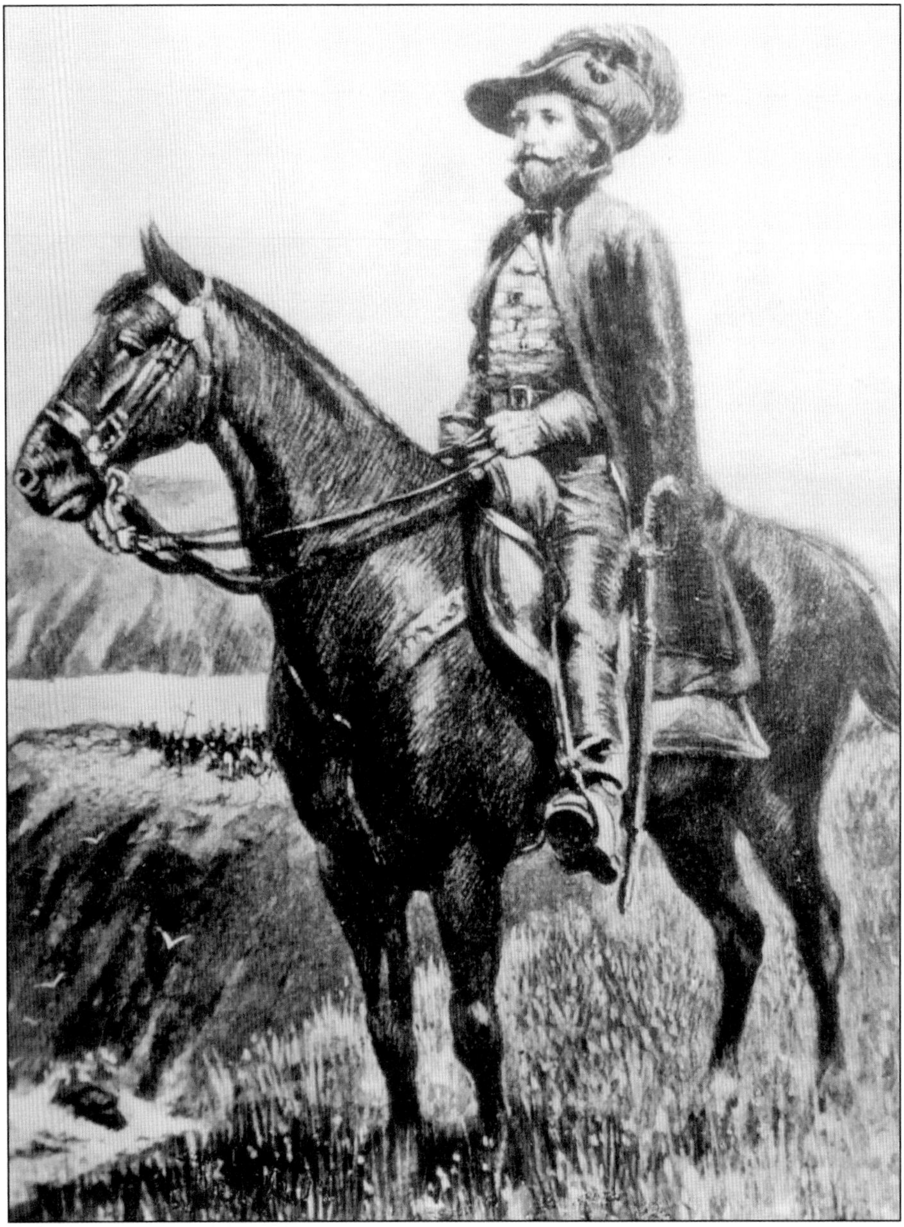

JUAN BAUTISTA DEANZA. Explorer Juan Bautista DeAnza passed through the Jurupa area twice during his explorations of Alta California. According to his diary, on his first journey in 1774, Anza reached a valley with "a good river which was given the name Santa Anna." He found the river to be a problem as it had steep banks and a swift current. The Anza party made camp along the river "near a place where there was a village of heathen . . . whose number would be more than 60." Two years later, Anza passed through the area again, leading a group of 240 settlers on their way to found the colony of San Francisco. On December 31, 1776, they reached the Santa Ana River. Father Font, a priest with Anza's party, also kept a diary. He said the Jurupa Valley was "a fertile and beautiful country, with rose bushes, grapevines, blackberry bushes, and other plants which by their verdue is pleasing to the sight." (Courtesy Riverside County Library System, Louis Robidoux Library.)

JUAN BANDINI. On September 28, 1838, well after Mexico had gained control of California, Governor Alvarado granted the 32,000-acre Jurupa Rancho to Juan Bandini. Bandini, born in Peru, came to California about 1820. In his 1840 book, *Two Years Before the Mast*, Bandini was described by Richard Henry Dana: "He had a slight and elegant figure, moved gracefully, danced and waltzed beautifully, spoke the best of Castilian with a pleasant and refined voice and accent, and had, throughout, the bearing of a man of high birth and figure." (Courtesy Steve Lech.)

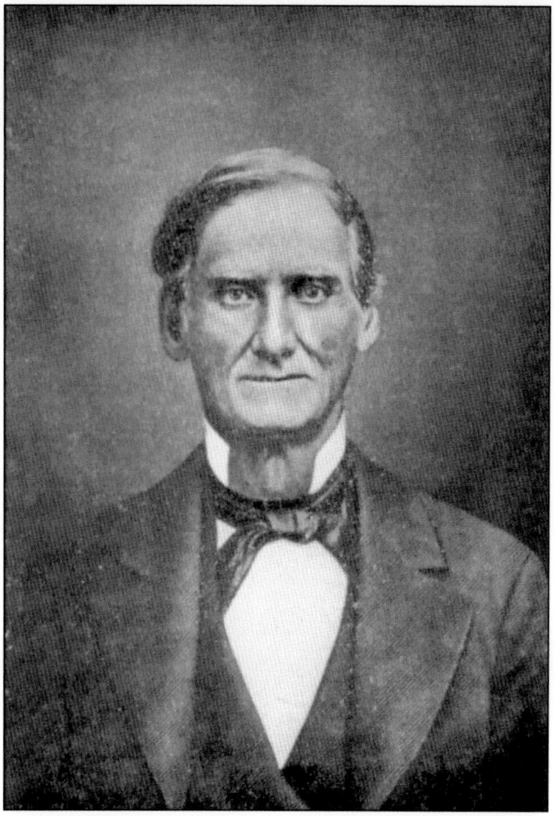

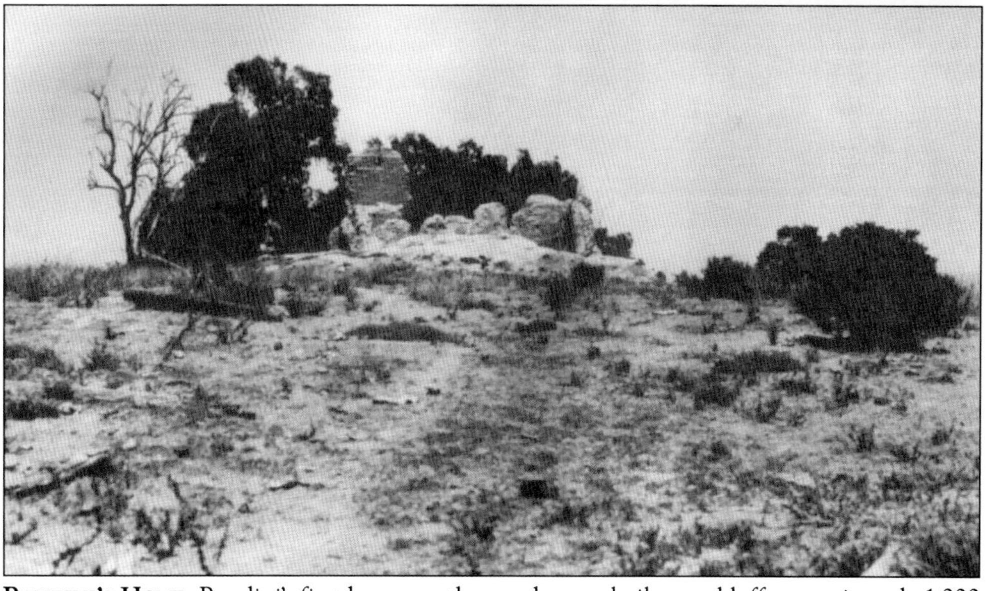

BANDINI'S HOME. Bandini's first home on the rancho was built on a bluff approximately 1,000 feet west of Hamner Boulevard, half a mile north of the Hamner Bridge over the Santa Ana River. His second home, whose ruins are shown here, was located on the Rancho Rincon, 4,500 choice acres of the Prado Basin. It was situated about three-and-a-half miles downriver of the first house, also on a bluff above the Santa Ana River. (Courtesy Steve Lech.)

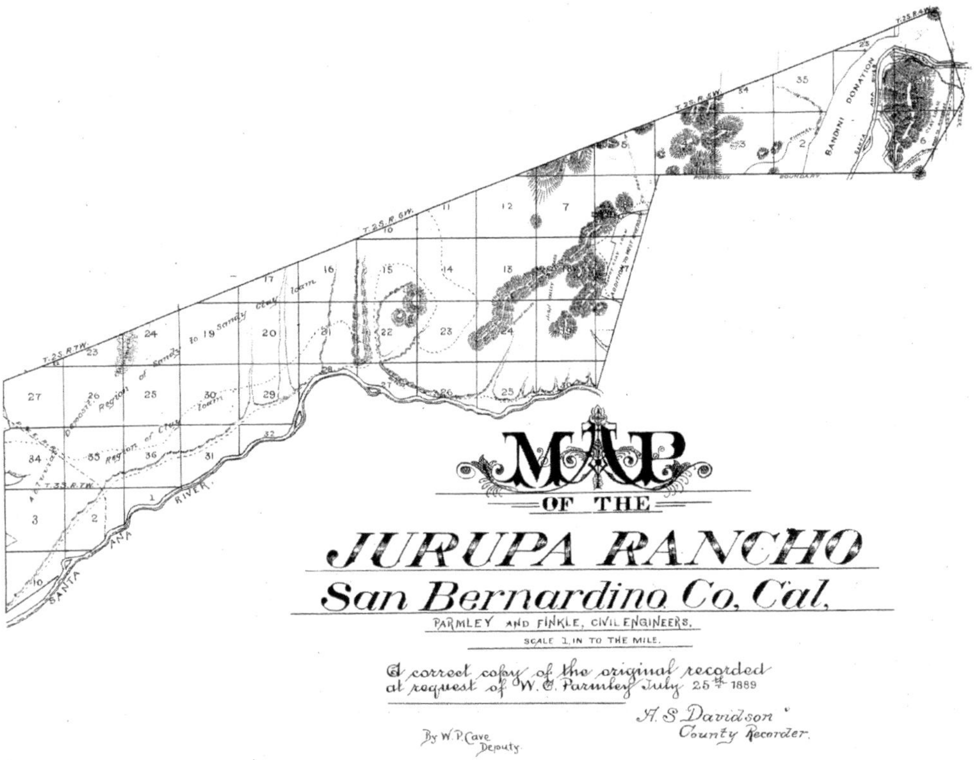

Jurupa Rancho. This map shows the uniquely shaped Jurupa Rancho that was granted to Juan Bandini. (Courtesy Steve Lech.)

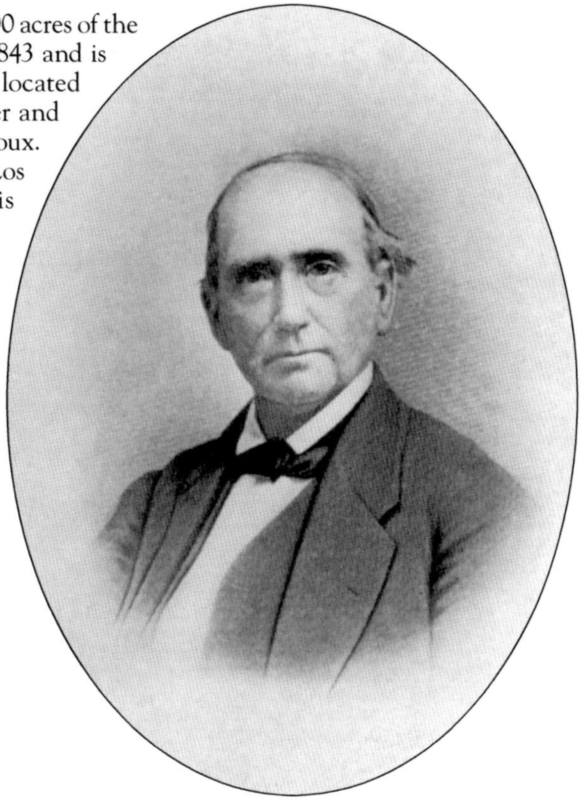

BENJAMIN WILSON. Wilson bought 6,700 acres of the Rancho Jurupa from Juan Bandini in 1843 and is believed to have built an adobe home located about a mile from the Santa Ana River and Mount Rubidoux, in present-day Rubidoux. Wilson later became the first mayor of Los Angeles. That city's Mount Wilson is named for him. (Courtesy Steve Lech.)

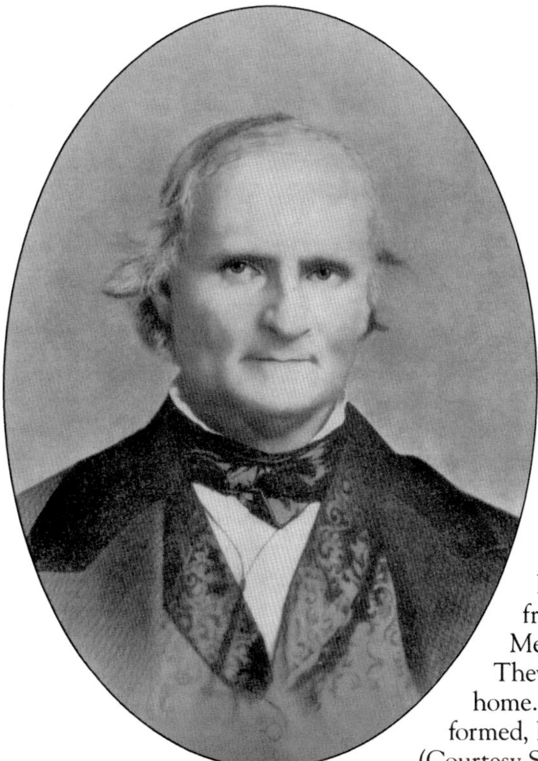

LOUIS ROBIDOUX. In 1844, Robidoux bought Wilson's portion of the Jurupa Rancho. Born near St. Louis in 1796, the one-time fur trader spoke as many as seven languages. He grew up on the American frontier and married Guadalupe Garcia in New Mexico before making his way to California. They raised seven children at their Jurupa Rancho home. When the County of San Bernardino was formed, he became one of its first three supervisors. (Courtesy Steve Lech.)

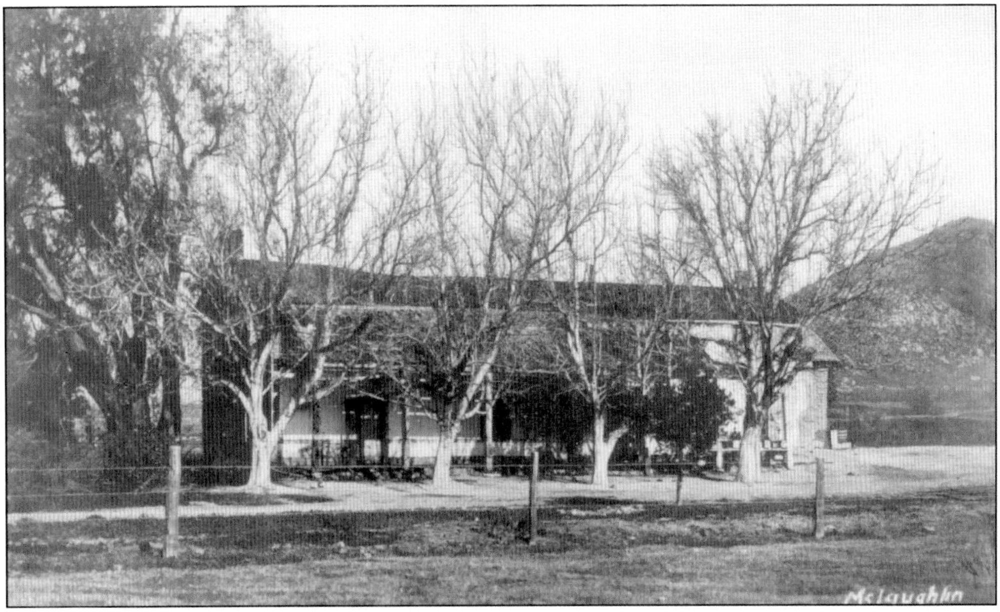

ROBIDOUX'S HOME. The adobe home built by Benjamin Wilson was part of the rancho bought by Louis Robidoux. After Robidoux's purchase, the area became known as the Robidoux Rancho. This picture of the house, taken about 1890, shows Rattlesnake Hill in the background. Notice that the house faced the Santa Ana River. The home was located where the Stater Brothers Market is now, at the northeast corner of Rubidoux and Mission Boulevards in Rubidoux. (Courtesy Steve Lech.)

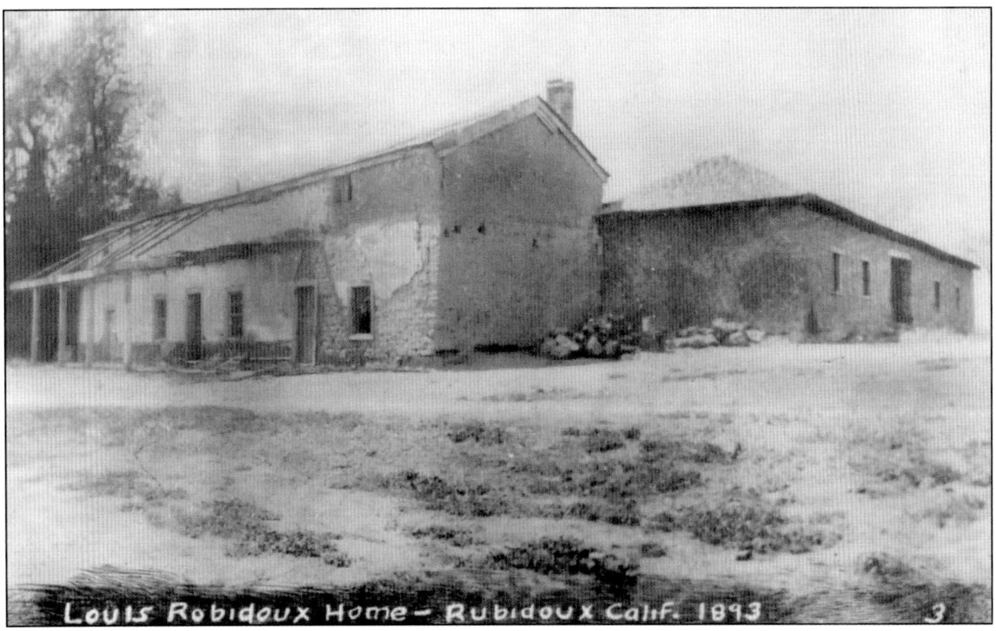

LOUIS ROBIDOUX HOME. This *c.* 1897 photograph shows the Robidoux winery, right, in relationship to the house on the left. The Robidoux house was at the crossroads of several important trails. Thus, the family was always kept abreast of area news as well as becoming known for their hospitality. (Courtesy Steve Lech.)

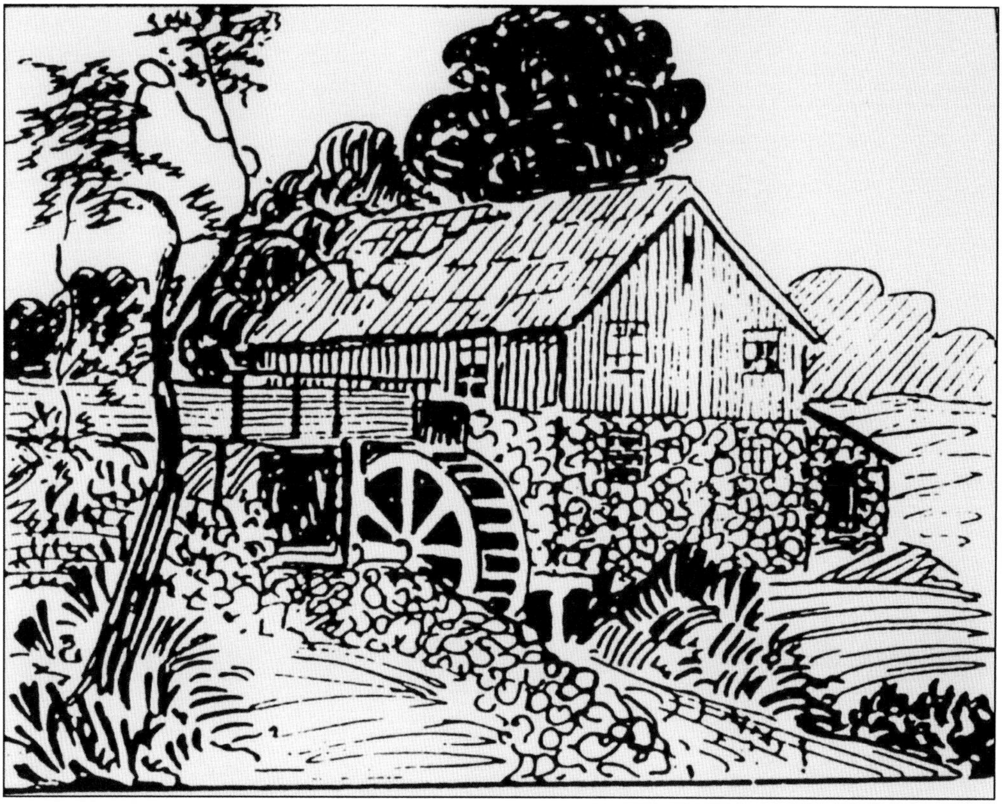

ROBIDOUX GRIST MILL. Louis Robidoux built a gristmill on the Jurupa Rancho. It was probably the only functioning mill in Southern California at that time. The mill supplied flour to the Mormon Battalion, commanded by Gen. Stephan Kearney, when it occupied Los Angeles in 1847. Water for the mill probably came from a canal that flowed from the Santa Ana River. Prior to 1862, the river ran much closer to the mill's location. Above is a sketch of the gristmill, based on the memories of Heber Parks, who saw the ruins of the mill when he moved to Jurupa as a boy in 1868. (Courtesy Riverside County Library System, Glen Avon Library.)

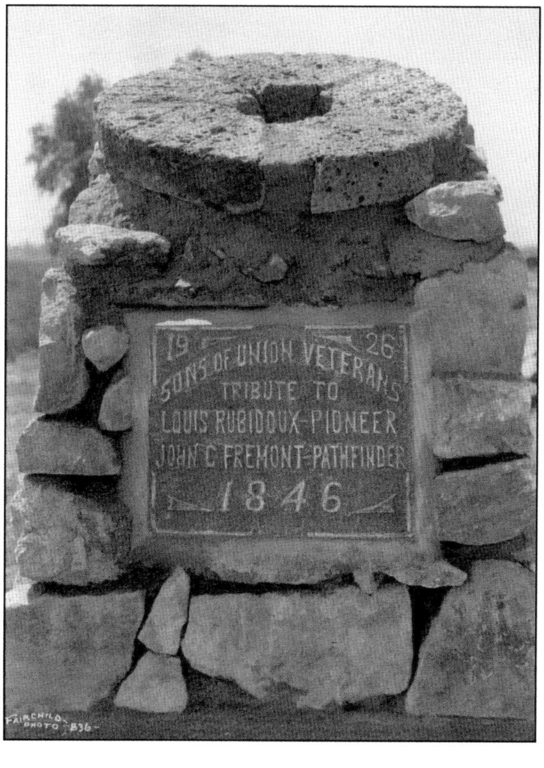

GRIST MILL MONUMENT. The mill was located near today's Molino Way and Fort Street, where this historical monument is placed. The monument includes one of the gristmill stones. Another stone is located at Riverside's Mission Inn. (Courtesy Riverside Metropolitan Museum.)

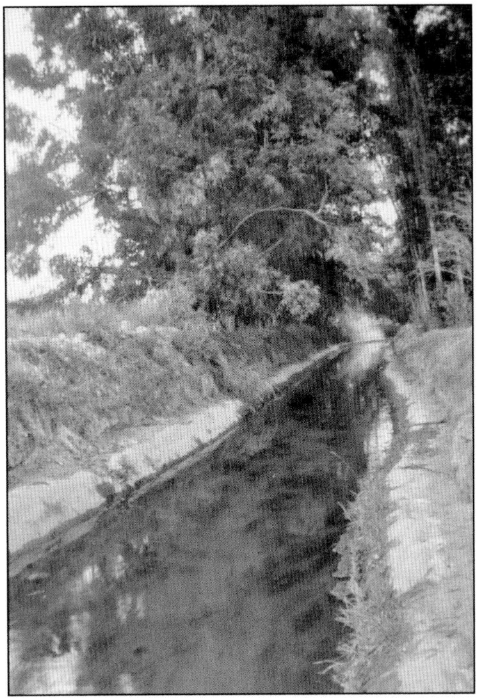

JURUPA DITCH. The Jurupa Ditch may date to as early as 1843–1845, when Benjamin Wilson reportedly dug a ditch to carry water for irrigation. After buying Wilson's property in 1848, Louis Robidoux probably continued to use the same ditch to irrigate his land and provide water to his gristmill. Following Robidoux's death in 1868, new owners, including Cornelius Jensen, formed a water association and filed the first formal claim for water rights. In 1902, the owners of the Jurupa Ditch incorporated as the Jurupa Ditch Company. This company continues to provide water to its shareholders to this day. Portions of the ditch are now piped underground. One of the best places to see the ditch today is along the south side of Riverview Drive, south of Limonite Avenue. (Courtesy Riverside Metropolitan Museum.)

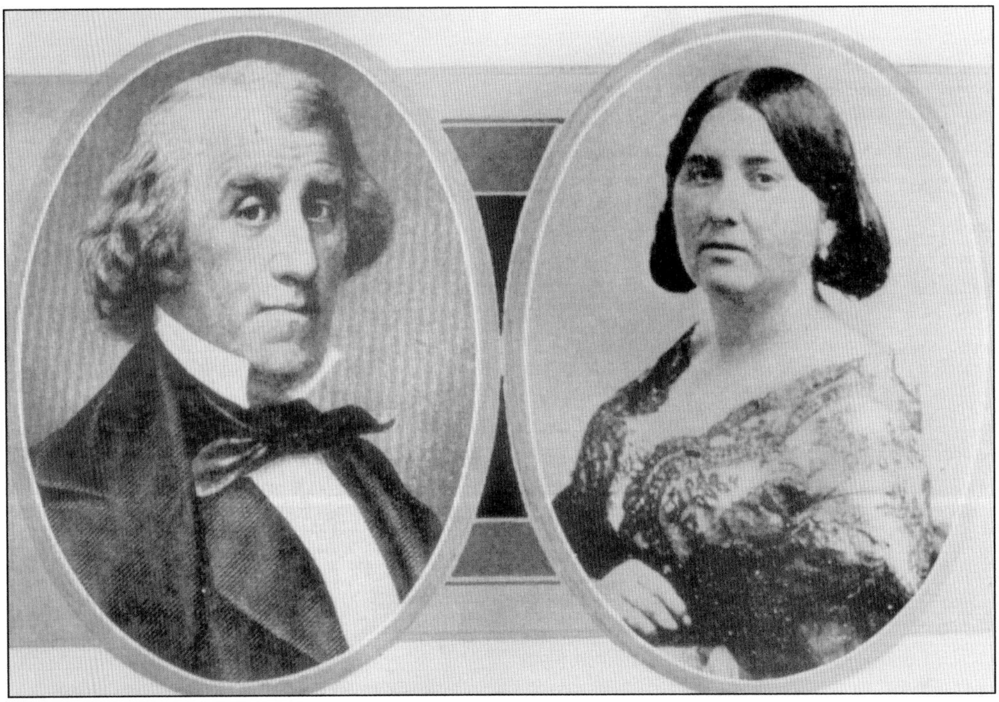

ABEL AND ARCADIA STEARNS. In 1829, Stearns arrived in California. He soon adopted Mexican citizenship and converted to Catholicism. At age 44, he married Juan Bandini's daughter Arcadia, who was 30 years his junior. In 1857, Stearns bought the remainder of the Jurupa Rancho from his father-in-law and continued maintaining it as a ranch until his death in 1871. (Courtesy Riverside County Library System, Louis Robidoux Library.)

ARTHUR PARKS. Before Louis Robidoux died in 1868, he began selling off small, ranch-size portions of his land. The first buyer was Arthur Parks. He was an ex-Mormon from England who came to Jurupa by way of Utah and San Bernardino. He and his wife, Mary Ann, had eight children. Parks became a lawyer and conducted most of the legal business for the citizens of the new community of Riverside across the Santa Ana River. He was also very active in the community. Parks served as justice of the peace, road supervisor, clerk of elections, and as a school board member. (Courtesy Ida Parks Condit family.)

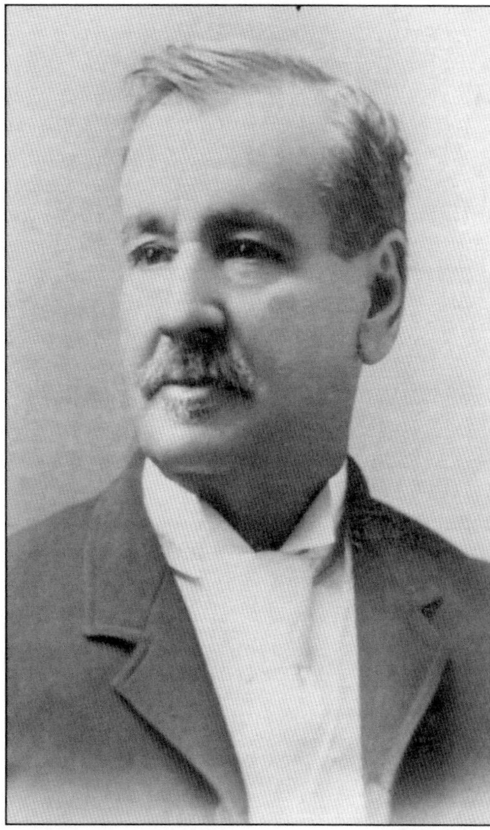

ARTHUR PARKS HOME. This is the home and property of Arthur Parks, *c.* 1883. The first part of the home, built in 1867, was adobe. A large wooden addition was added to the front of the house about 1875. The home was located at what is now 5560 Thirty-fourth Street. In 1974, it was demolished. (Courtesy Riverside County Library System, Glen Avon Library.)

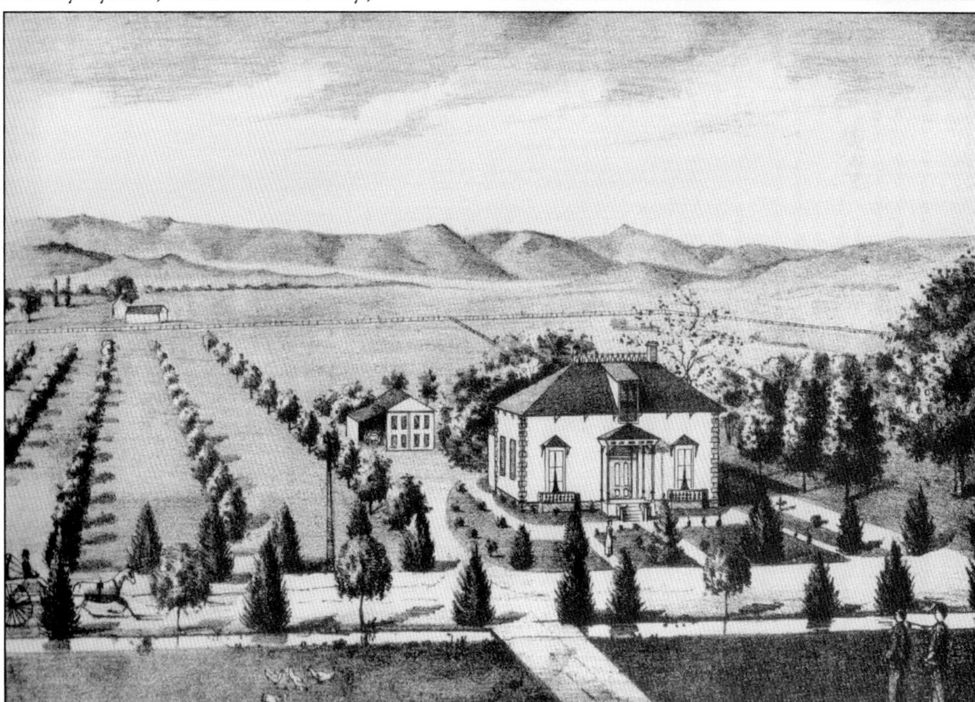

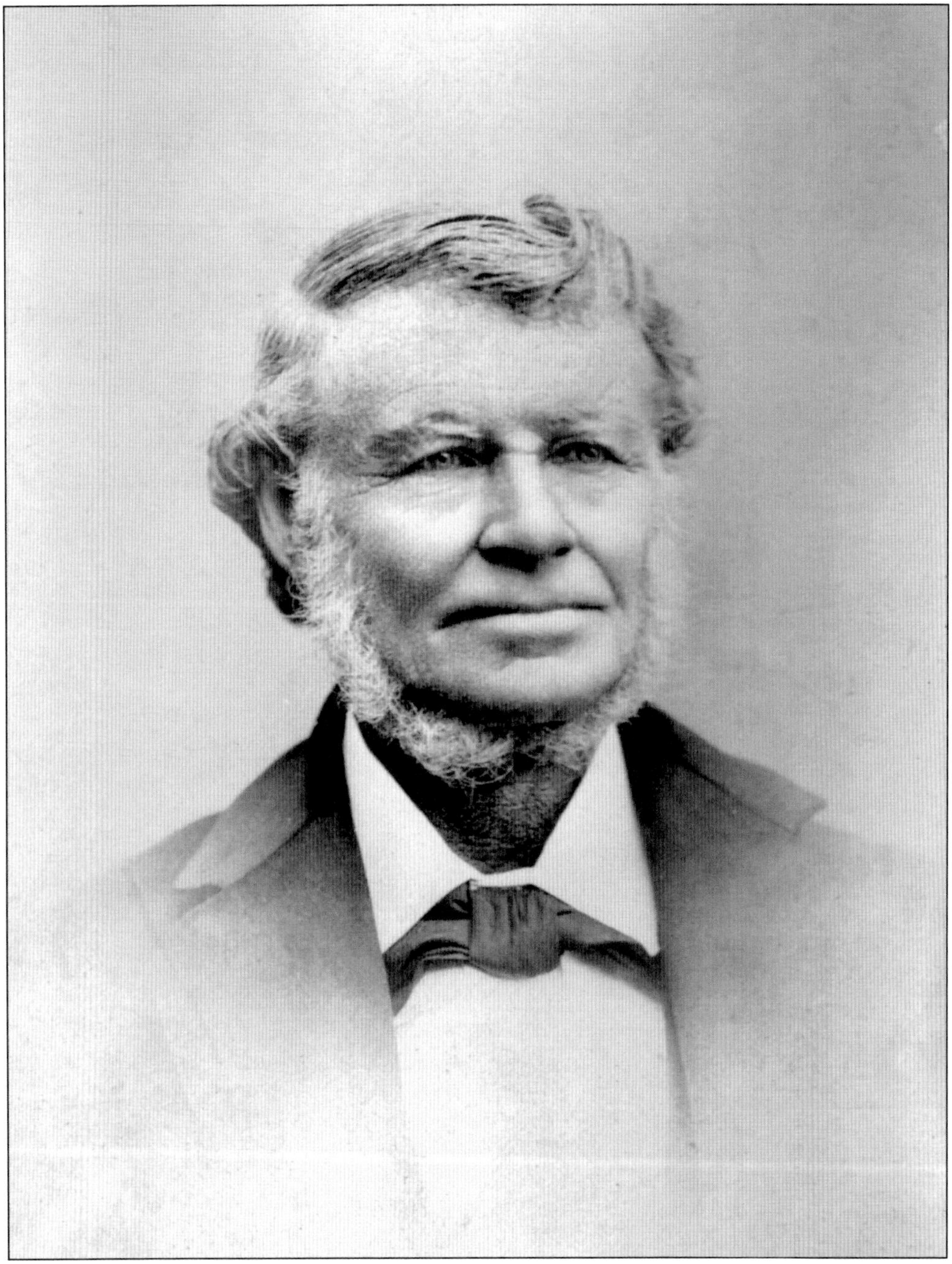

CORNELIUS JENSEN, C. 1865. Born on the Island of Sylt off the coast of Denmark in 1815, Jensen went to sea at an early age. He eventually rose to the rank of captain, serving on a trading vessel that pulled into San Francisco Bay in 1848. His crew abandoned the ship due to "gold fever" and Captain Jensen had his cargo shipped to the gold country where he opened a store to trade with the miners. He was encouraged to come south by some prominent citizens who had traveled north to sell hides. In 1851, he moved to the area. He was well known and respected both in Agua Mansa, where he lived first, and at his home in Jurupa. He served a total of nine one-year terms as county supervisor between 1856 and 1877. (Courtesy Riverside Metropolitan Museum.)

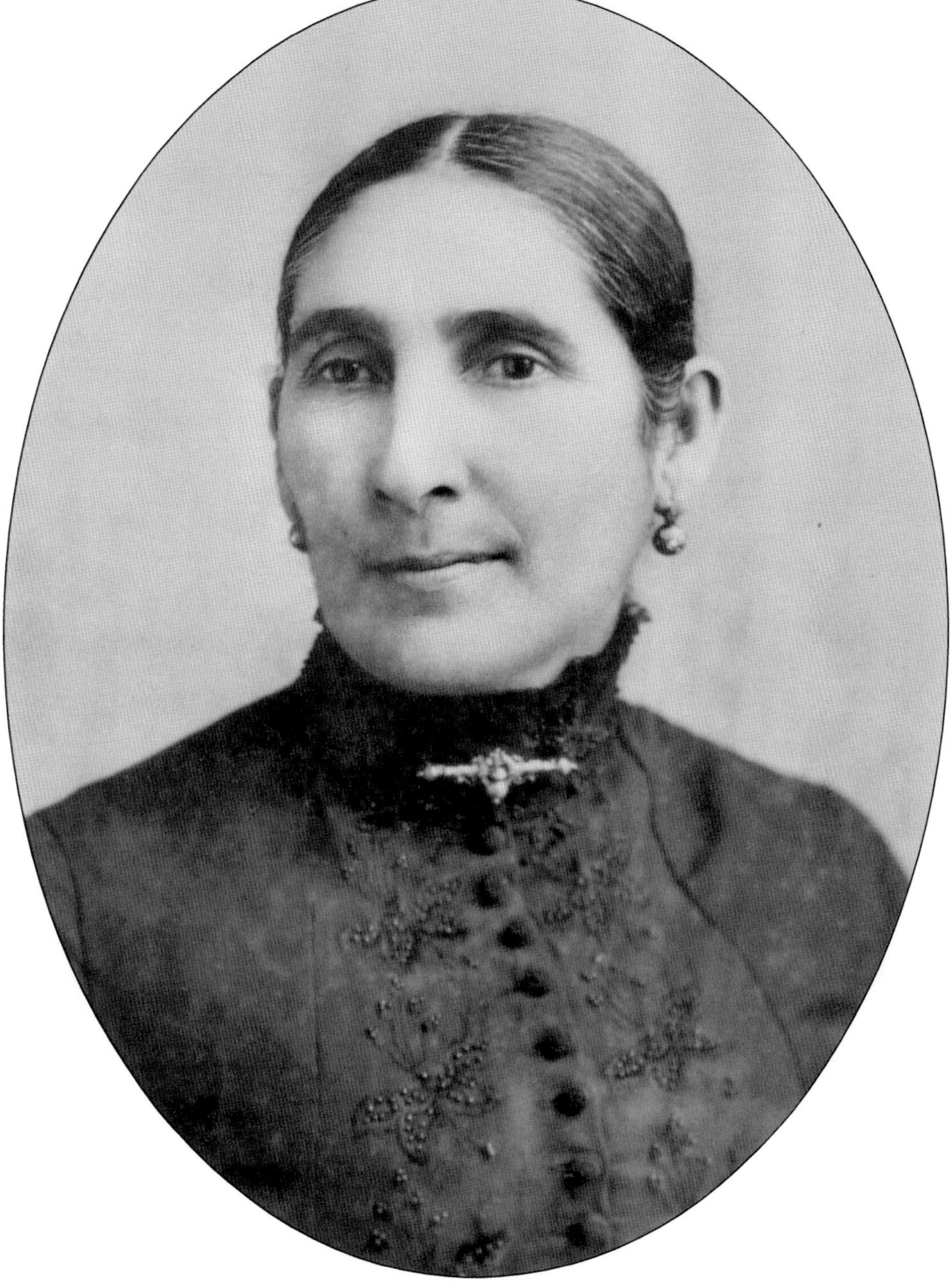

MERCEDES ALVARADO JENSEN, C. 1865. Born in 1837, Mercedes was the daughter of Francisco and Juana Maria Alvarado, a prominent Californio family. In 1854, Mercedes and Cornelius Jensen were married in the Catholic church in Agua Mansa. Since the Alvarados didn't live in the area at the time, the wedding celebration was held at the home of Louis Robidoux. Mercedes and her new husband initially settled in Agua Mansa, where they lived for approximately 13 years. After the flood of 1862 destroyed virtually all of Agua Mansa, Jensen decided to purchase 100 acres of the Robidoux Rancho. The purchase was recorded on September 15, 1865. (Courtesy Riverside Metropolitan Museum.)

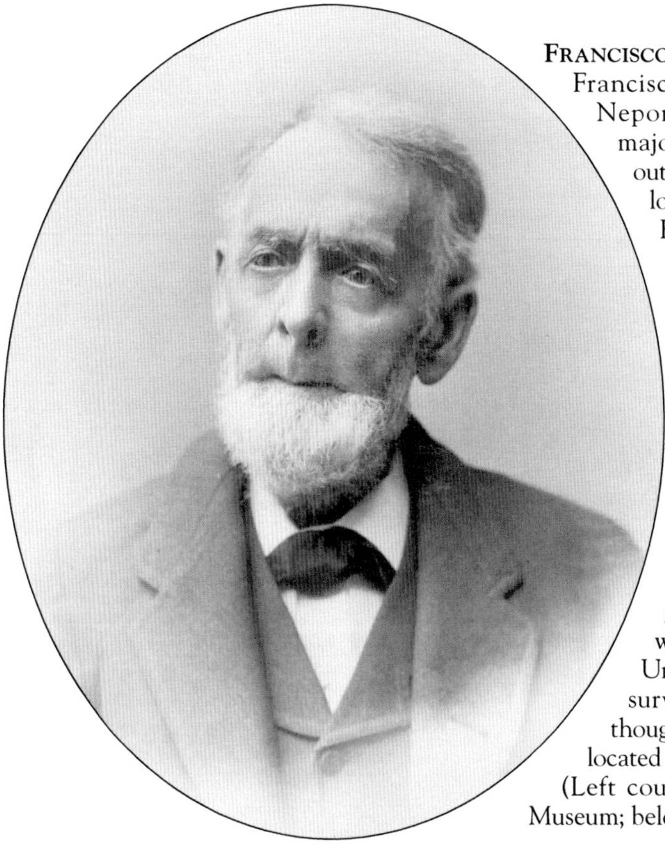

FRANCISCO ALVARADO. Mercedes father, Francisco Alvarado, was the son of Nepomuceno Alvarado, the last majordomo of the Assistencia, an outpost of the Mission San Gabriel, located in what is now Redlands. He was born in 1816 or 1817. In 1867, he and his wife, Juana Maria Avila, purchased 12 acres from Louis Robidoux that adjoined Jensen's property to the north. There they built an adobe and wood home in 1870. The photograph below shows the home in 1940 before it was extensively remodeled. Note the severely pruned rose bush in front of the middle column of the porch. General Sherman gave it to the Alvarados in 1875 when he came to call on them. Unfortunately the rose bush didn't survive the pruning. This home, though significantly remodeled, is still located on what is now Riverview Drive. (Left courtesy Riverside Metropolitan Museum; below courtesy Jensen family.)

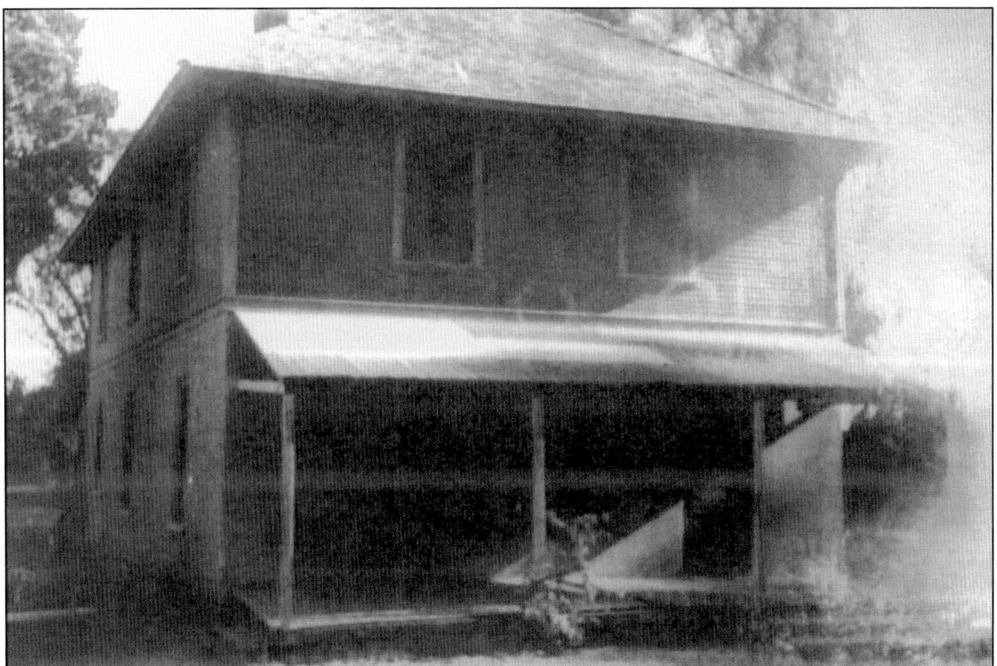

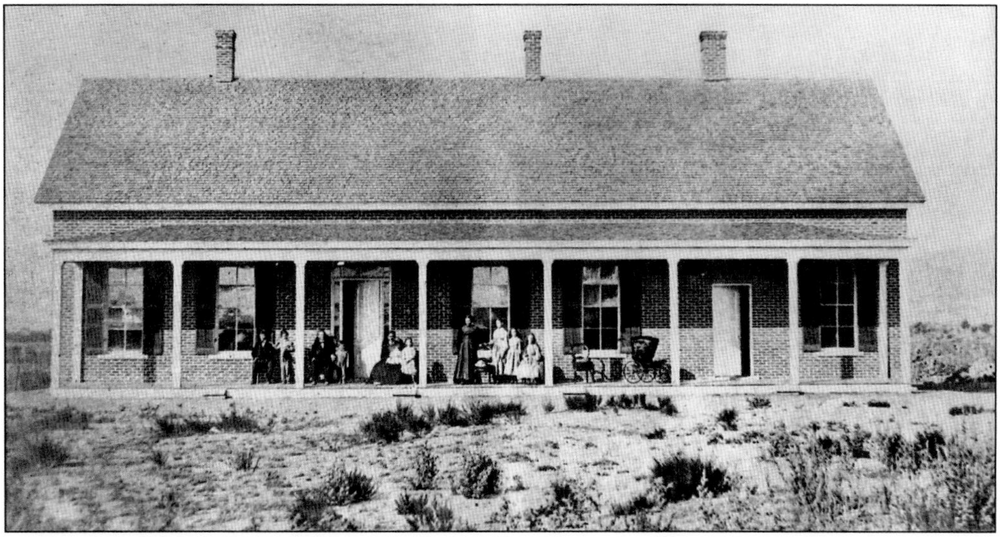

CORNELIUS JENSEN HOME. The Jensen home, built in 1868–1870, was unique in many ways. It was the first kiln-fired brick building constructed in what is now Riverside County. It was made in an architectural style found in Jensen's birthplace on the Island of Sylt. However, probably due to his wife Mercedes influence, it had a front porch which is uncommon on Sylt but very common in California. Thus the house became a marriage of the cultures of the Danish sea captain and his Californio wife. On his ranch, which grew to over 300 acres, grapes were grown for wine and raisins. Other parts were planted in apricots and oranges. Jensen also raised sheep, cattle, and horses, primarily on other property he owned. (Courtesy Jensen family.)

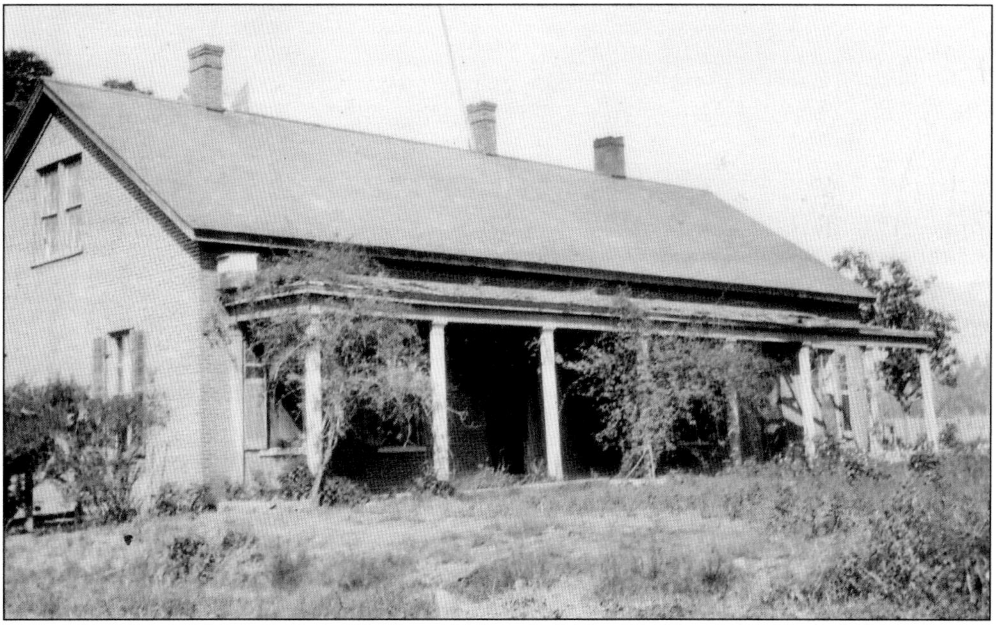

JENSEN HOME, C. 1935. Brick for the Jensen home was manufactured on site by Chinese laborers from clays available on the ranch. Rocks for the foundation and lime for mortar came from the Jensen Quarry, now part of the Riverside Cement Company, in the hills north of the house. The beams were hauled by a team of oxen from the sawmills in the San Bernardino Mountains. (Courtesy Jensen family.)

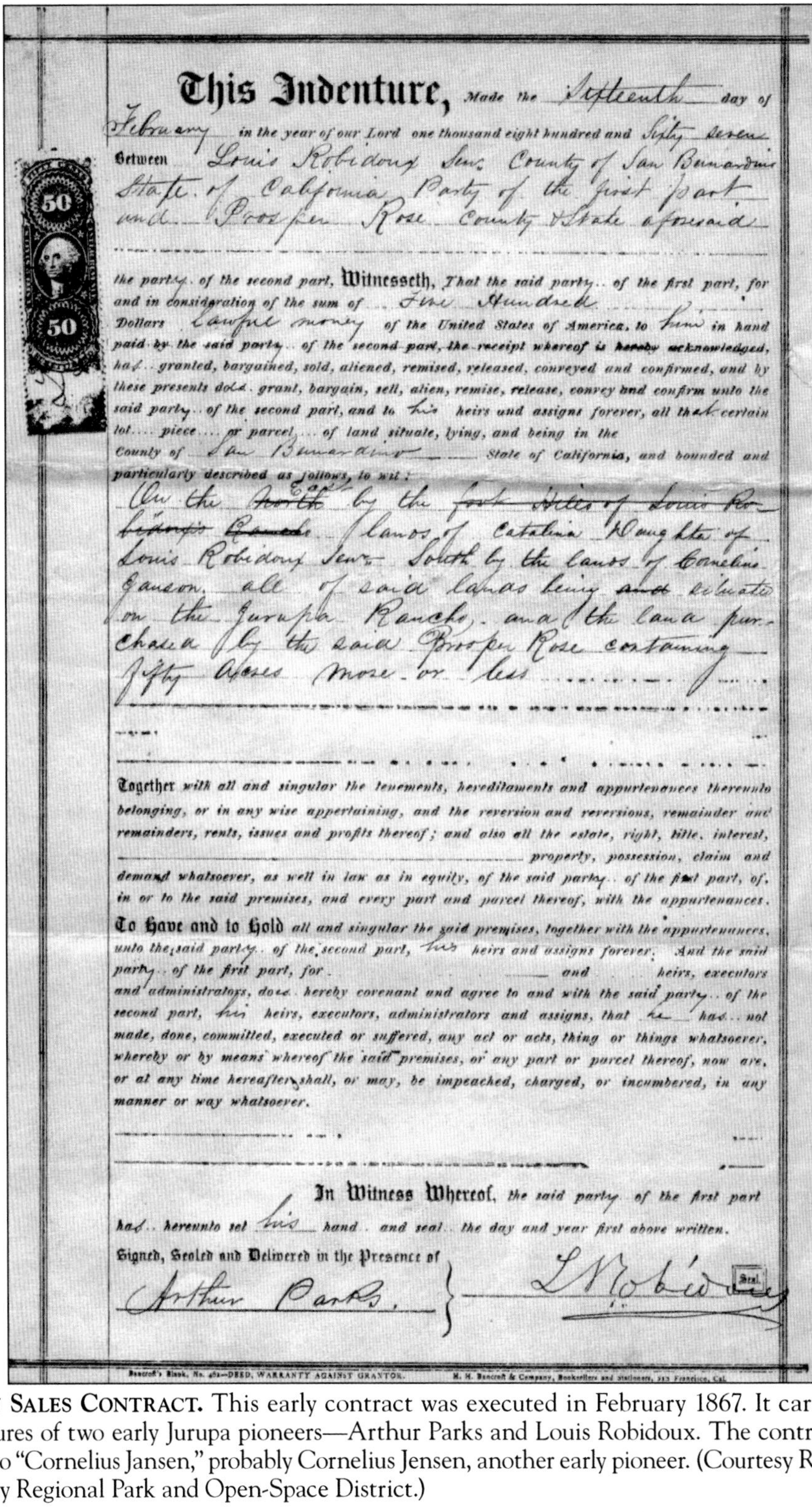

This Indenture, Made the Sixteenth day of February in the year of our Lord one thousand eight hundred and Sixty seven Between Louis Robidoux Senr. County of San Bernardino State of California Party of the first part and Prosper Rose County & State aforesaid

the party of the second part, Witnesseth, That the said party of the first part, for and in consideration of the sum of Five Hundred Dollars lawful money of the United States of America, to him in hand paid by the said party of the second part, the receipt whereof is hereby acknowledged, has granted, bargained, sold, aliened, remised, released, conveyed and confirmed, and by these presents does grant, bargain, sell, alien, remise, release, convey and confirm unto the said party of the second part, and to his heirs and assigns forever, all that certain lot.... piece.... or parcel.... of land situate, lying, and being in the County of San Bernardino State of California, and bounded and particularly described as follows, to wit:

On the ~~North~~ East by the ~~foot Hills of Louis Robidoux's Rancho~~ lands of Catalina Daughter of Louis Robidoux Senr. South by the lands of Cornelius Jansen all of said lands being ~~and~~ situated on the Jurupa Rancho. and the land purchased by the said Prosper Rose containing fifty Acres more or less

Together with all and singular the tenements, hereditaments and appurtenances thereunto belonging, or in any wise appertaining, and the reversion and reversions, remainder and remainders, rents, issues and profits thereof; and also all the estate, right, title, interest, property, possession, claim and demand whatsoever, as well in law as in equity, of the said party of the first part, of, in or to the said premises, and every part and parcel thereof, with the appurtenances.

To Have and to Hold all and singular the said premises, together with the appurtenances, unto the said party of the second part, his heirs and assigns forever. And the said party of the first part, for and heirs, executors and administrators, does hereby covenant and agree to and with the said party of the second part, his heirs, executors, administrators and assigns, that he has not made, done, committed, executed or suffered, any act or acts, thing or things whatsoever, whereby or by means whereof the said premises, or any part or parcel thereof, now are, or at any time hereafter shall, or may, be impeached, charged, or incumbered, in any manner or way whatsoever.

In Witness Whereof, the said party of the first part has hereunto set his hand and seal the day and year first above written.

Signed, Sealed and Delivered in the Presence of

Arthur Parks. L. Robidoux [Seal]

Bancroft's Blank, No. 452—DEED, WARRANTY AGAINST GRANTOR. H. H. Bancroft & Company, Booksellers and Stationers, San Francisco, Cal.

EARLY SALES CONTRACT. This early contract was executed in February 1867. It carries the signatures of two early Jurupa pioneers—Arthur Parks and Louis Robidoux. The contract also refers to "Cornelius Jansen," probably Cornelius Jensen, another early pioneer. (Courtesy Riverside County Regional Park and Open-Space District.)

Two

Landmarks and Events

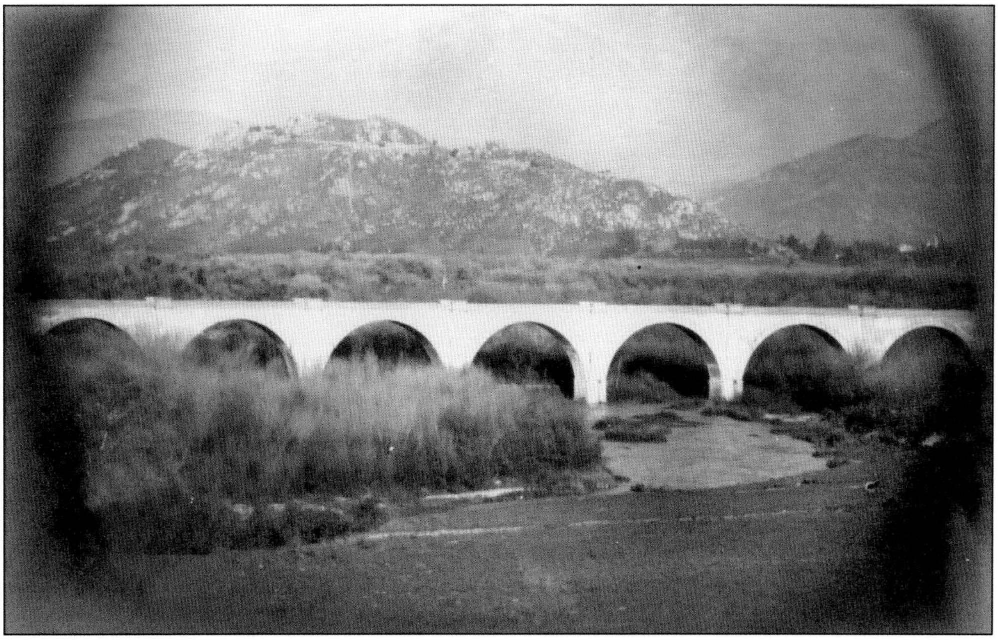

Mount Rubidoux. This distinctive landmark is located between Rubidoux and the City of Riverside. A favorite hiking spot over the years, it was named for early pioneer Louis Robidoux. This view was taken from below the Union Pacific Railroad Bridge, which crosses the Santa Ana River near Van Buren Boulevard. (Courtesy Glenn Wenzel.)

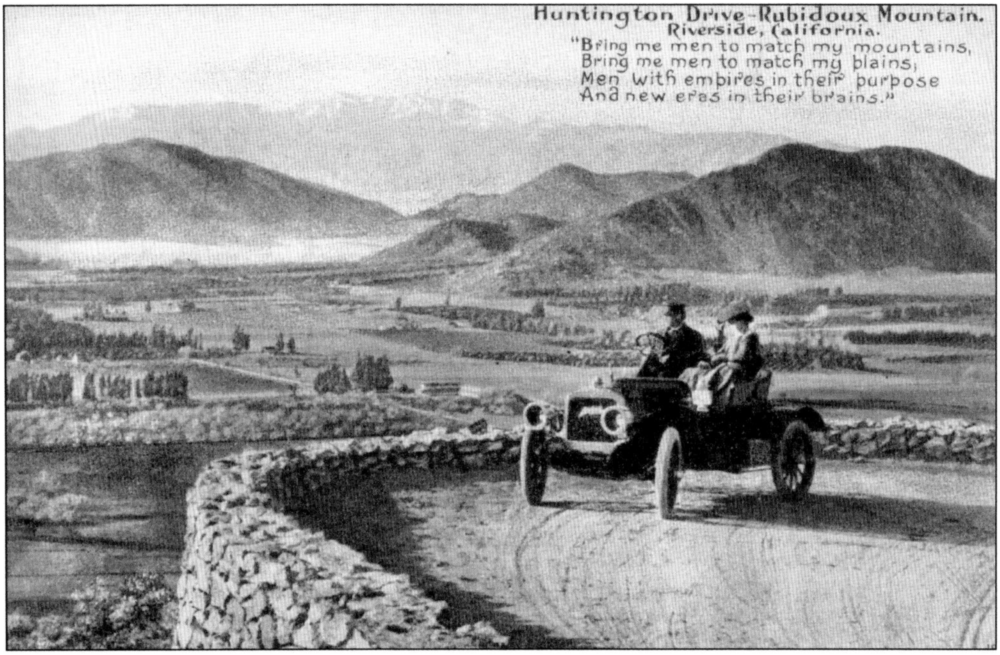

Views of Jurupa. These early 1900 postcards were designed to highlight one of the places visitors to Riverside could enjoy. They also show a panoramic view of West Riverside from Huntington Drive on Mount Rubidoux. In the view with the two cars, it appears that the Louis Robidoux home can be seen in the distance. (Courtesy Steve Lech.)

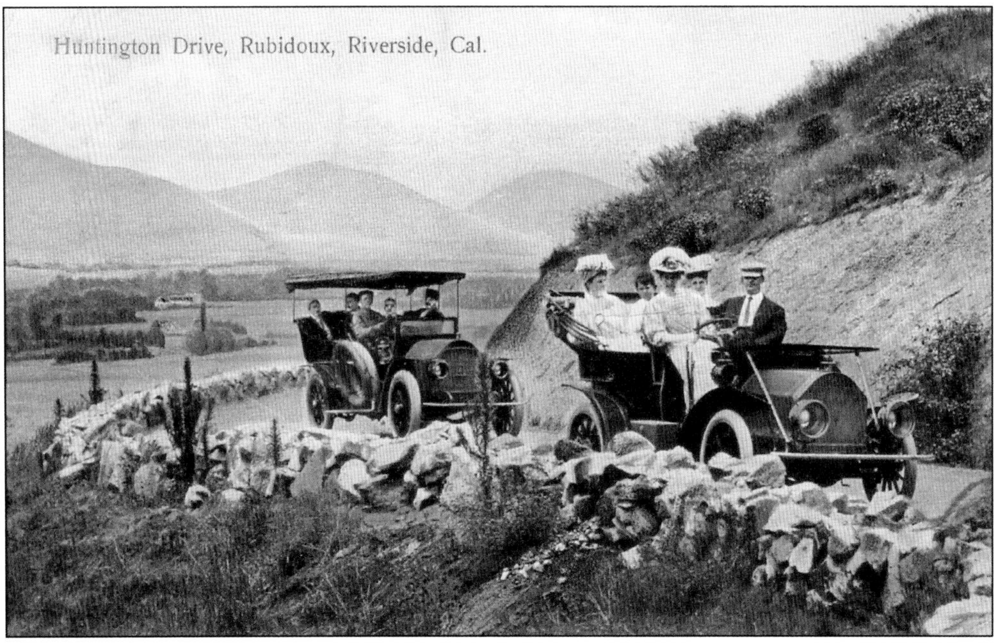

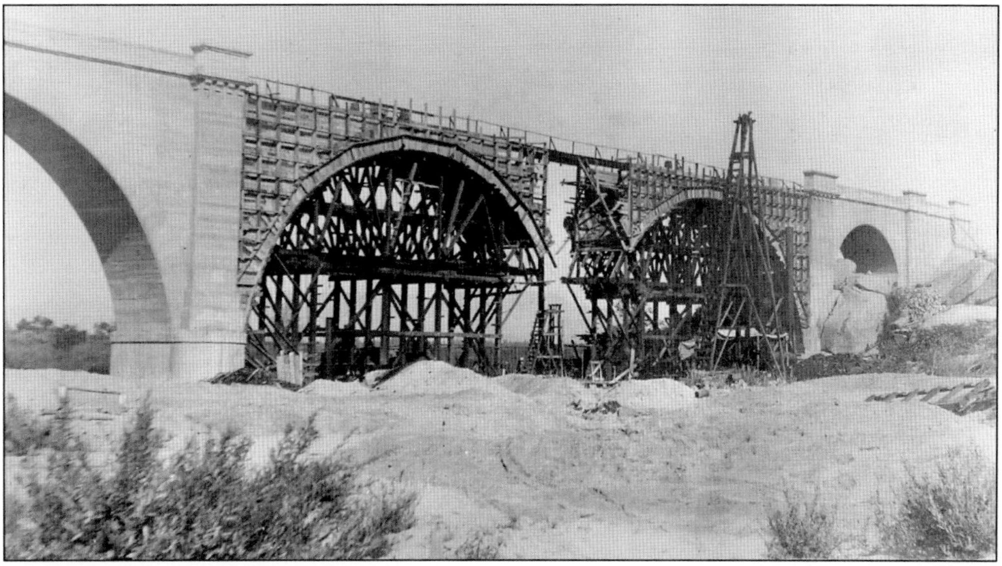

CONSTRUCTION OF RAILROAD BRIDGE. Construction began in 1902 on the world's first continuous concrete bridge, needed to cross the Pedley narrows of the Santa Ana River for the San Pedro, Los Angeles, and Salt Lake Railroad (now part of Union Pacific.) Quicksand caused almost immediate construction delays. An even greater problem developed when it was discovered that the bedrock under Pier No. 7, near the eastern bank, was 90 feet under the riverbed. It took 11 months to solve this engineering problem before pouring cement at the bedrock level could begin. (Courtesy Riverside Metropolitan Museum.)

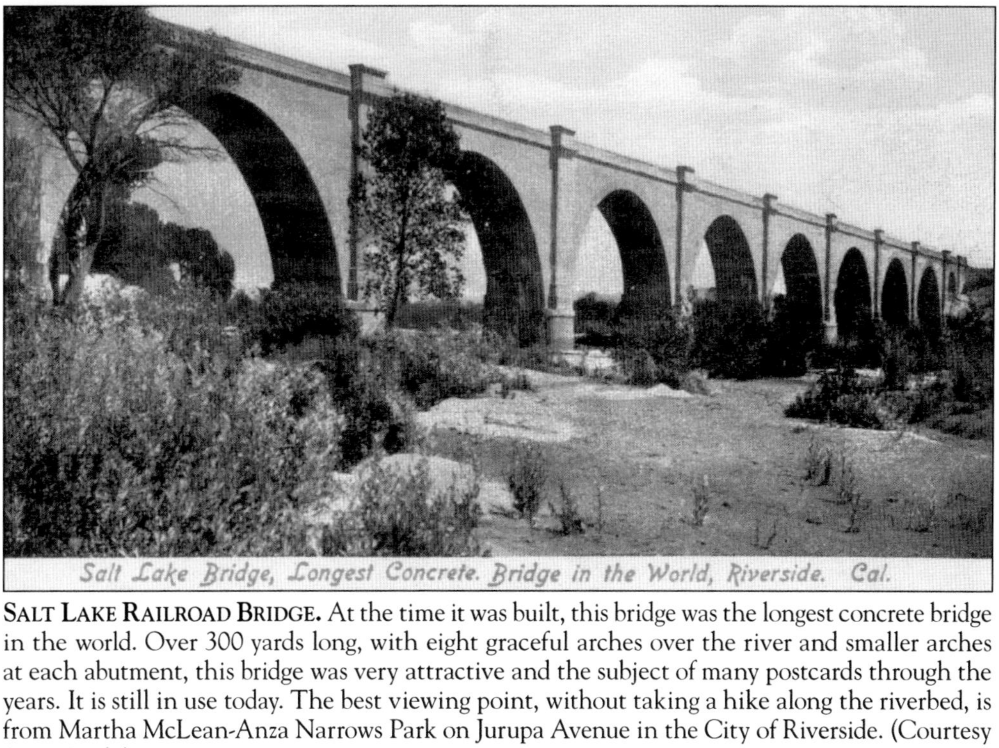

SALT LAKE RAILROAD BRIDGE. At the time it was built, this bridge was the longest concrete bridge in the world. Over 300 yards long, with eight graceful arches over the river and smaller arches at each abutment, this bridge was very attractive and the subject of many postcards through the years. It is still in use today. The best viewing point, without taking a hike along the riverbed, is from Martha McLean-Anza Narrows Park on Jurupa Avenue in the City of Riverside. (Courtesy Steve Lech.)

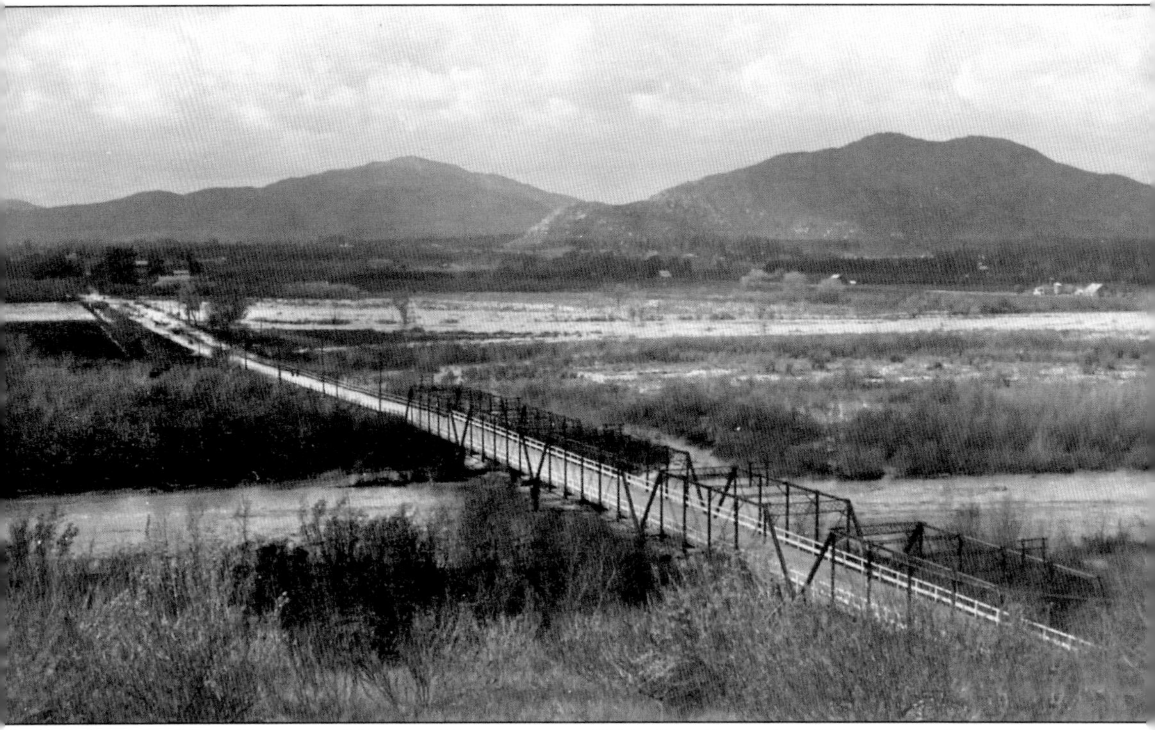

SANTA ANA RIVER AT MISSION BOULEVARD, 1911. The Santa Ana River carved two channels along the riverbed through the West Riverside area before the levee was built to contain the river. The first channel ran along the base of Mount Rubidoux where the present river runs. The second channel ran in the vicinity of today's Wallace Street. (Courtesy Riverside Metropolitan Museum.)

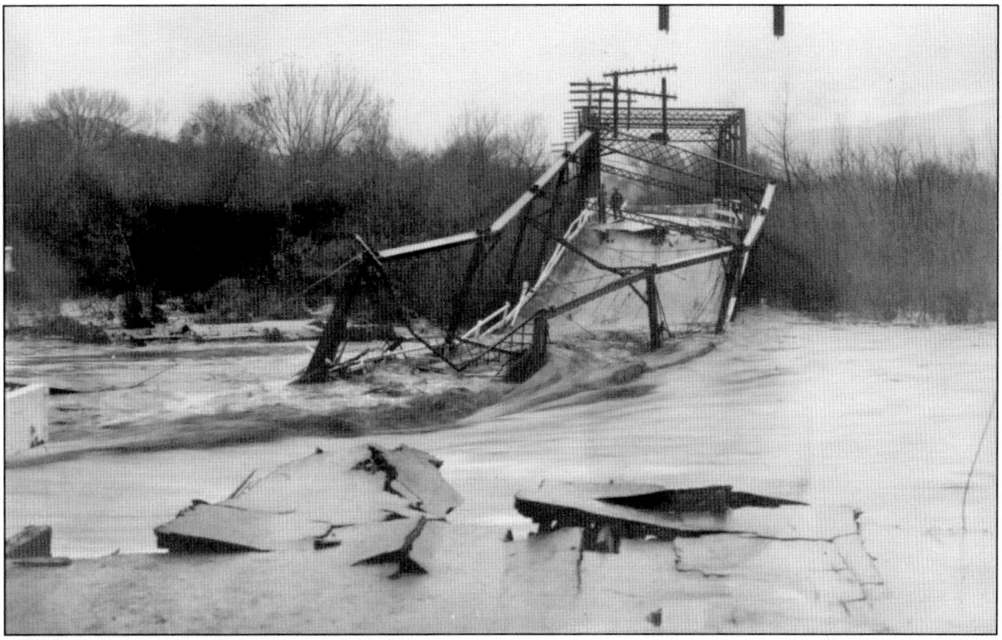

1916 FLOOD. The 1916 flood of the Santa Ana River was the first major flood to be captured on film but was just another in the long history of Santa Ana flooding. This shows the bridge that crossed the river from Riverside to the Jurupa area after it was washed out. (Courtesy Steve Lech.)

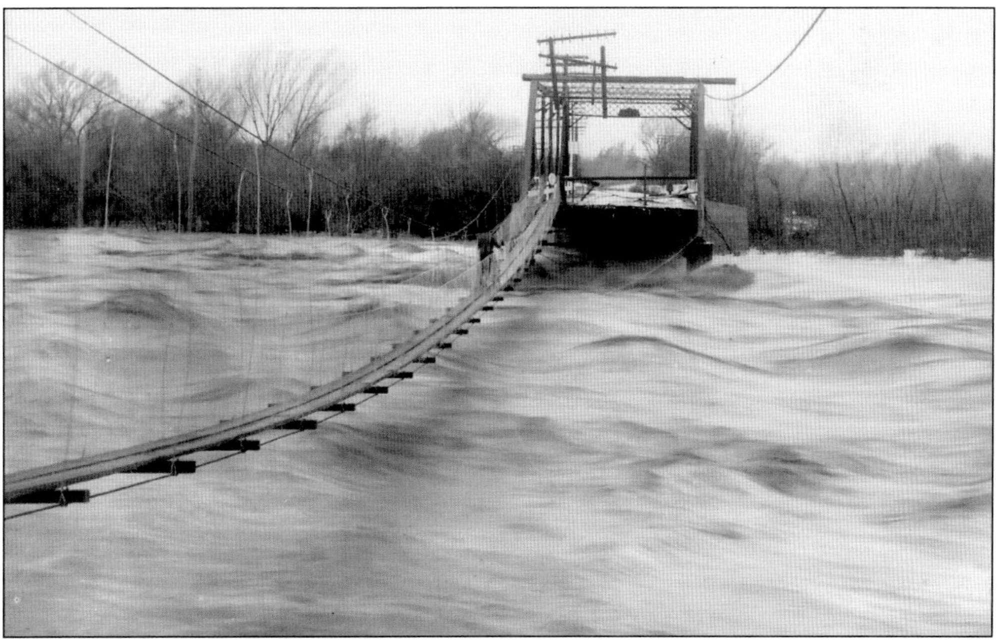

TEMPORARY BRIDGE. A temporary pedestrian bridge was constructed to cross the still raging Santa Ana River. Note the undeveloped nature of the river bottom on the Jurupa side of the bridge. (Courtesy Steve Lech.)

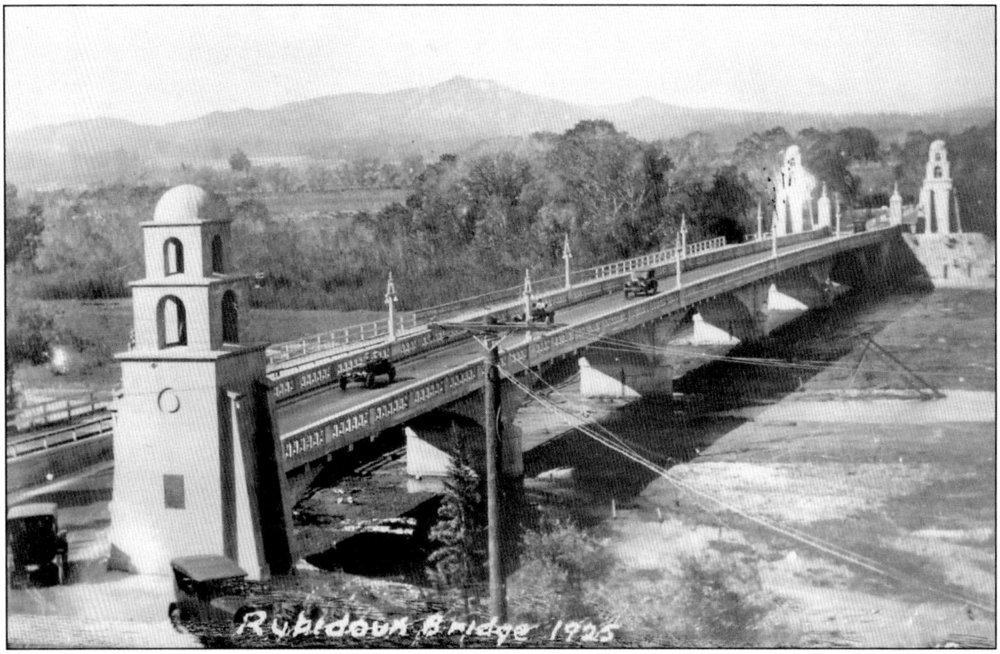

New Santa Ana River Bridge. In 1923, a newer, more picturesque bridge was constructed to cross the river. (Courtesy Riverside County Library System, Louis Robidoux Library.)

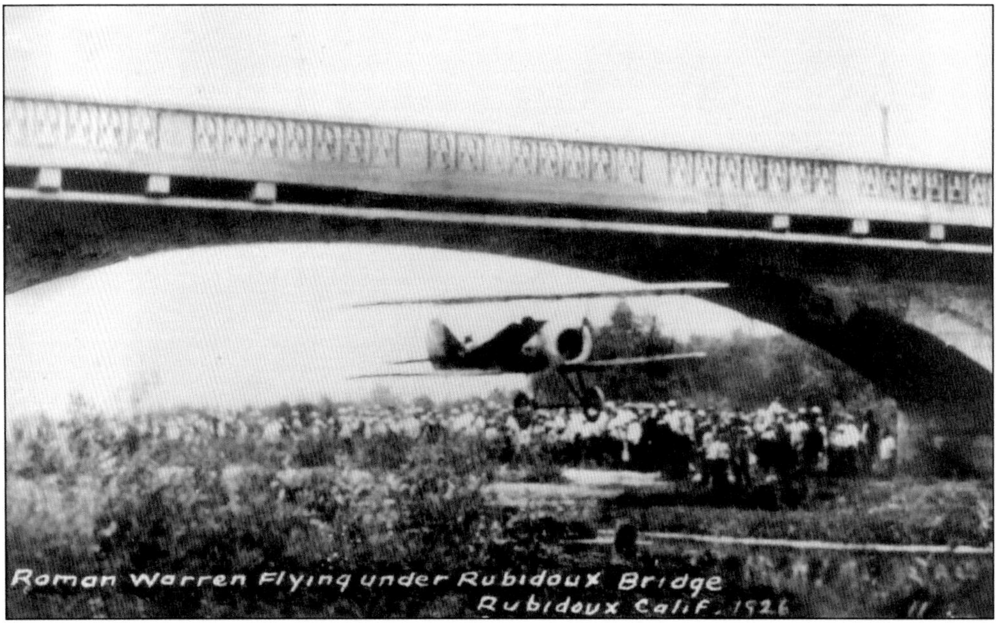

Flight under the Santa Ana River Bridge. On June 13, 1926, Roman Warren, known as the "Cowboy Aviator," accomplished his most famous feat—flying his plane under the 16-foot tall center arch of the West Riverside Bridge over the Santa Ana River. His motivation was publicity for his business of giving rides and flying lessons. Thousands watched the flight from both sides of the river and from Mount Rubidoux. The headline in the *Riverside Enterprise* on June 15, read, "Cowboy Aviator Bets Life and Wins." Film footage of that flight still amazes people today. (Courtesy Steve Lech.)

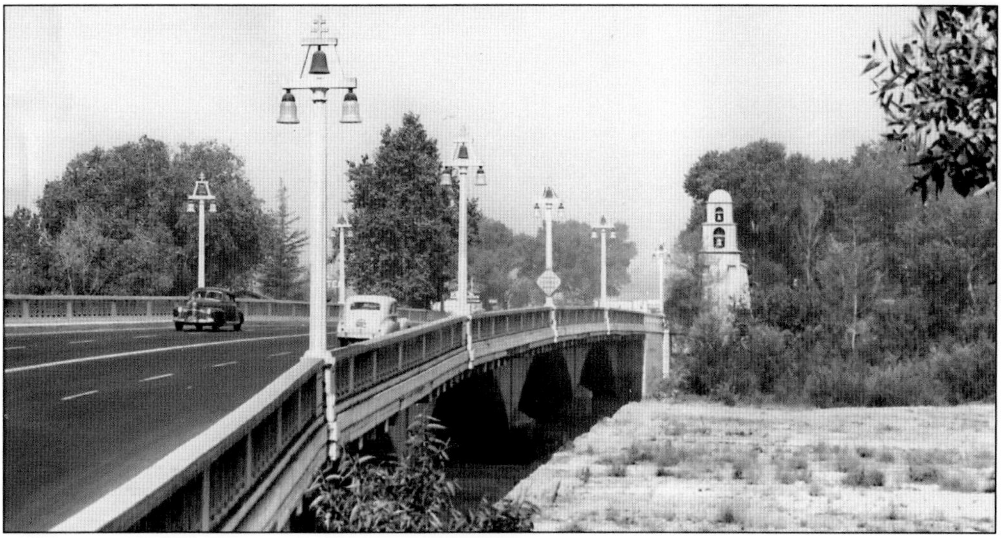

WIDENED BRIDGE. As more and more traffic used the bridge between Jurupa and Riverside, the two lanes it provided became outdated. In 1931, the bridge was widened to four lanes. This bridge also became outdated because it did not span a wide enough distance across the river and did not provide enough clearance under its length to allow for high-water events. A new bridge was constructed upriver and this bridge was removed in 1958. At the base of Mount Rubidoux, two of the bridge's towers still mark where it stood. (Courtesy Jurupa Mountains Cultural Center.)

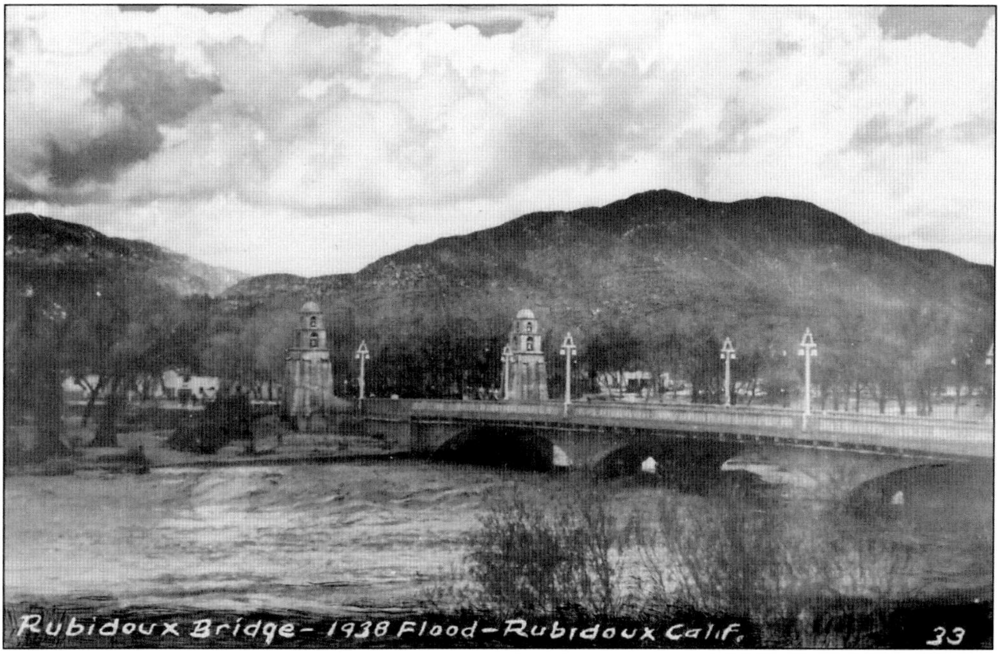

1938 FLOOD. The Santa Ana River Bridge is shown during the 1938 flood. The bridge to West Riverside was the only bridge on the Santa Ana River to survive, but it was closed to traffic for two weeks. One hundred fifty nine lives were lost in Southern California, 116 of them in Riverside County. The devastation caused by this flood prompted the formation of the Riverside County Flood Control and Water Conservation District as well as the building of the levees seen today in the Rubidoux area. (Courtesy Flabob Airport.)

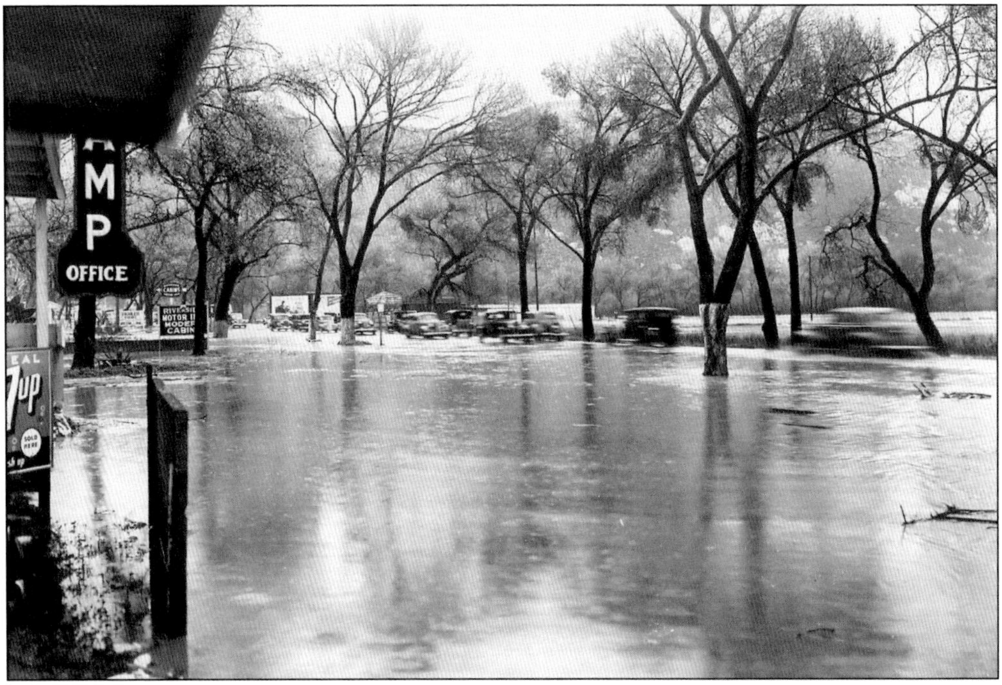

MARCH 1938 FLOOD. West Riverside was particularly hard hit by the 1938 flood. By that time, more development had occurred closer to the river. This shows an auto camp on Mission Boulevard with Mount Rubidoux in the background behind the trees. (Courtesy Riverside Metropolitan Museum.)

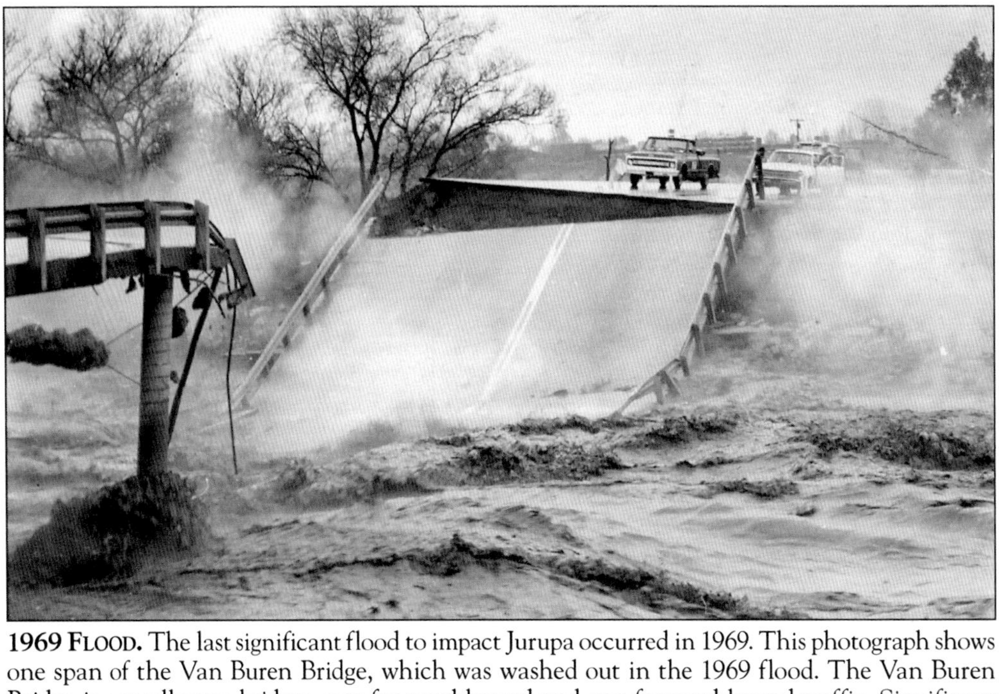

1969 FLOOD. The last significant flood to impact Jurupa occurred in 1969. This photograph shows one span of the Van Buren Bridge, which was washed out in the 1969 flood. The Van Buren Bridge is actually two bridges, one for northbound and one for southbound traffic. Significant flooding occurred in the Mira Loma area as well. Major flood control improvements have been built in Jurupa since that time. (Courtesy Louis Robidoux Nature Center.)

Three

SCHOOL LIFE

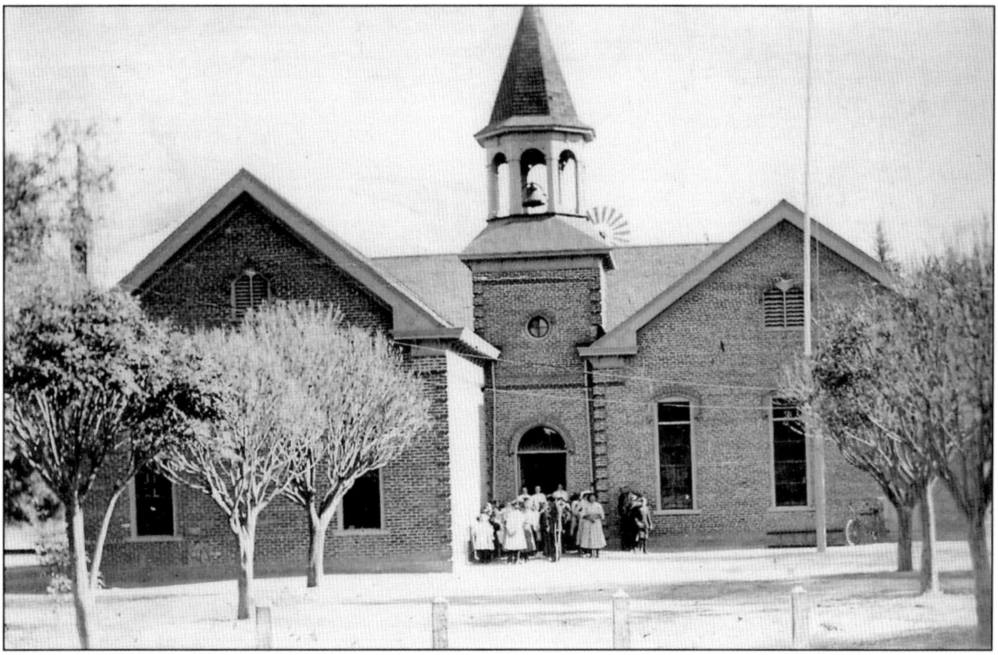

JURUPA SCHOOL. Initially the original families to settle the area, including the Parkses and the Jensens, hired tutors for their children. As more people settled on the land of the former Robidoux Rancho, the need for a school grew. In 1868, the Evans family donated seven acres for a school site on what is now Riverview Drive. The first school built on the site, the Jurupa School, was made from adobe and taught grades one through eight. It was replaced in 1888–1889 with the two-room brick building shown here. In 1915, the school and school district changed its name from Jurupa to West Riverside. The present West Riverside School is still located on this original school site. (Courtesy Jensen family.)

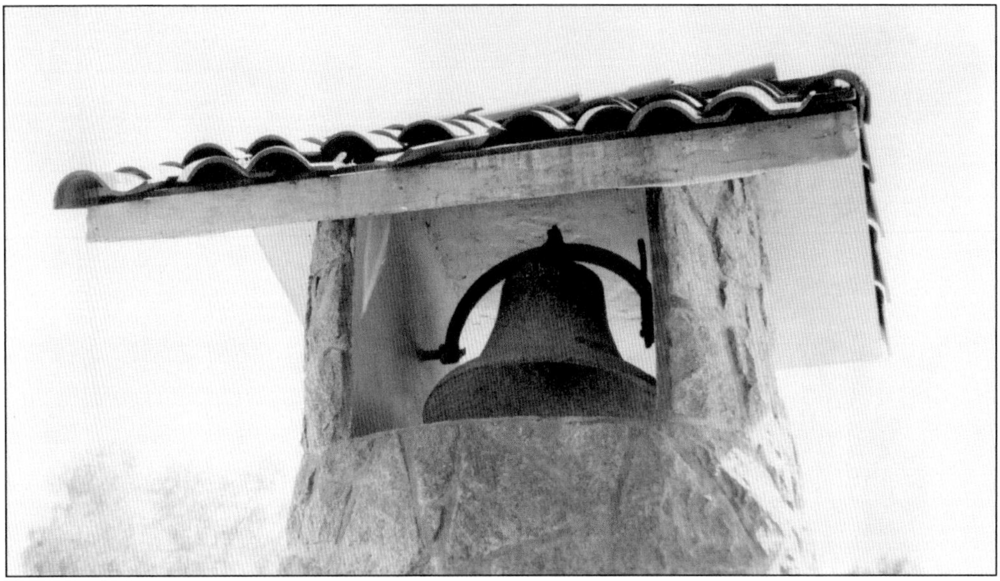

JURUPA SCHOOL BELL. This bell was purchased for the Jurupa School in 1889 at a cost of $87.50. The bell remained there until 1923 when the school was replaced by a Spanish-style reinforced concrete building with a red tile roof. In 1932, the Old Settlers' group paid to have a gray granite tower constructed at West Riverside School to hold the old school bell. The tower and bell are still located at West Riverside School. (Courtesy Jurupa Unified School District.)

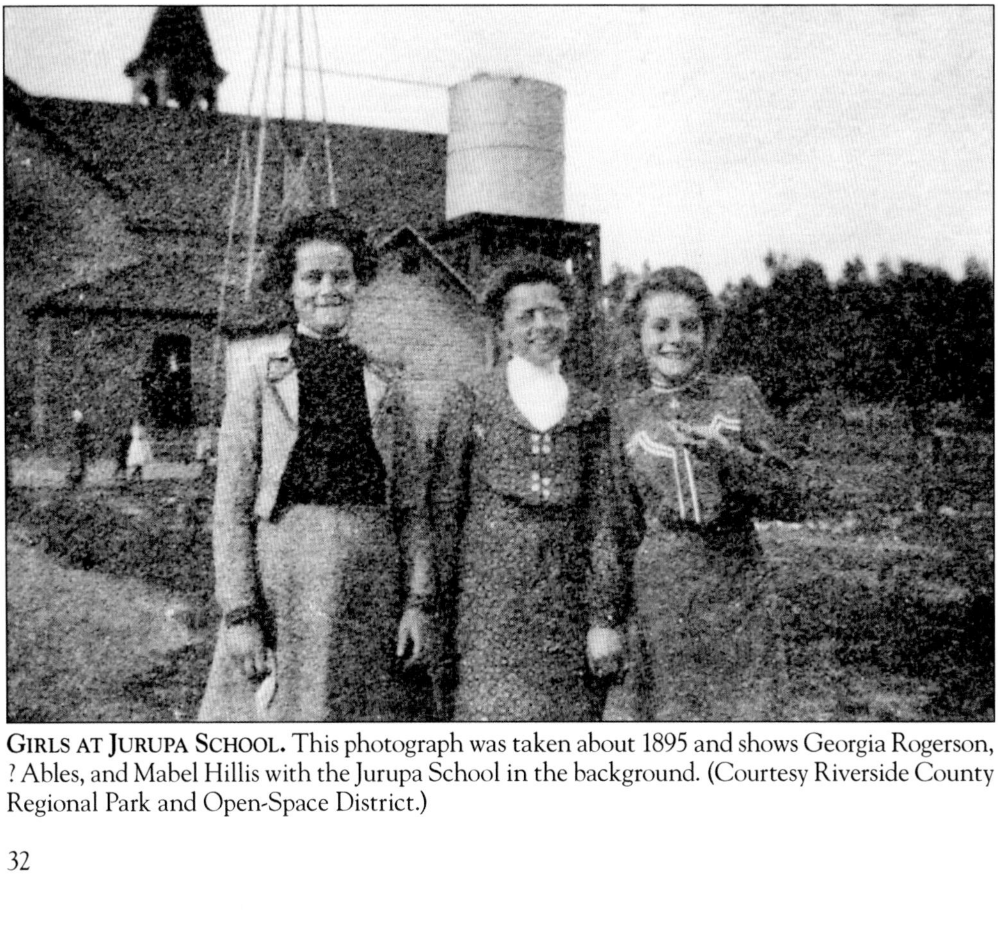

GIRLS AT JURUPA SCHOOL. This photograph was taken about 1895 and shows Georgia Rogerson, ? Ables, and Mabel Hillis with the Jurupa School in the background. (Courtesy Riverside County Regional Park and Open-Space District.)

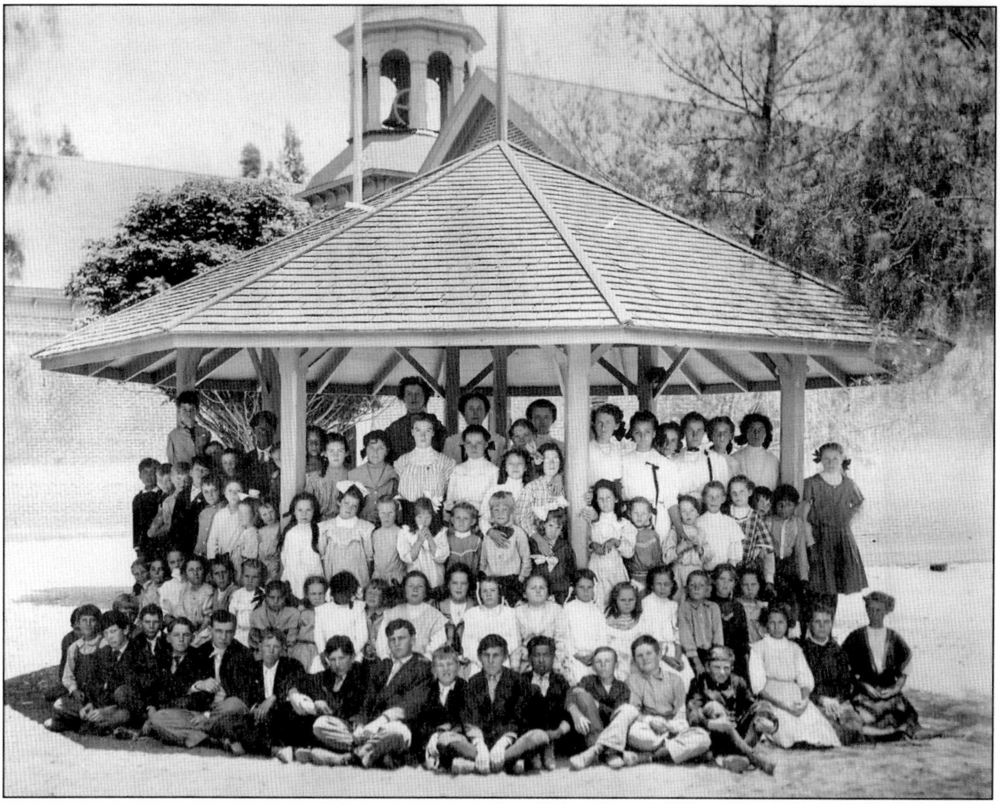

SCHOOL GAZEBO. Jurupa School students are shown here in 1909 gathered in and around the school gazebo. (Courtesy Jensen family.)

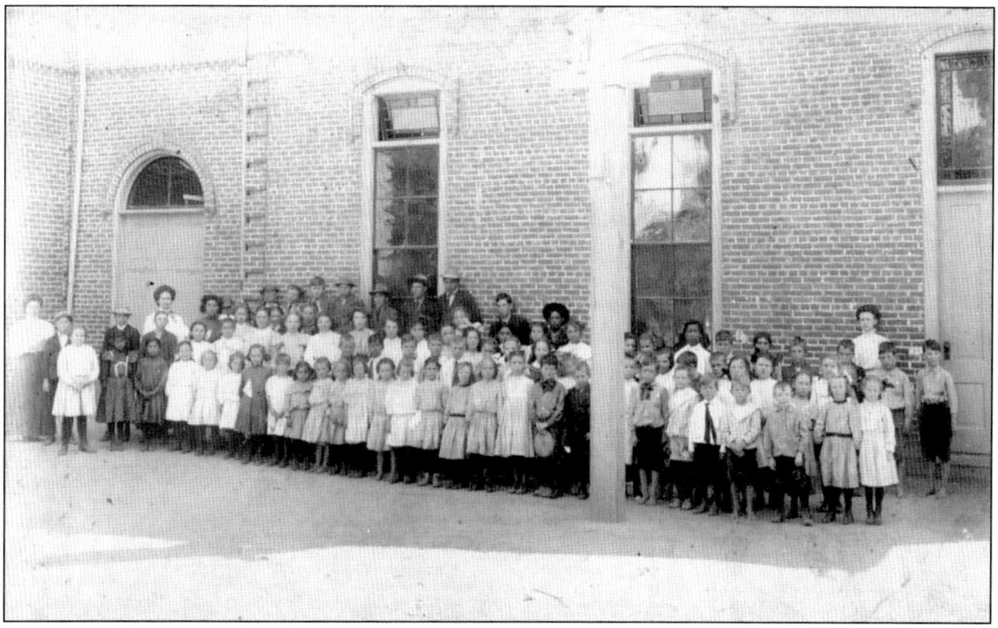

JURUPA SCHOOL. Jurupa School's population continued to grow. Here are students lined up outside the school in 1910. (Courtesy Jensen family.)

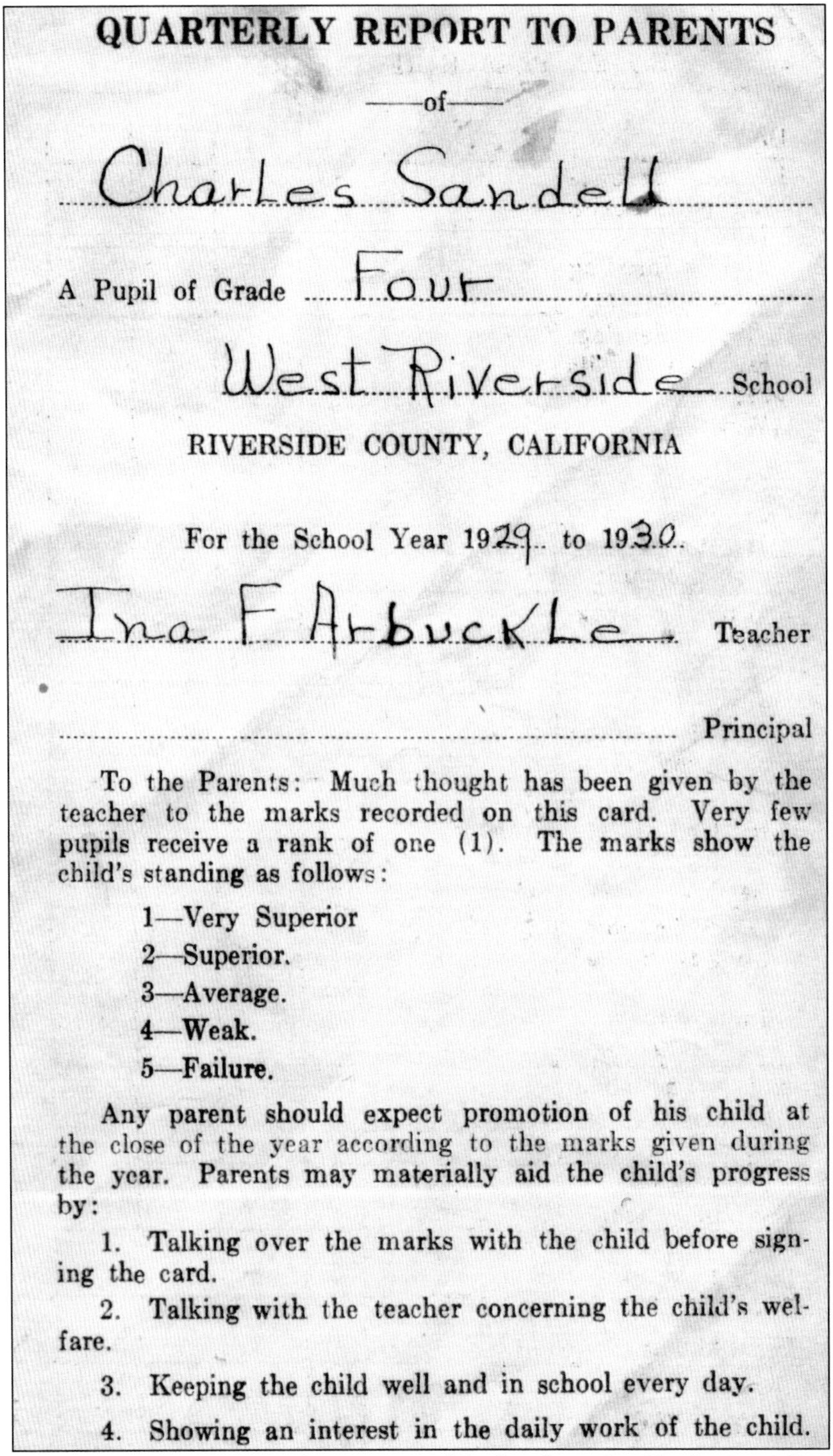

QUARTERLY REPORT TO PARENTS

—of—

Charles Sandell

A Pupil of Grade Four

West Riverside School

RIVERSIDE COUNTY, CALIFORNIA

For the School Year 1929 to 1930

Ina F Arbuckle Teacher

Principal

To the Parents: Much thought has been given by the teacher to the marks recorded on this card. Very few pupils receive a rank of one (1). The marks show the child's standing as follows:

1—Very Superior
2—Superior.
3—Average.
4—Weak.
5—Failure.

Any parent should expect promotion of his child at the close of the year according to the marks given during the year. Parents may materially aid the child's progress by:

1. Talking over the marks with the child before signing the card.
2. Talking with the teacher concerning the child's welfare.
3. Keeping the child well and in school every day.
4. Showing an interest in the daily work of the child.

WEST RIVERSIDE REPORT CARD. This report card for fourth-grader Charles Sandell was issued for the 1929–1930 school year. His teacher that year was Ina Arbuckle, for whom the elementary school on Packard Street in Rubidoux was later named. (Courtesy Janis Sandell McKee.)

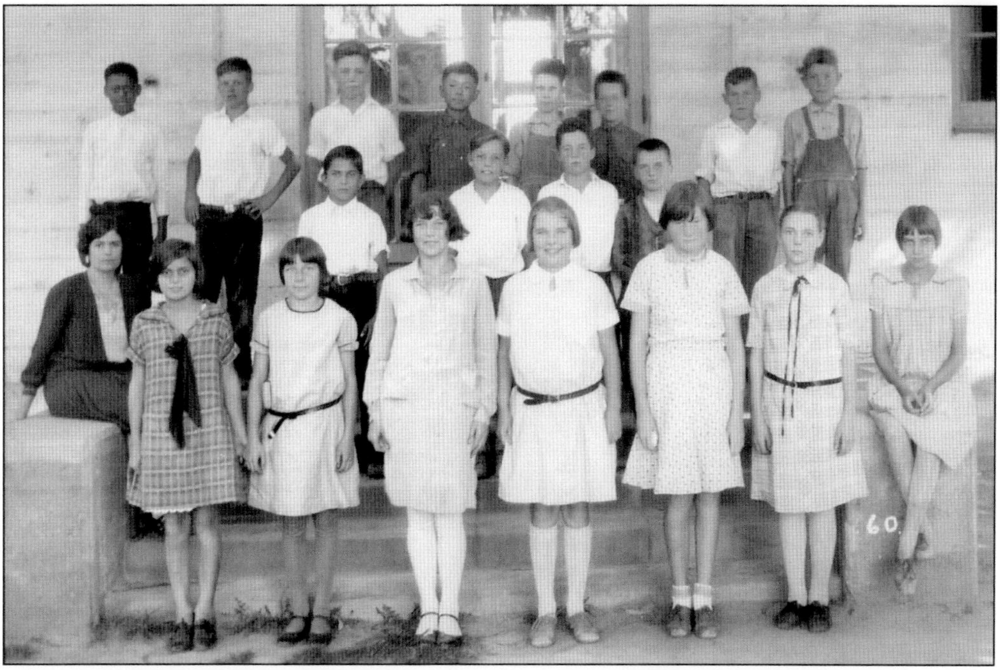

WEST RIVERSIDE SCHOOL. This photograph was taken in 1929. The schools name had been changed to West Riverside 14 years before. (Courtesy Jensen family.)

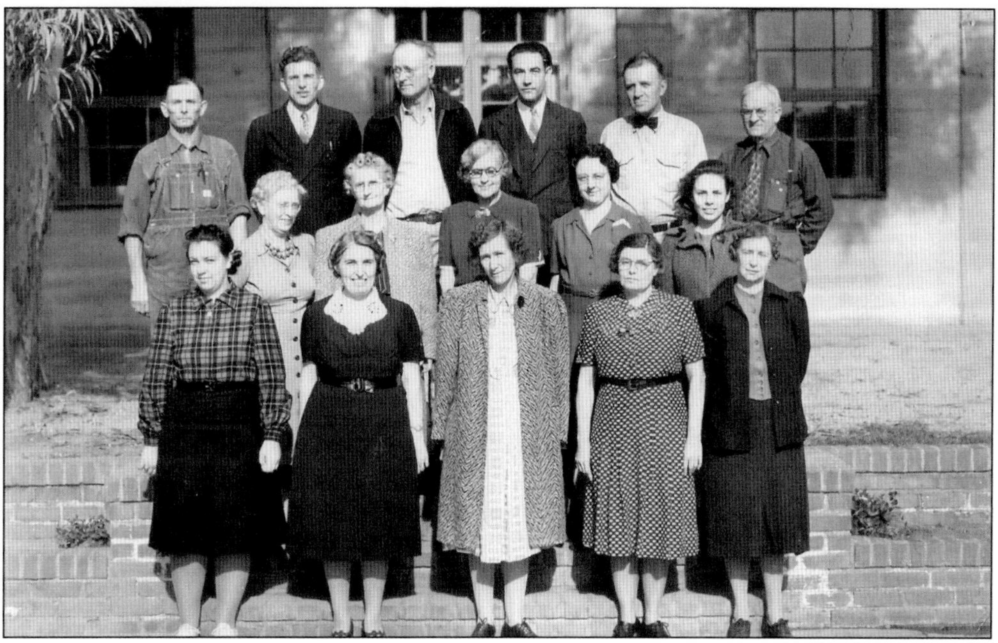

WEST RIVERSIDE SCHOOL STAFF, 1941. In 1941, teachers and staff of the West Riverside School, identified by their last name only, from left to right, are (first row) Bitz 1st grade; Arbuckle, 5th grade; Fauste, cafeteria; Hall, vice principal and 6th grade; and Vickerson, 1st grade; (second row) Wright 3rd grade; Scott, cafeteria; Withrow, 4th grade; LaRue, 4th grade; and Brink, office; (third row) Fauste, janitor; Miller, principal; Scott, janitor; Bailey, 7th grade; Brink, bus driver; and Yeager, manual training. (Courtesy Jurupa Unified School District.)

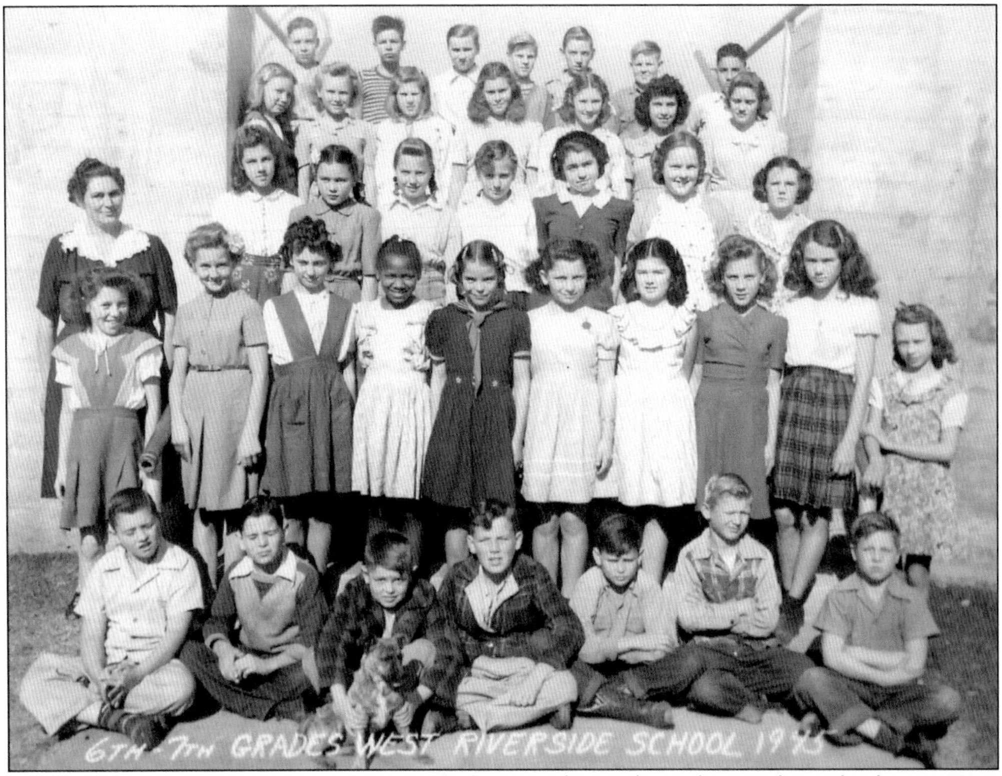

WEST RIVERSIDE SCHOOL, 1945. In 1945, this was the sixth- and seventh-grade class at West Riverside School. (Courtesy Dorothy Thorson Evans.)

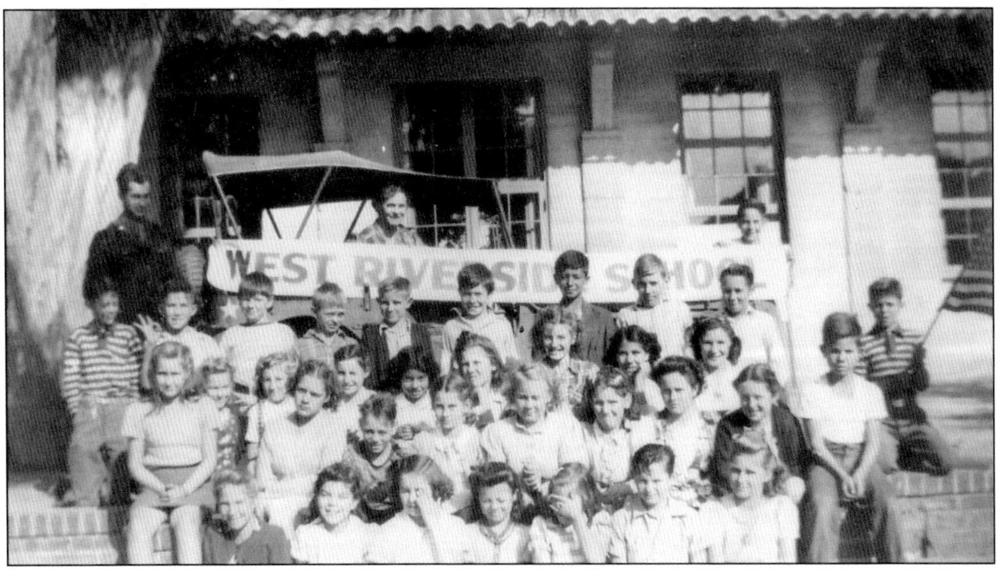

JEEP AT WEST RIVERSIDE SCHOOL. During World War II, West Riverside School held a scrap metal drive. The students collected as much scrap metal as they could, saving even the aluminum off of gum wrappers. When they had collected enough money, they bought a jeep for the army. When the brand new jeep was brought to the school, every child got a ride, and every class had their picture taken with it. This is the fifth-grade class of Eva Engelauf. (Courtesy Engelauf/Flowers families.)

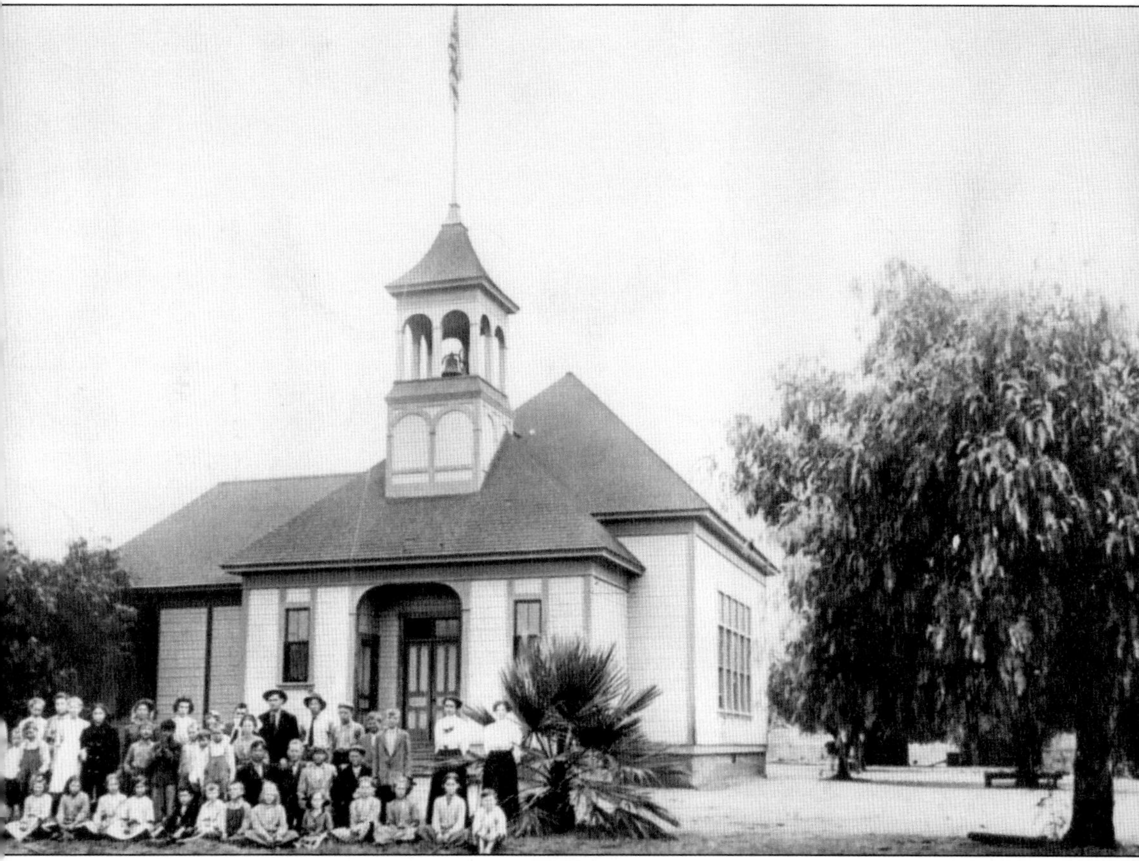

GLEN AVON SCHOOL. When the first school building on Tyrolite Street became inadequate, John R. Johnston deeded two acres on Pyrite Street to the newly organized West Riverside School District for a new school. The deed was recorded on November 19, 1894. A new wooden schoolhouse, shown here, was built during 1895. It was a one-room school, with a cloakroom at the entry facing Pyrite Street. The school and school district's name was changed to Glen Avon in 1909 after the community voted to change its name from West Riverside. (To avoid confusion, these early pictures of the West Riverside School will be identified by the later name of Glen Avon School.) (Courtesy Jurupa Unified School District.)

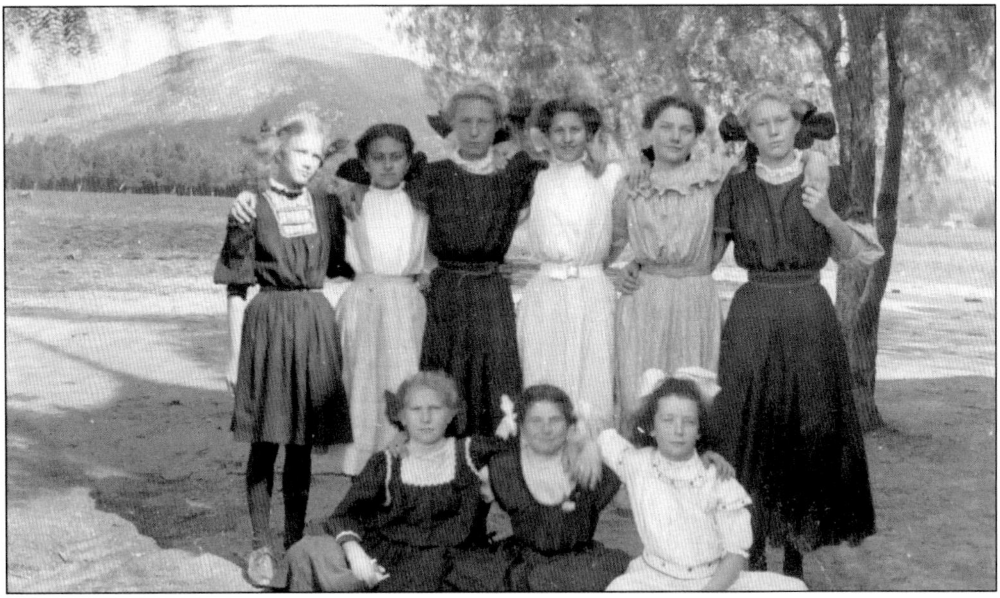

GLEN AVON SCHOOL, 1908–1909. These two photographs show students at Glen Avon School the year that the community changed its name from West Riverside to Glen Avon. The following September, the school and school district followed suit and changed their names as well. (Courtesy Riverside Metropolitan Museum.)

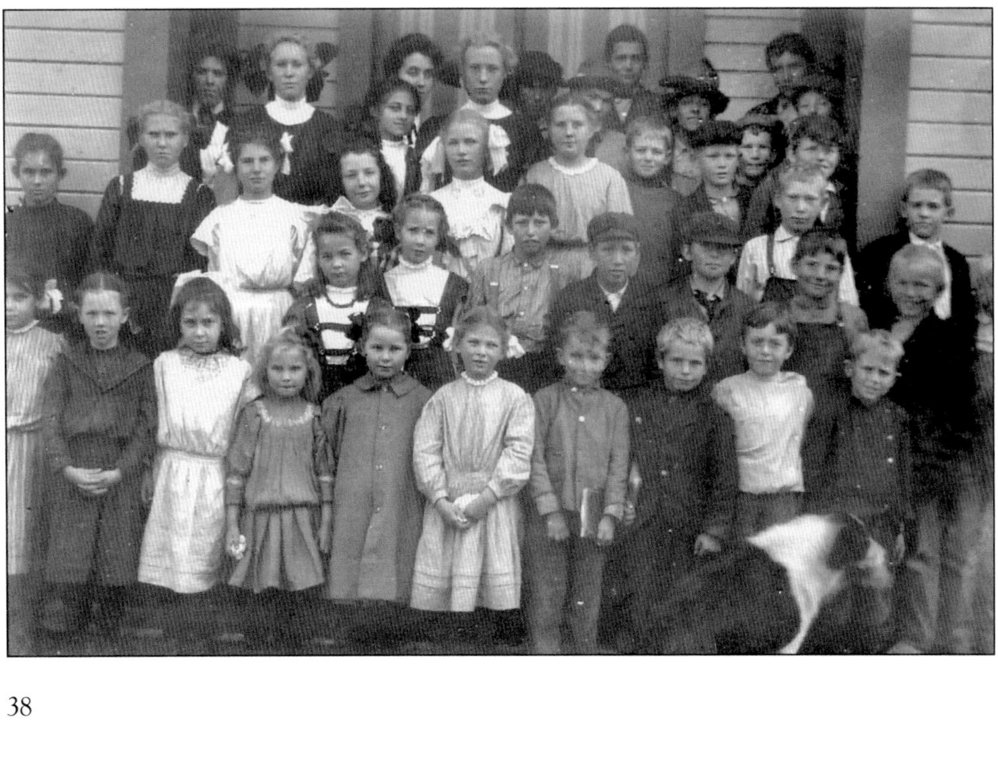

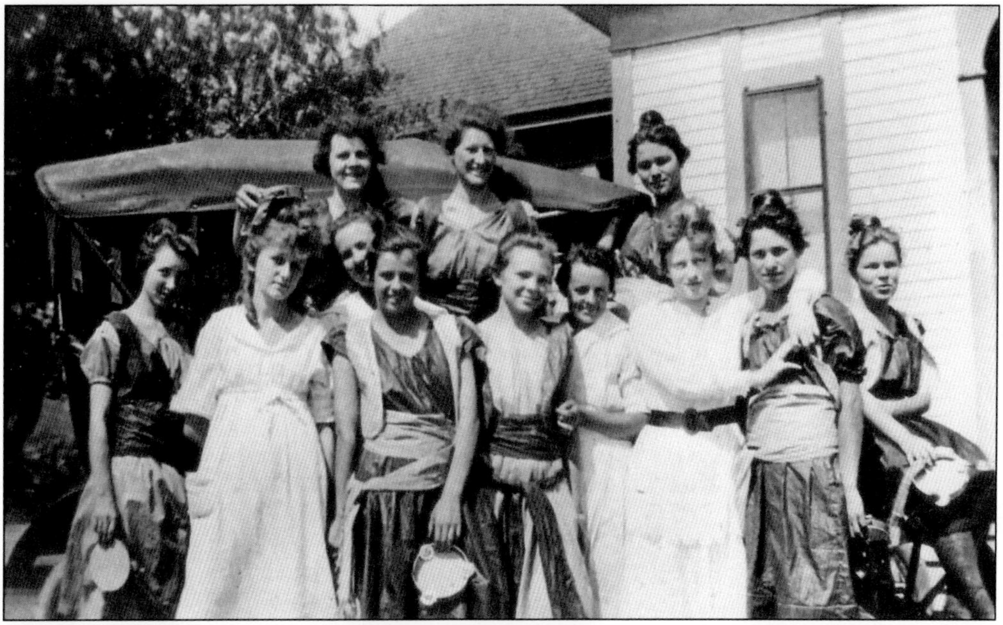

TAMBOURINE BAND. This is the girl's tambourine band in 1918 at Glen Avon School. (Courtesy Jurupa Mountains Cultural Center.)

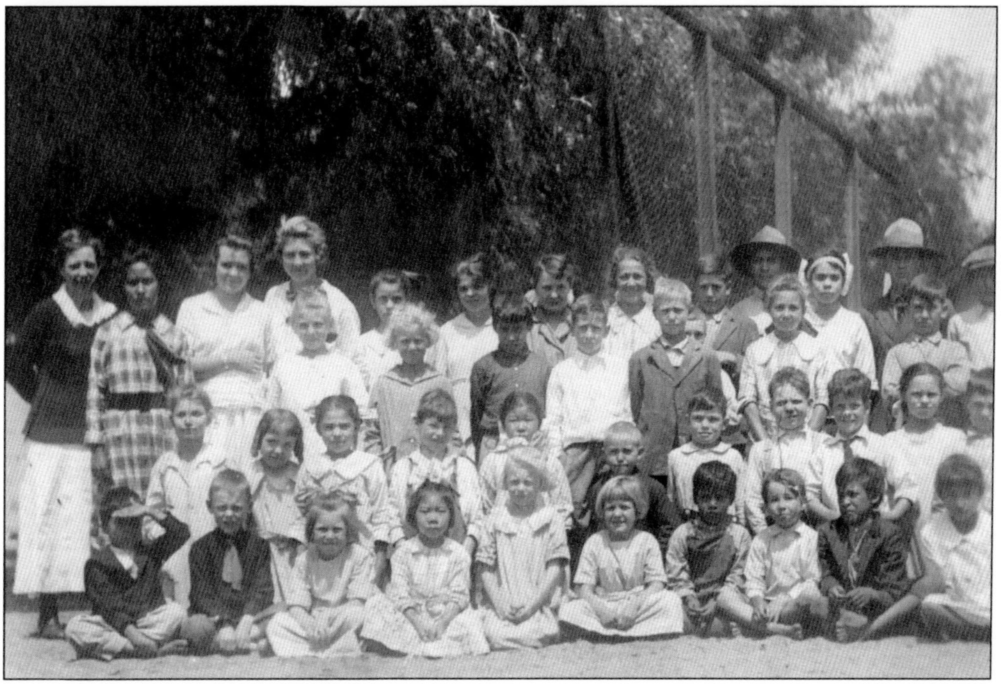

STUDENT BODY OF GLEN AVON SCHOOL, 1919. Donated to the Jurupa Unified School District, this photograph from an early scrapbook shows members of the student body. School enrollment in 1919 was 57 with students divided into grades one through eight. The bell in the school's bell tower was paid for through subscription among the school's patrons. It later developed a crack, and when citizens were urged to donate metal for ammunition during World War I, the bell was sold for scrap. (Courtesy Jurupa Unified School District.)

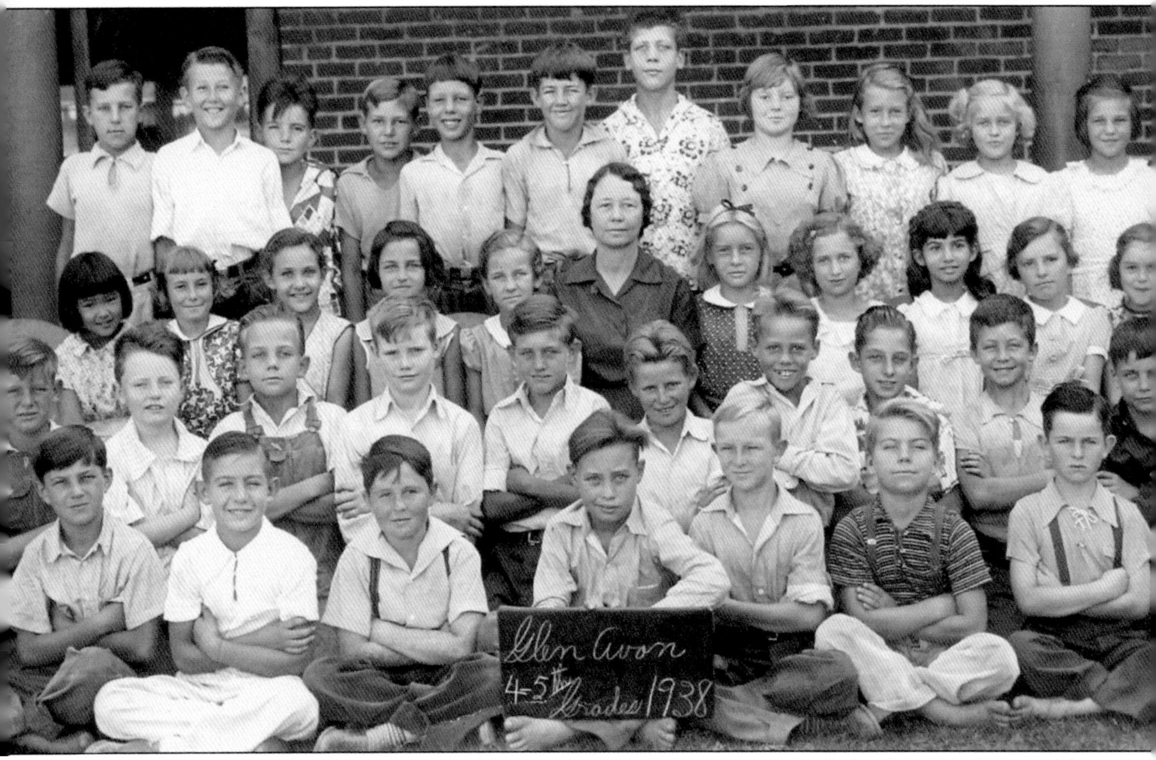

GLEN AVON SCHOOL. This 1938 photograph shows the second- and third-grade class at Glen Avon School. By 1921–1922, 113 children were attending the school. The school building built in 1895 was not large enough to accommodate that many children. In 1922, a new school was built. It was a brick building with four classrooms, an office, a kitchen, and an auditorium—all laid out in U shape. The school had a red tile roof, giving it a Spanish architectural style. As the Glen Avon School District continued to grow, this school expanded with additional classroom wings. The present Glen Avon School eventually replaced the 1922 school. (Courtesy Cates family.)

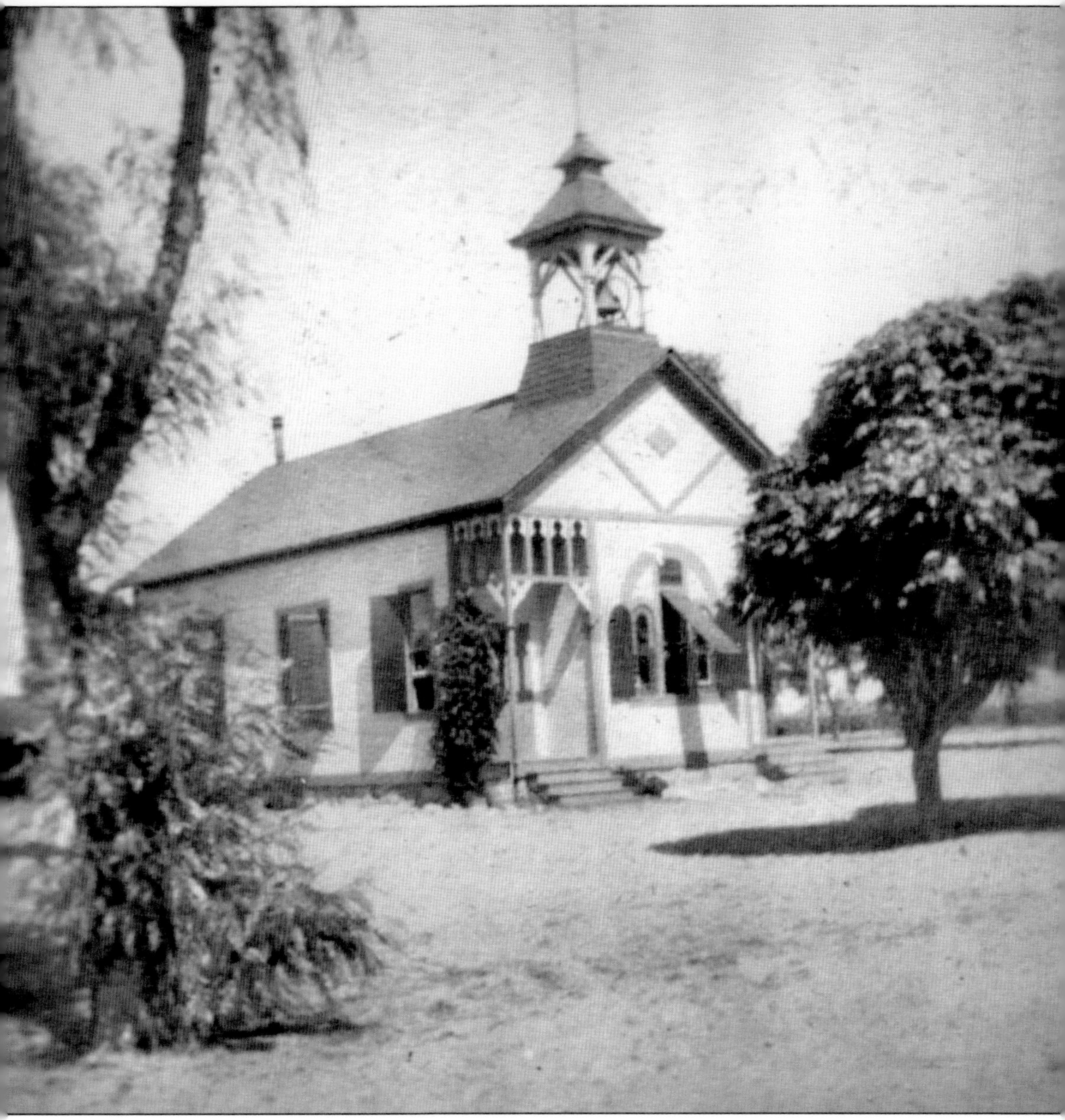

Pleasant Valley School. In 1888, A. J. Stadler donated land for a school in what is now the Mira Loma area. Lumber and labor were donated by the men of the district to build the school, which was named Pleasant Valley School. When Riverside County was formed in 1893 from portions of San Bernardino and San Diego Counties, it contained another Pleasant Valley School District in the Winchester area. Because two districts in the same county couldn't have the same name, the Jurupa area Pleasant Valley School District changed its name to that of its election precinct—Union. It included children from both Riverside and San Bernardino Counties so it was a joint district, becoming Union Joint School. Built in 1892, this school was located where Etiwanda currently intersects the 60 Freeway. (Courtesy Jurupa Unified School District.)

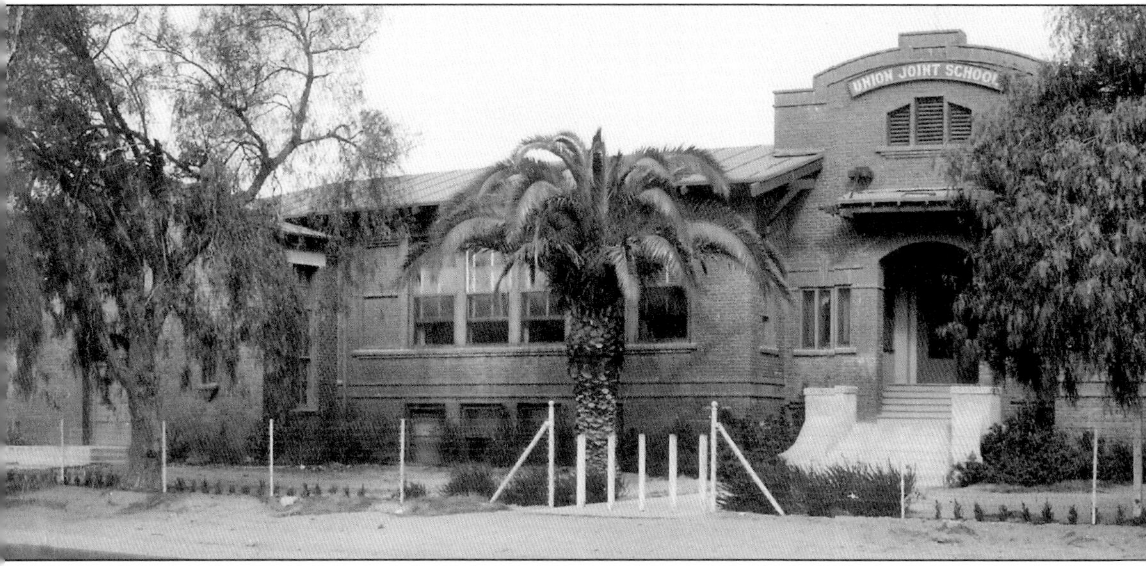

UNION JOINT SCHOOL. Growth in the student population caused a new Union Joint School to be built in 1915. It had a Mission Revival style of architecture. An auditorium and more classrooms

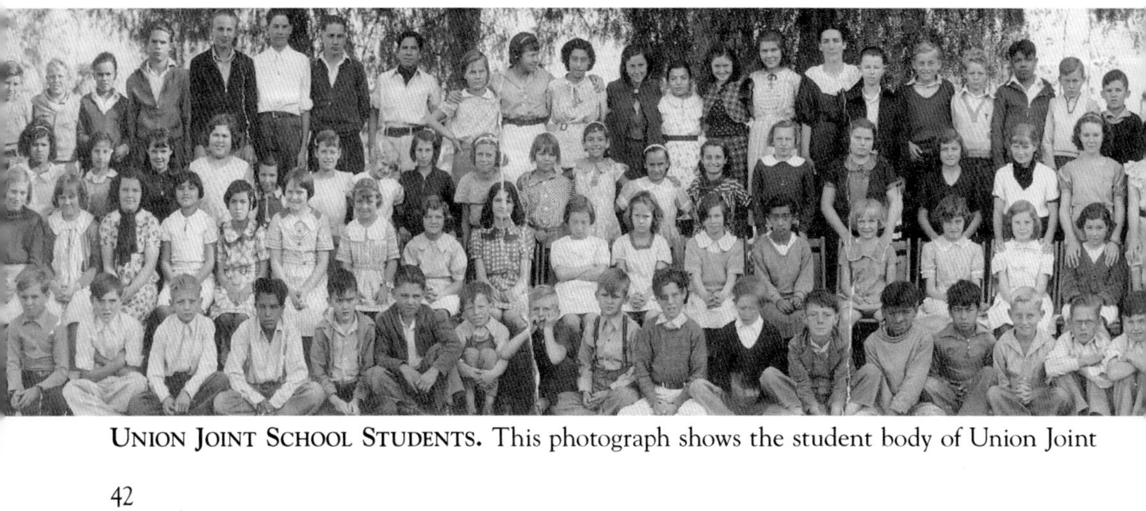

UNION JOINT SCHOOL STUDENTS. This photograph shows the student body of Union Joint

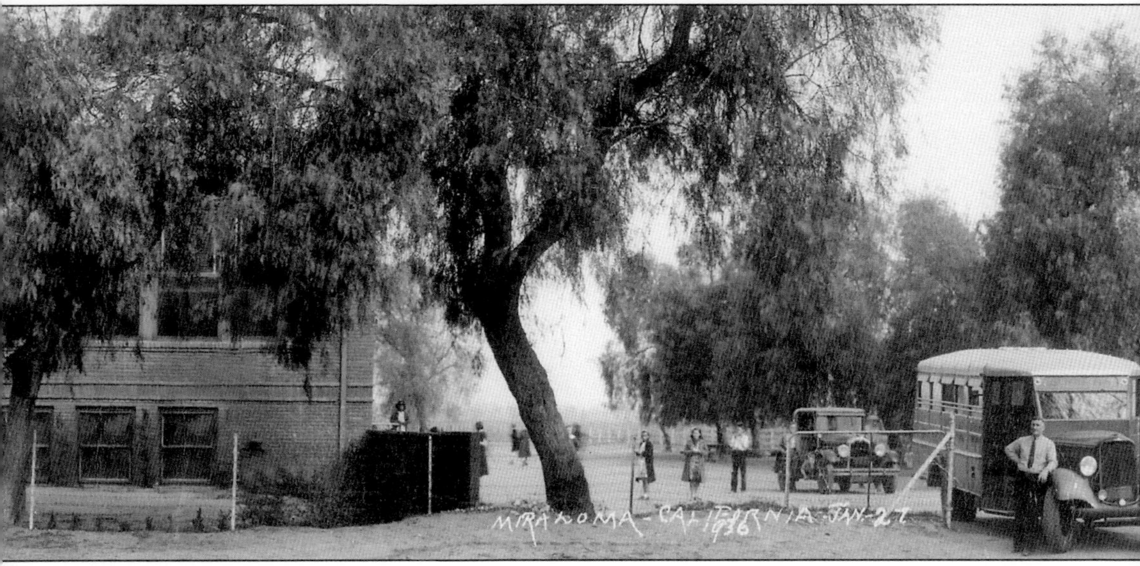

were added later. This photograph shows the school in 1936. The school was sold by the district in 1959 and demolished in 1989. (Courtesy George Miller family.)

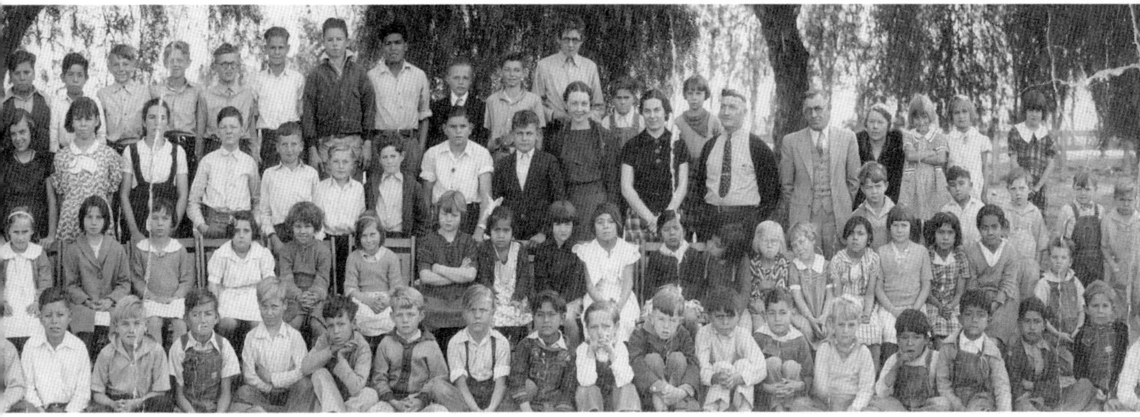

School, c. 1936.

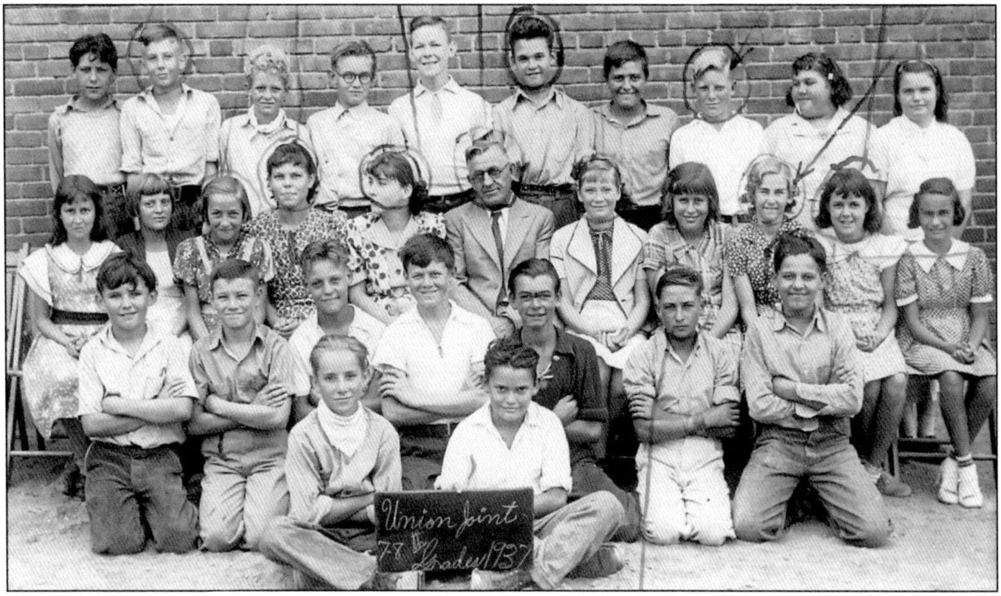

UNION JOINT SCHOOL, 1937. This is the seventh- and eighth-grade class at Union Joint School in Mira Loma. (Courtesy Cates family.)

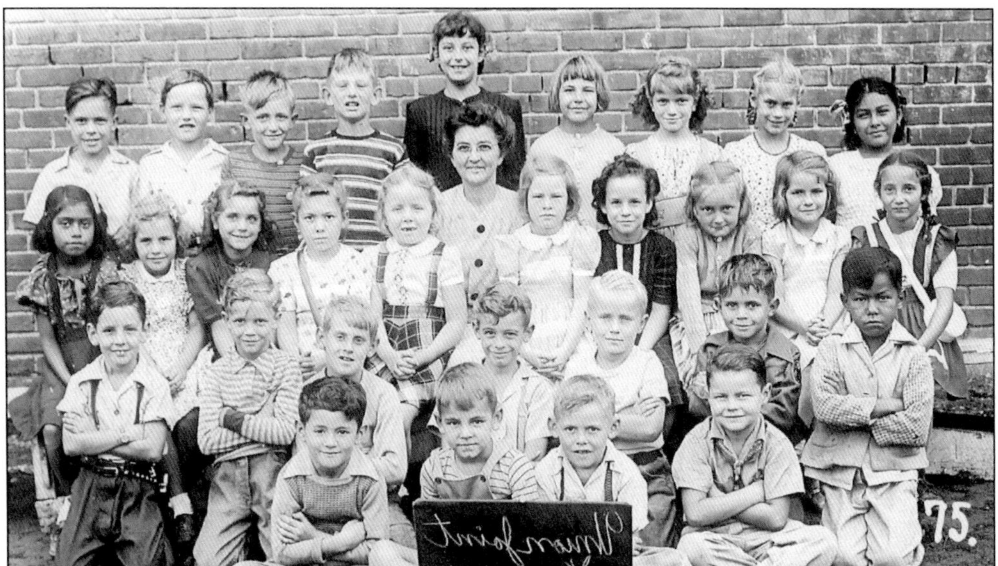

SECOND- AND THIRD-GRADE CLASS. Mrs. Raymer's second- and third-grade class at Union Joint School is pictured here in 1946. (Courtesy Ethel Chavez Sanborn.)

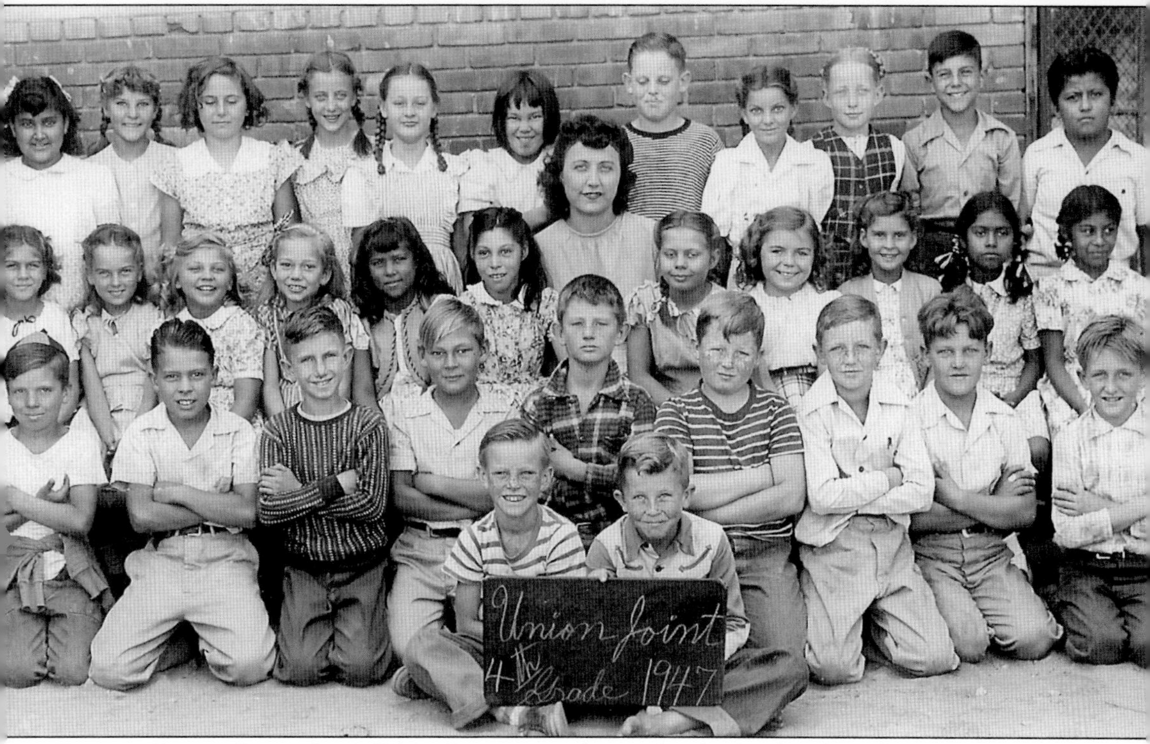

FOURTH-GRADE CLASS. In 1947, Mrs. Raymer was the teacher for this fourth-grade class at Union Joint School. (Courtesy Ethel Chavez Sanborn.)

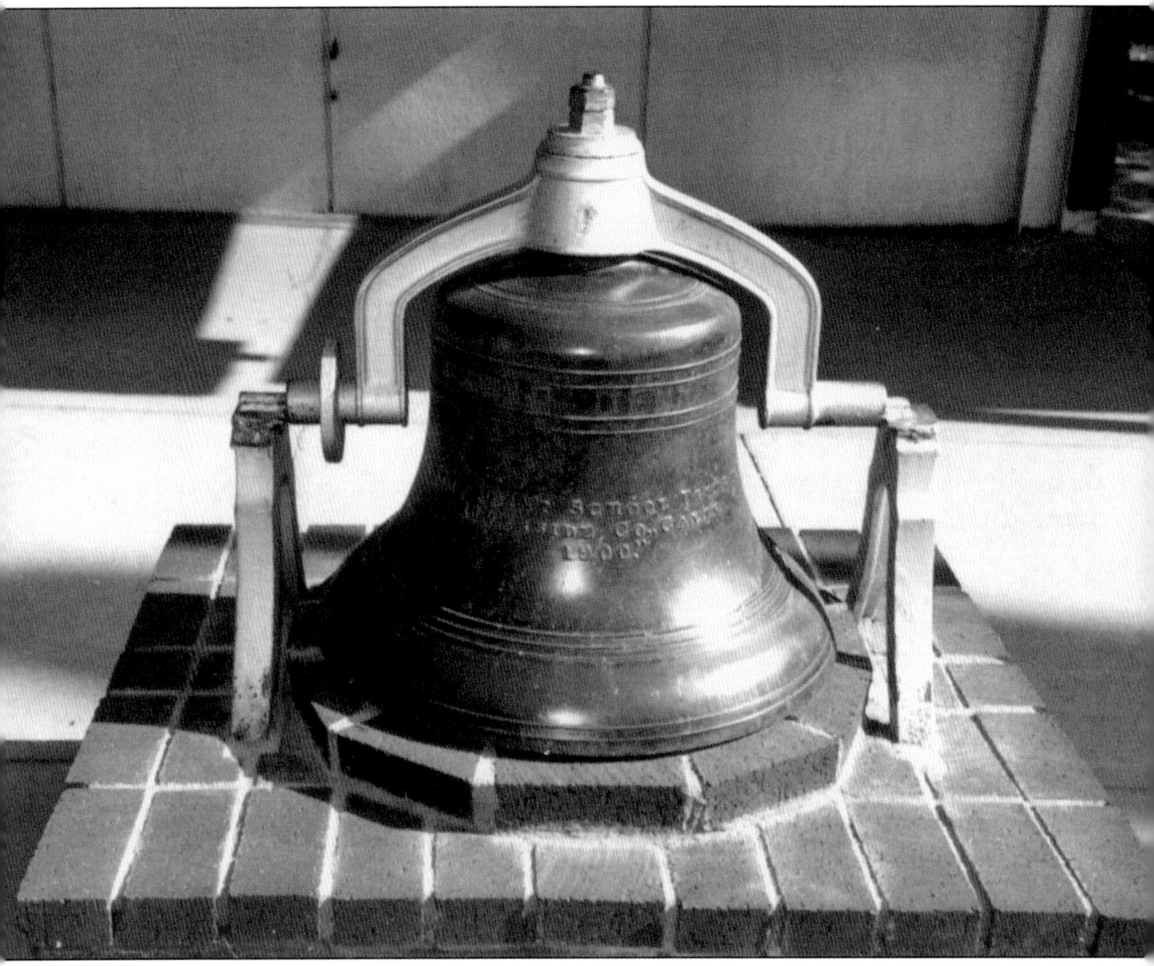

UNION JOINT BELL. The Union School was replaced by Mission Bell School on Conning Street in Glen Avon. The bell from Union School, dated 1900, was placed at the new school, giving the school its name. (Courtesy author.)

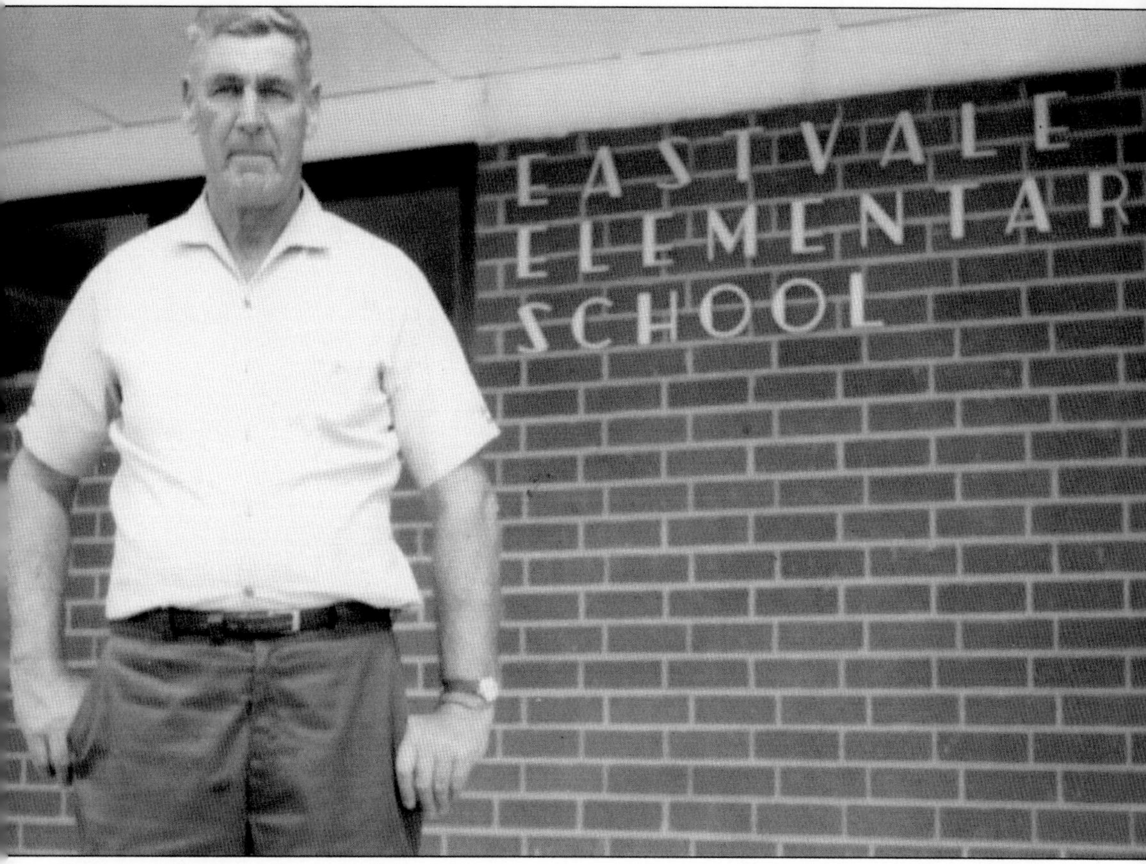

EASTVALE SCHOOL. Eastvale School District was named as one of the 52 districts in existence when Riverside County was formed in 1893. The Eastvale School was located on Cleveland Avenue between Orange Street and Schleisman Road. In 1947, it became part of the Corona Unified School District, now the Corona/Norco Unified School District. The two-room Eastvale School was used until 1958 when a new Eastvale School opened. Incorporating it as part of the new Eastvale Elementary School, a portion of the school built in 1958 will still serve students of Eastvale. This photograph, taken in 1976, shows Marcel De Leenheer, an Eastvale student from the 1920s, in front of the 1958 Eastvale School. The origin of the Eastvale name is not known. (Courtesy Martha Vanderham.)

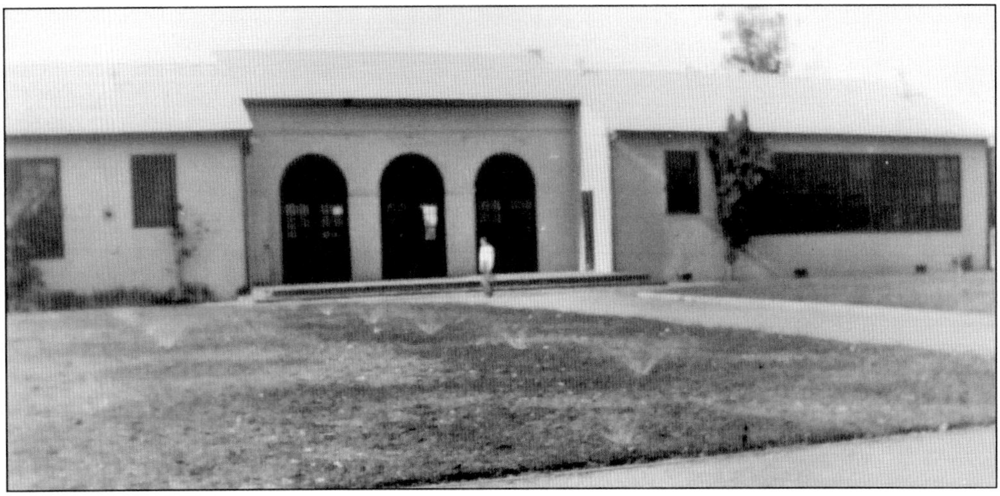

PEDLEY SCHOOL. Around 1911, a one-room schoolhouse was built in Pedley, located at the southeast corner of Limonite Avenue and Archer Street. When it became too small, it was replaced in 1930 by this three-room schoolhouse. The middle room was an auditorium with a stage and the other two rooms were used for classes. A 1930 publication of the County Superintendent of Schools showing the boundaries of all county school districts called this the Jurupa Heights School District. Sometime between 1930 and 1953, the name of the school district was changed to Pedley. (Courtesy Julie and Del Coats.)

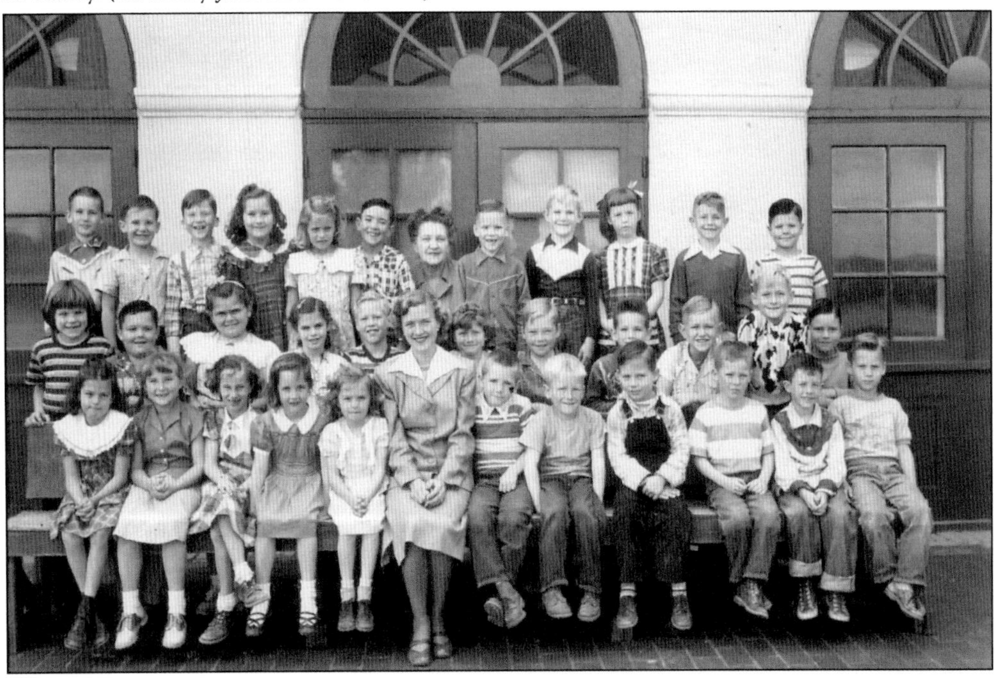

PEDLEY SCHOOL CLASS. This is the first- and second-grade class of Pedley School in 1951–1952. Due to the size of the class, two teaches shared the classroom. In the front row is Mrs. Nelson and in the back row is Mrs. Chapman. Note the fan-shaped windows. These three windows were a distinctive feature of the 1930 Pedley School. Sam's Western Wear was later built on the site of the old Pedley School but incorporated the old school building. The school windows can still be seen inside the store. (Courtesy Julie and Del Coats.)

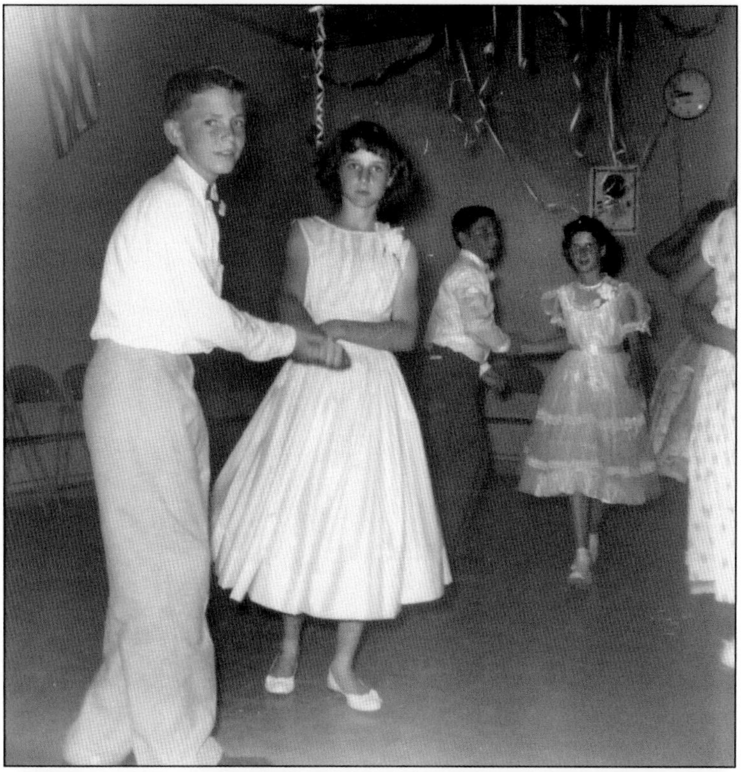

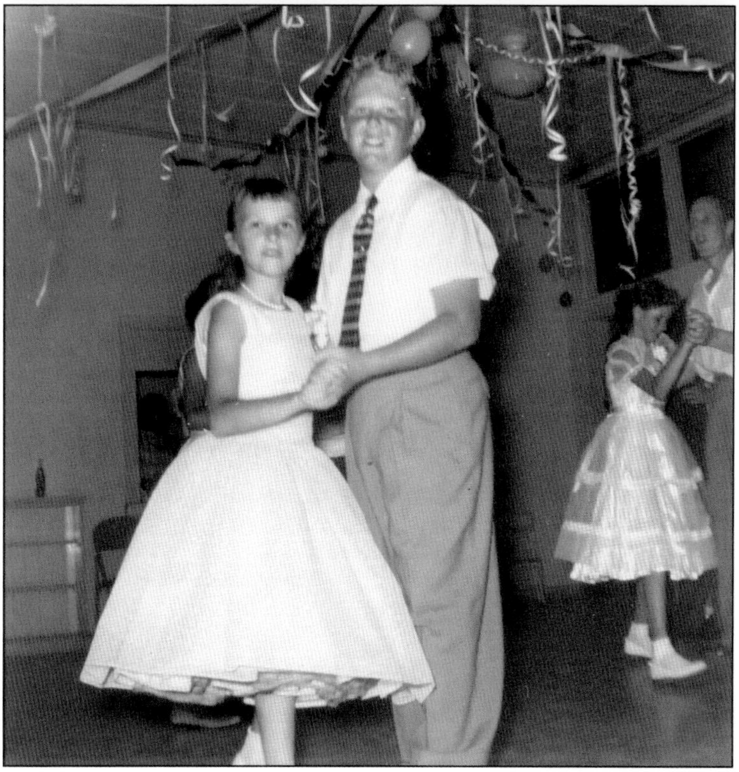

SIXTH-GRADE GRADUATION DANCE. The 1956–1957 sixth-grade class at Pedley Elementary School celebrated the end of their elementary school years with a dance. The top photograph shows Rick Coats dancing with Rheta Lee Blevins. The bottom photograph shows Carolyn Todd and Terry Bockman. (Courtesy Julie and Del Coats.)

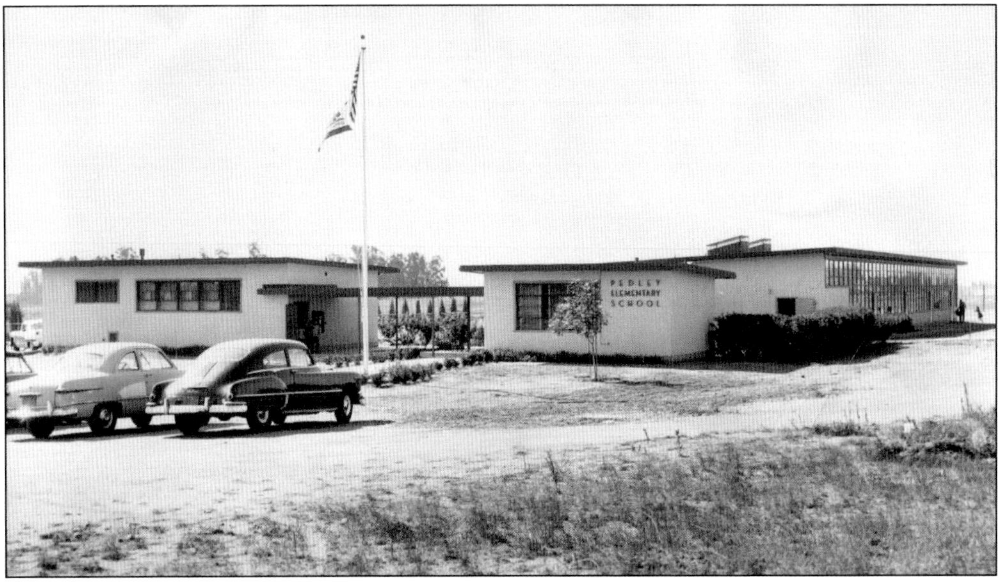

New Pedley School. The three-room Pedley School built in 1930 became more crowded and planning for a new school was undertaken. The new school, built in the mid-1950s, had something the old school did not have—an office with a desk for the school secretary. At the old school, the secretary had to sit at a table in the kitchen. This photograph, taken during the 1957–1958 school year, shows the office to the right with the school's name on it. (Courtesy Julie and Del Coats.)

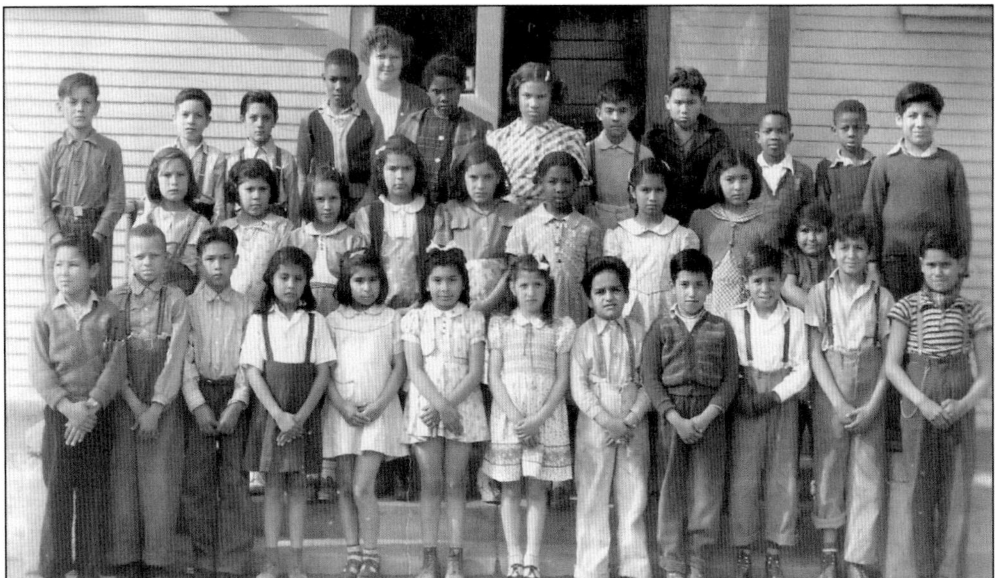

Belltown School Class, 1942. First subdivided in 1907, and further subdivided in 1914 and 1924, Belltown, named by and for the original subdivider, N. R. Bell, was primarily populated by Mexican immigrant families and their descendants—especially before World War II. There were also a very small number of Italian and African American families. Belltown School, located on Hall Avenue across from the Our Lady of Guadalupe Catholic Church, was built in 1920. It closed in 1956 and its students moved to the new Ina Arbuckle School in Rubidoux. (Courtesy Bermudez family.)

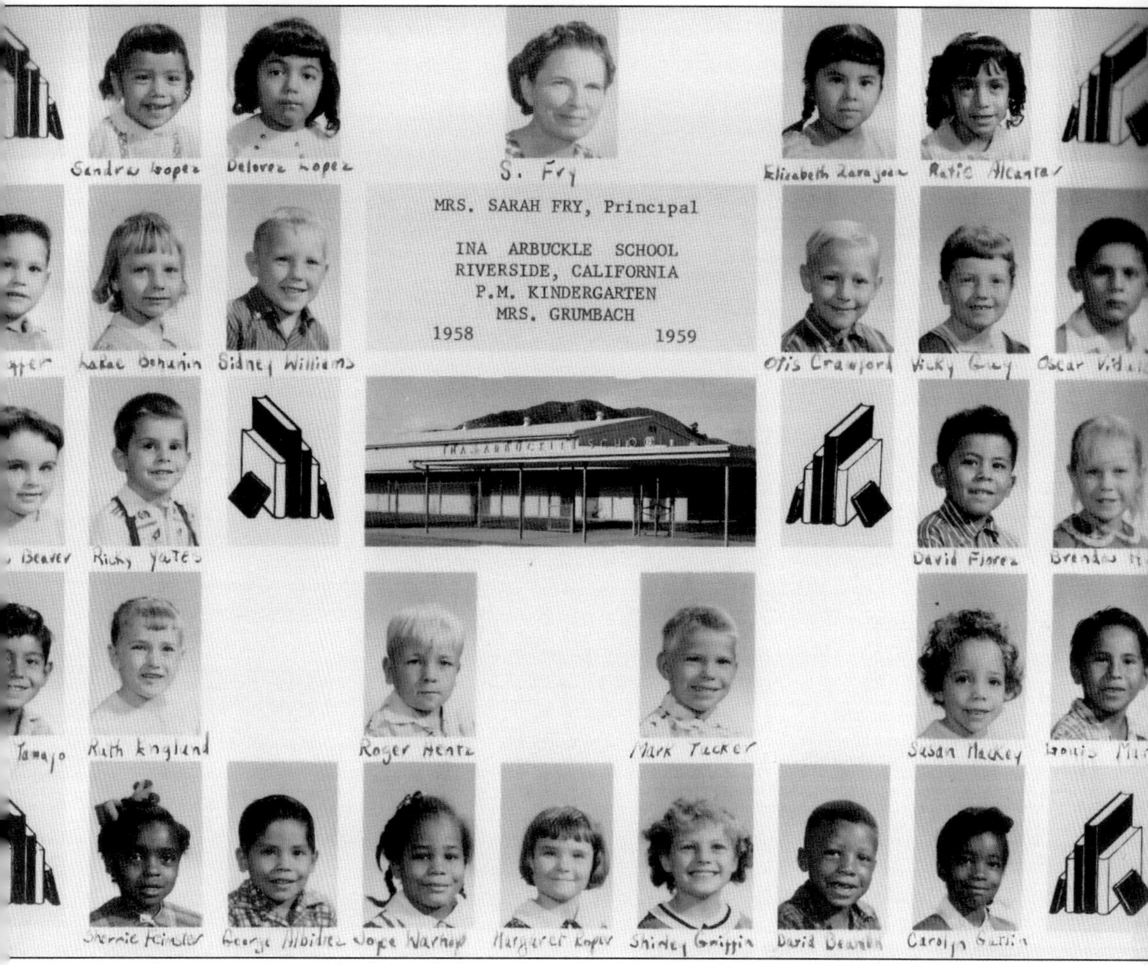

INA ARBUCKLE SCHOOL. This photograph shows Mrs. Grumbach's P.M. kindergarten class during the 1958–1959 school year at Ina Arbuckle School. The students in this class reflect the diversity of the population in the Rubidoux area in the late 1950s. (Courtesy Ina Arbuckle School.)

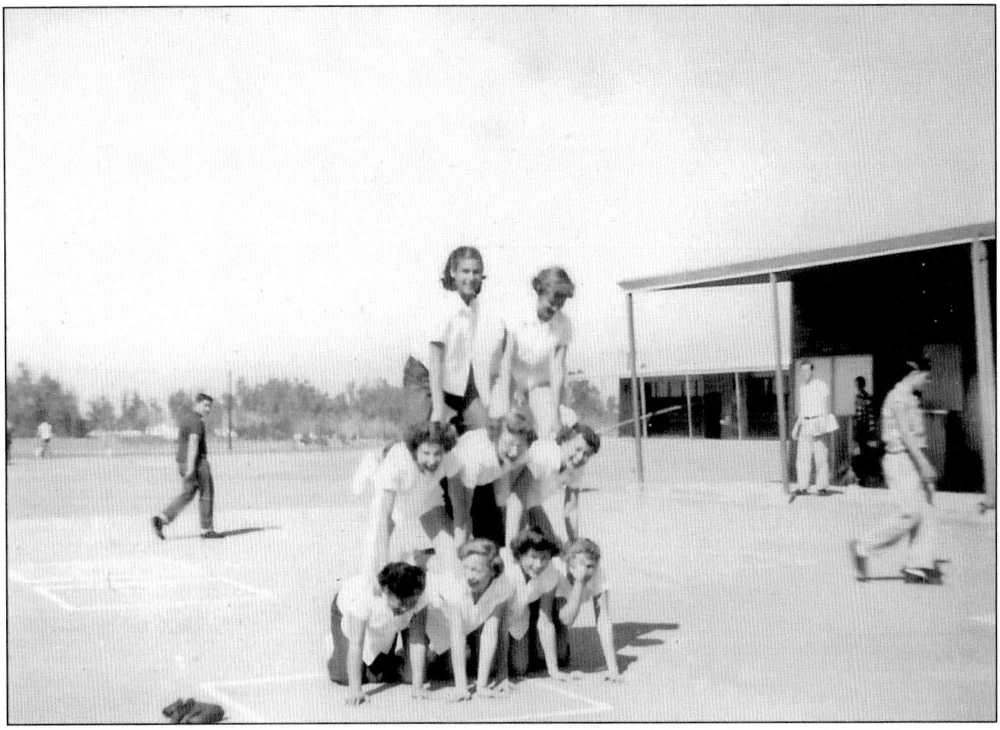

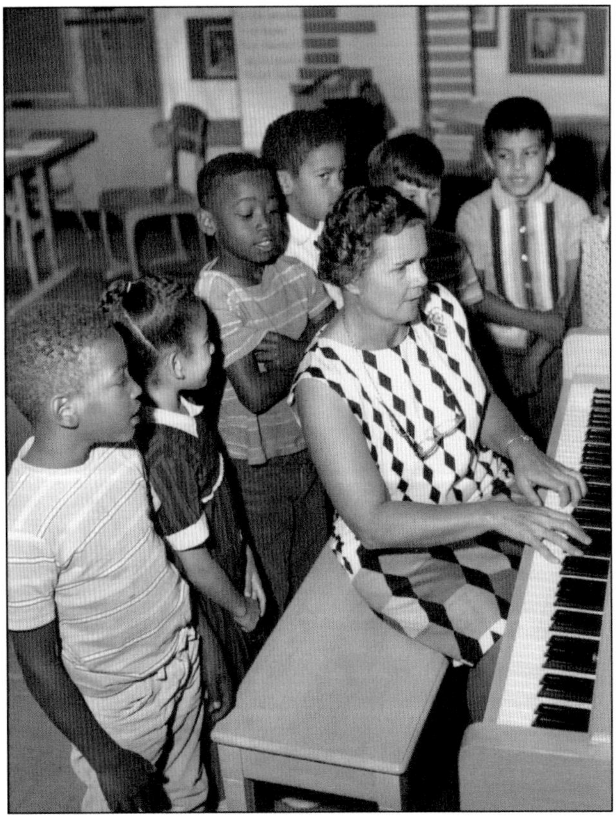

JURUPA JUNIOR HIGH SCHOOL. Before 1949, Jurupa students had to go by bus to Riverside to attend junior high and high school. Parents were very happy when Jurupa Junior High opened on the south side of Galena Street and the long bus ride could be postponed until high school. This 1953 photograph shows girls in Miss Openshaw's physical education class. Pictured in the pyramid, from left to right, are (first row) Lola Inaba, Zoe Oxford, Kate Barragan, and Deanna Spridgeon; (second row) Paula Woolfolk, Joan Van Allen, and Carolyn Wendelin; (third row) Rhea Diehl and Joyce Petmecky. (Courtesy Ethel Chavez Sanborn.)

SCHOOL LIFE IN THE 1960S. This photograph is from the files of the Jurupa Unified School District. (Courtesy Jurupa Unified School District.)

Four

Community Life

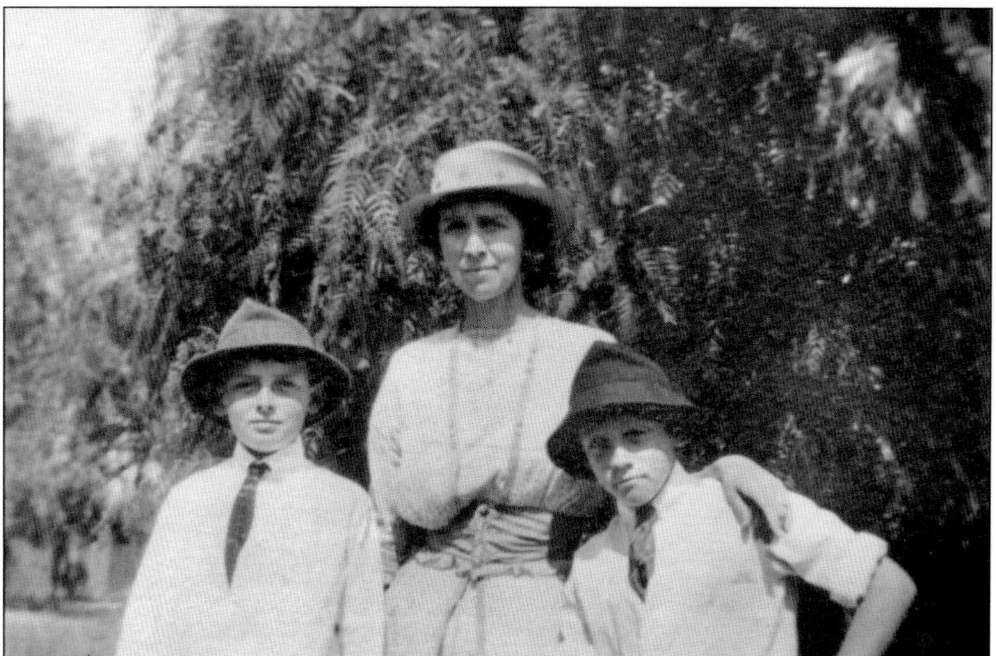

West Riverside Friendship Circle. This photograph shows the second president of the West Riverside Friendship Circle, Mrs. C. N. Sheldon, and her two sons. This woman's group was founded in 1912 and continued until 1977. It was organized by a few women who felt the need for more social life in the community. At their first meeting, they sewed together a quilt that was given to a underprivileged family in the area. (Courtesy Riverside County Regional Park and Open-Space District.)

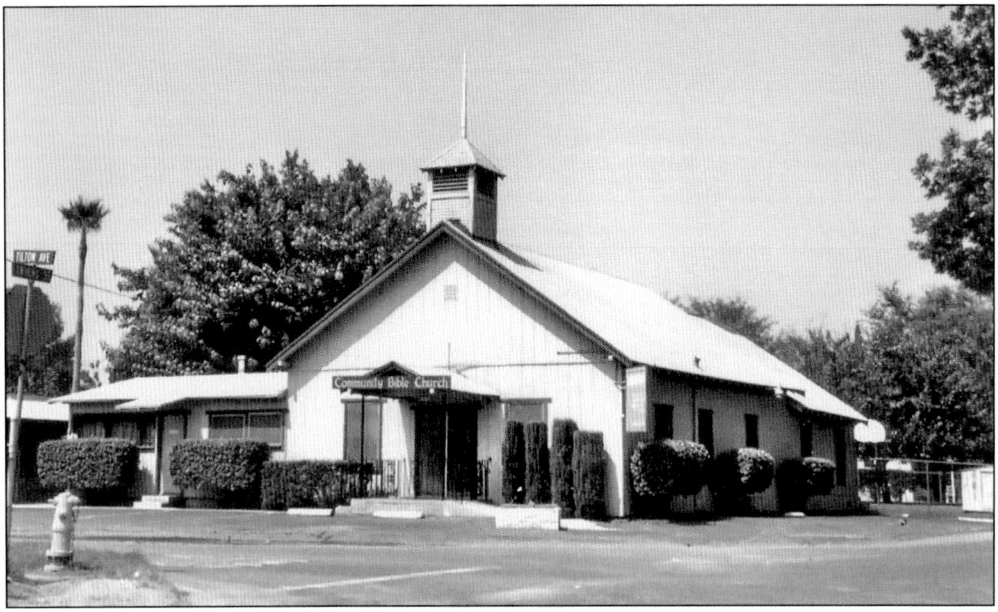

FORT FREMONT COMMUNITY CHURCH. Around 1900, a Sunday school was started and its members met in the Jurupa School. In 1925, it was moved to a commercial building on Mission Boulevard in West Riverside, closer to the families moving into the Fort Fremont subdivision. The Sunday school grew and in 1927 bought property at the corner of Tilton and Twining Streets. There a small building was built and called Fort Fremont Sunday School. Beginning in the early 1940s, ministers were brought in to preach on a regular basis. In early 1945, it formally organized as Fort Fremont Community Church. It is now known as Community Bible Church. (Courtesy author.)

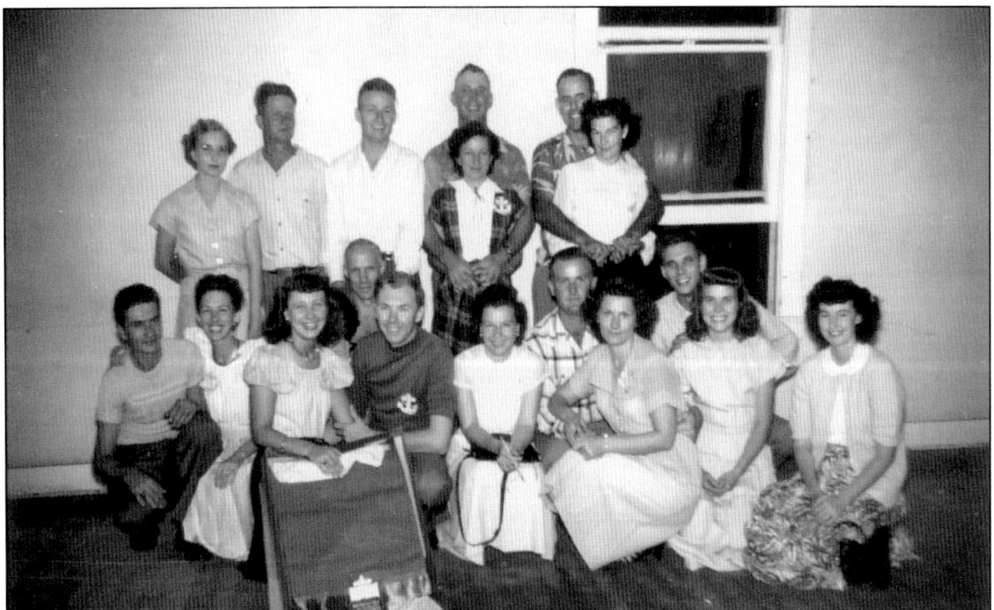

MARINER'S CLUB, 1950. This adult club was formed at the Fort Fremont Community Church to perform community service. (Courtesy Ruby Dickinson.)

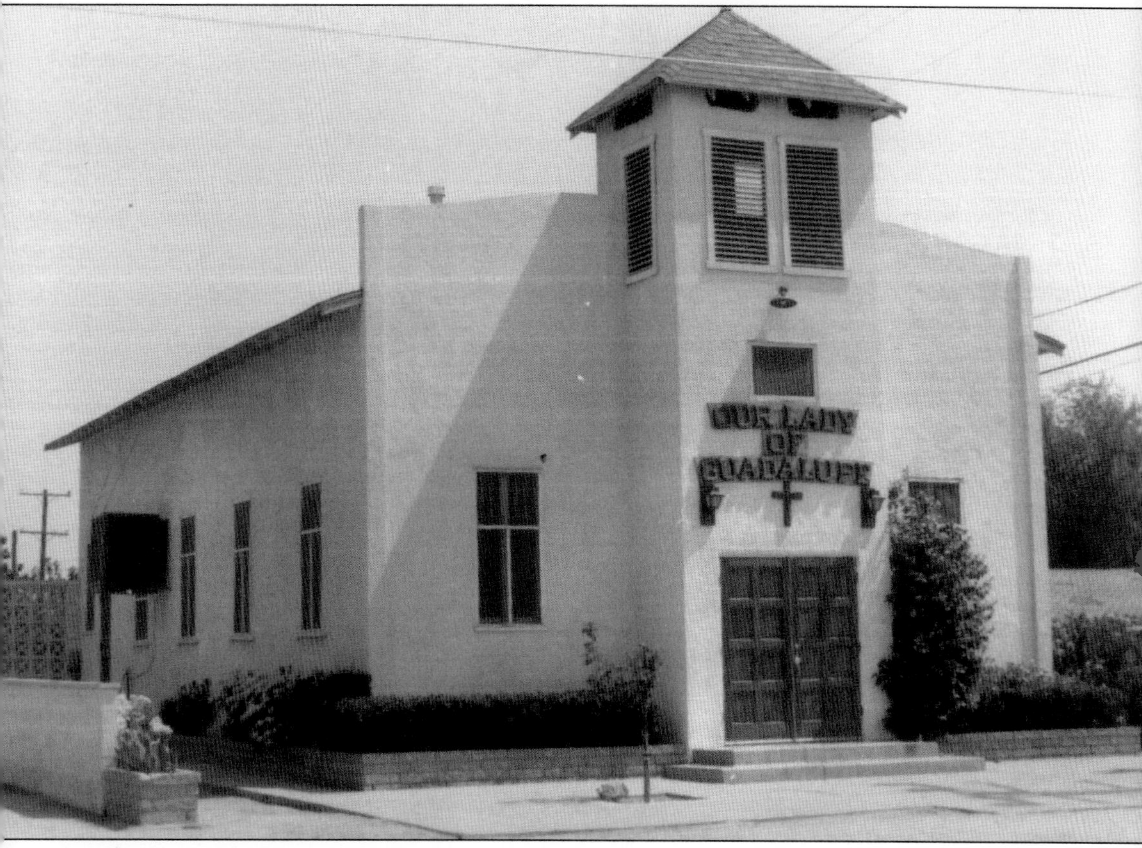

OUR LADY OF GUADALUPE CHURCH. In 1927, Our Lady of Guadalupe Church was founded in Belltown on Hall Avenue. At that time, the Catholic Diocese was responding to an influx of Mexican immigrants who came to this area after the Mexican Revolution. A total of three churches were built, all named Our Lady of Guadalupe. The three churches were located in Belltown, Highrove, and Riverside's eastside. The Belltown church remains an active mission church. (Riverside County Regional Park and Open-Space District.)

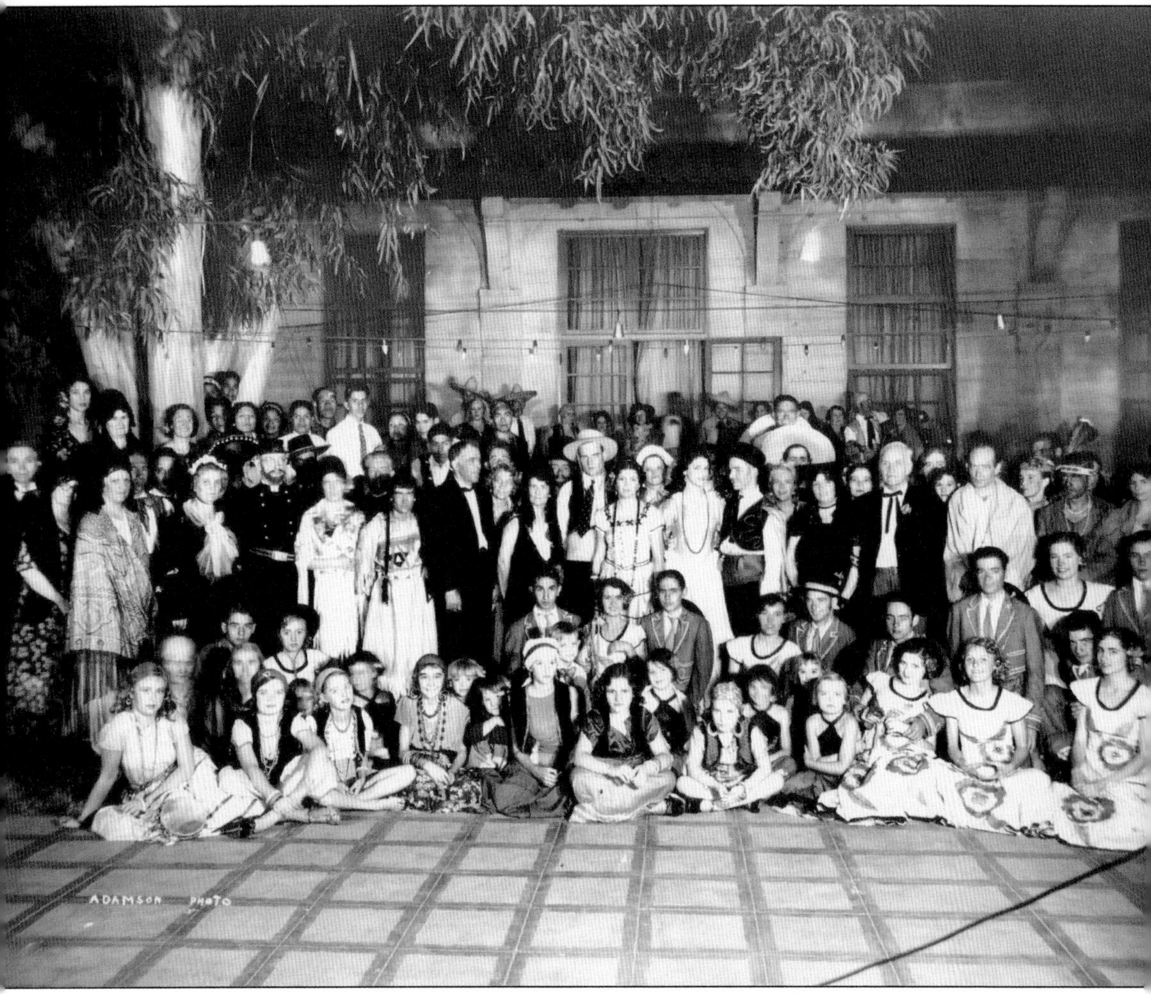

WEST RIVERSIDE HARVEST FESTIVAL, 1933. The Harvest Festival Association was founded in 1932 during the Great Depression. The Riverside County Fair had merged with the Los Angeles County Fair in Pomona so West Riverside community members decided to start their own fair. They named it the Harvest Festival and had it on the grounds of West Riverside School. After its success in 1932, it was decided in 1933 to make it an annual affair and to add a historical pageant. The first pageant, whose cast is shown here, was written by C. C. Ball of Glen Avon and was called the "Coming of Louis Robidoux and Gen. John Fremont." (Courtesy Jurupa Mountains Cultural Center.)

"West Riverside"
Words and music by Jessie Wright

Verse I
Under a sky of azure, where balmy breezes hide-
Kissed by golden sunshine- our bonny West Riverside;
Land of the citrus orchards- Past lovely homes we ride-
Place of events historic, is our West Riverside.

Chorus
Our own West Riverside; we love, we love you so,
Our hearts are satisfied, no matter where we go-
Our own West Riverside, we love here to abide
The grandest place to know- West Riverside.

Verse II
Green is our fertile valley- For fruit we never want-
Long years ago lived Rubidoux, and the soldiers of Fremont-
Fields full of sweet alfalfa- By Flying Port our pride;
With Bridge of many Blossoms so near West Riverside.

Chorus

Verse III
Just off our Mission Highway, our school our youth doth guide-
Beaming its benediction over our West Riverside-
Place for a jolly party- From far and near they ride,
Business and fun aplenty in our West Riverside.

Chorus

Verse IV
Far-famed for fun aplenty is Harvest Festival
From four great farming districts in gala style come they all-
Vegetables fruit and flowers are seen in lovely booths-
Night sees the lovely drama, that none our hist'ry lose.

Chorus

HARVEST FESTIVAL SONG. An original song was composed by Jesse Wright that was included as part of the Harvest Festival pageant. These are the words to that song. (Courtesy Jurupa Mountains Cultural Center.)

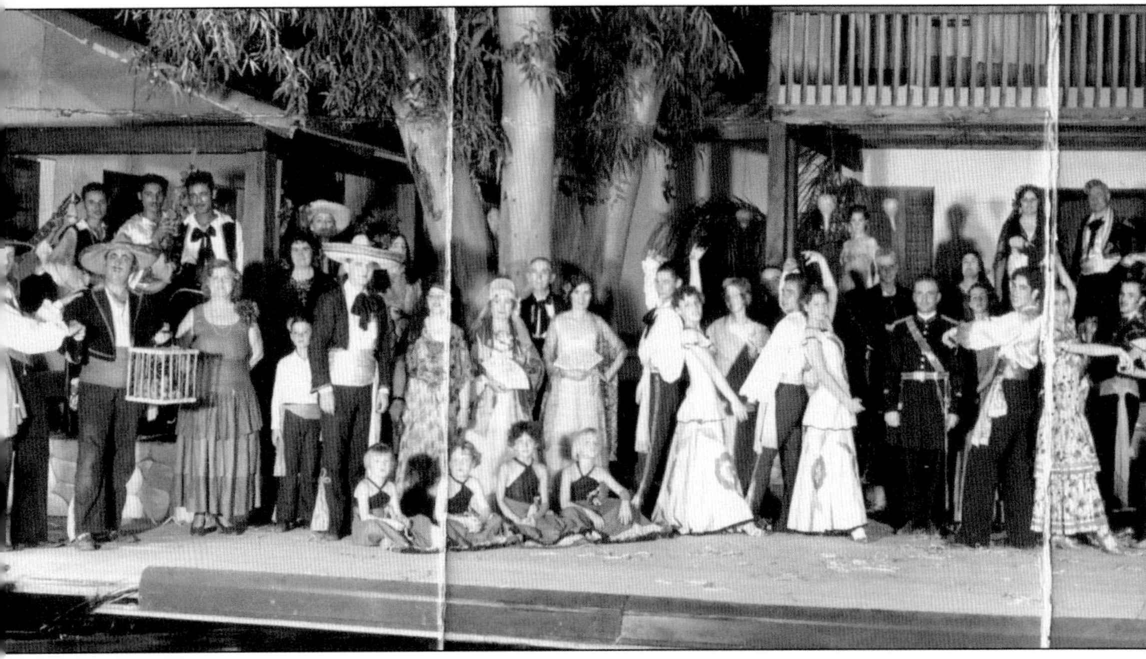

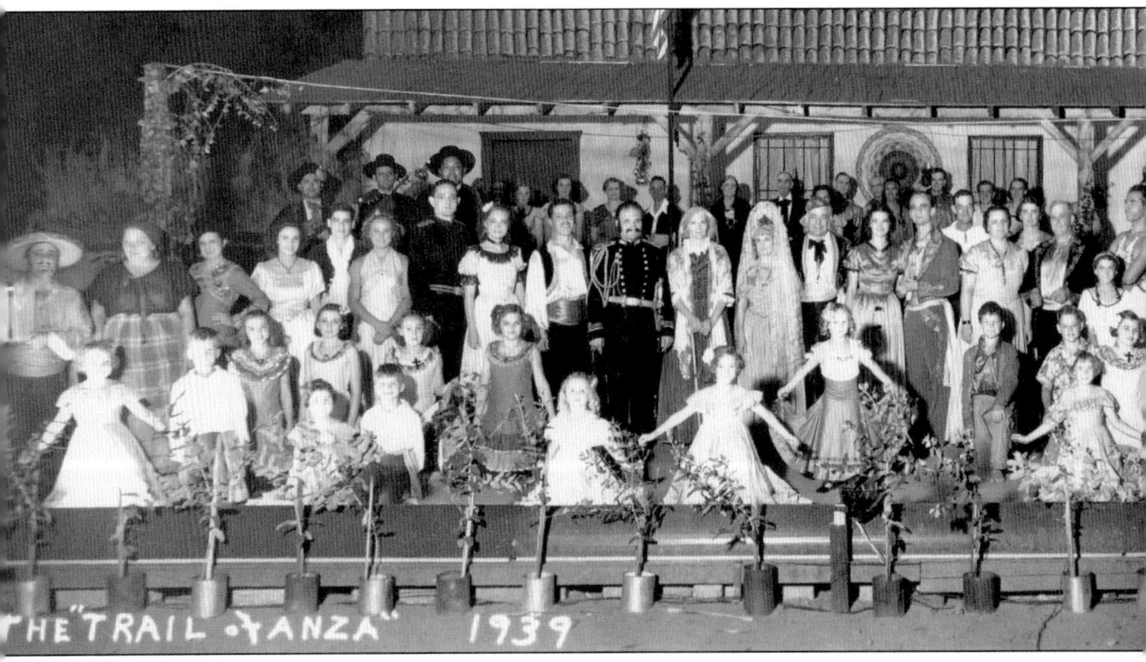
THE "TRAIL of ANZA" 1939

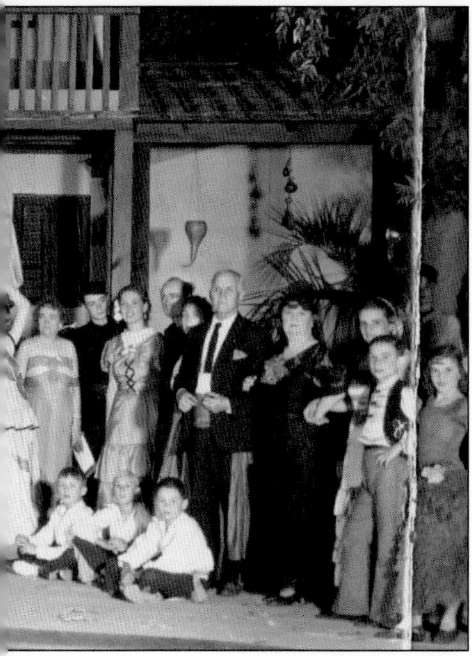

West Riverside Harvest Festival. This is the cast of the 1936 Harvest Festival pageant. In 1935, the pageant was renamed "The Trail of DeAnza," and well-known local citizens such as Roman Warren and Tom Clay played roles in the show. Warren played Pio Pico and Clay, Louis Robidoux. (Courtesy Jurupa Mountains Cultural Center.)

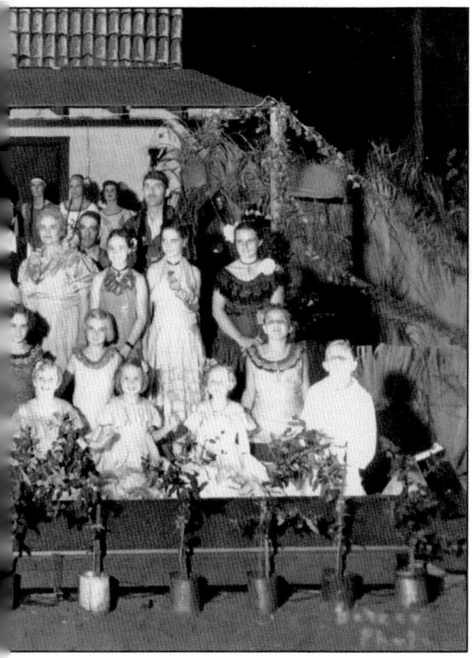

Harvest Festival, 1939. By 1939, the Harvest Festival and its pageant had moved to its permanent home on property purchased on the north side of Mission Boulevard, now the location of the Jurupa Mountains Cultural Center. Many families participated in the pageant every year. Dorothy Thorson Evans remembers her parents making exhibits and her mother making her costumes. She is pictured in the front row near the center, the blonde girl in the white dress. Her sister Yolanda is in the front row, third from the right. (Courtesy Dorothy Thorson Evans.)

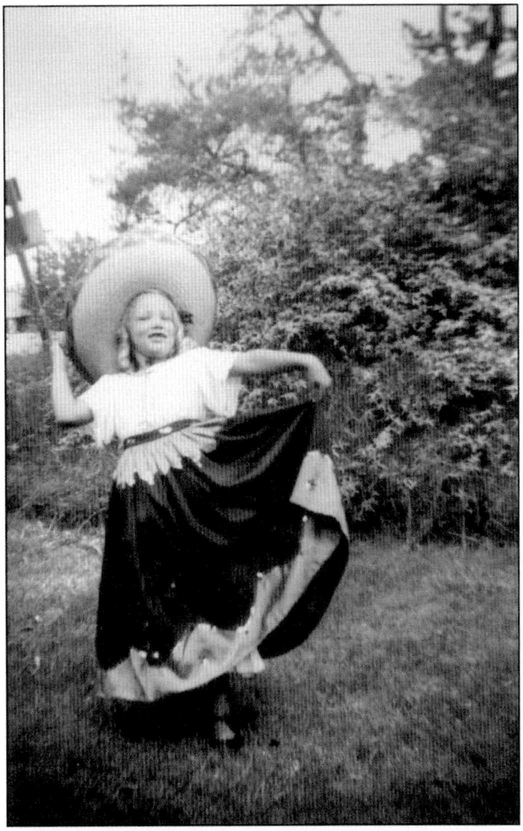

Harvest Festival Dancer. In the early 1940s, Dorothy Thorson is wearing the costume her mother made her for a dance number in the Harvest Festival. (Courtesy Dorothy Thorson Evans.)

Harvest Festival, 1948. These ladies are helping set up the Harvest Festival on the property purchased by the Harvest Festival Association. Pictured here, from left to right, are unidentified, unidentified, Marie Scott, unidentified, and Marcia Engelauf. (Courtesy Engelauf/Flowers families.)

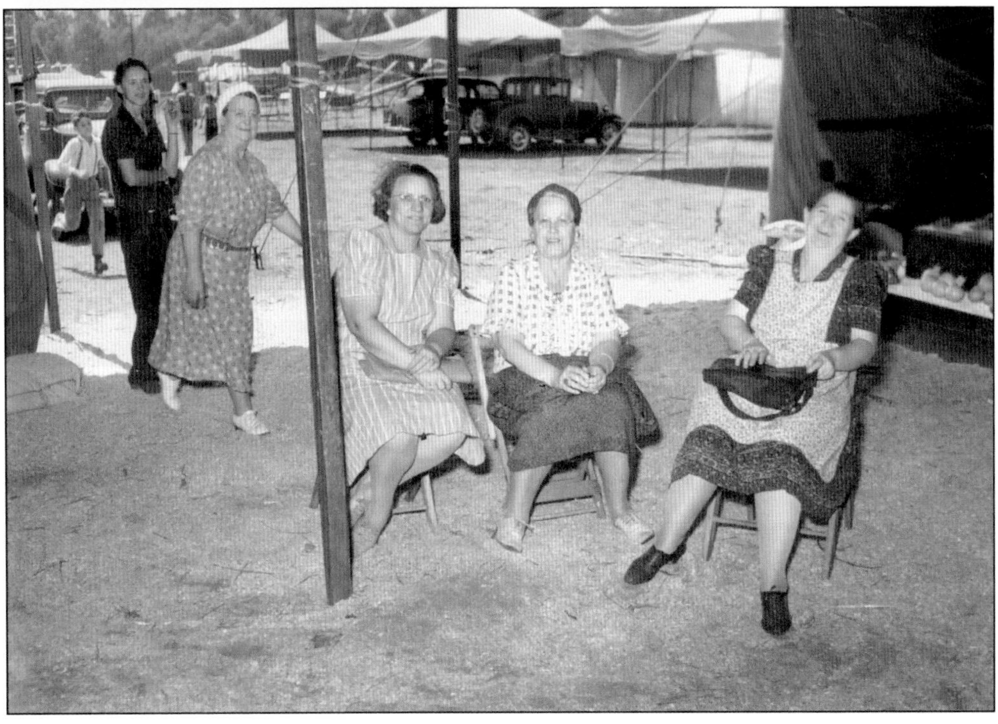

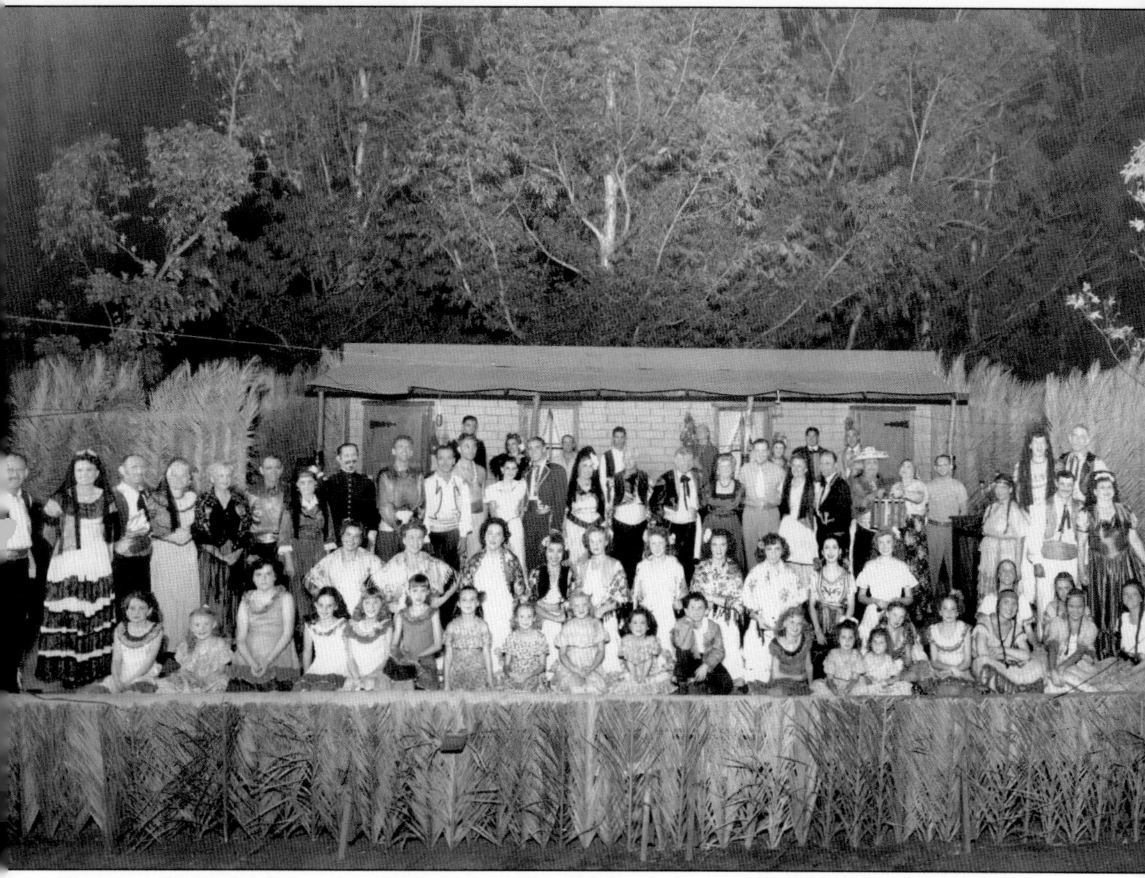

Harvest Festival Pageant, 1949. During World War II, the Harvest Festival and pageant were suspended. In 1949, the Harvest Festival Association decided to revive the pageant so "newcomers" could learn about the area's history. (Courtesy Engelauf/Flowers families.)

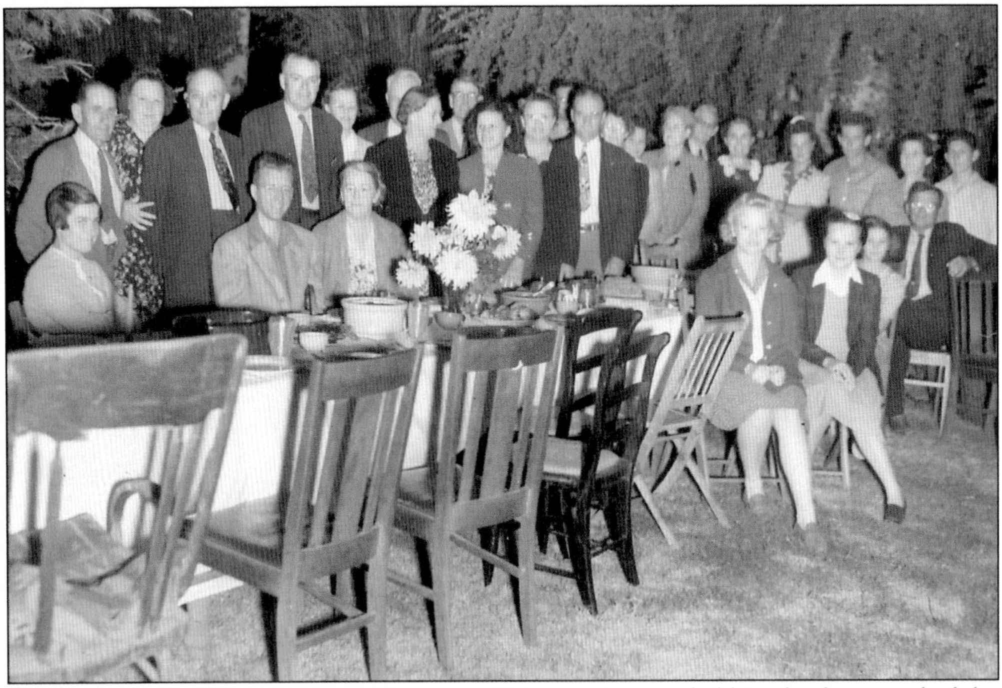

HARVEST FESTIVAL COMMITTEE MEETING. This meeting was held in the front yard of the Engelauf home on Thirty-fourth Street. First there would be a potluck dinner, then a social hour that included singing old songs like "The Old Gray Mare," and finally the adults would get down to the business of planning the next Harvest Festival. (Courtesy Engelauf/Flowers families.)

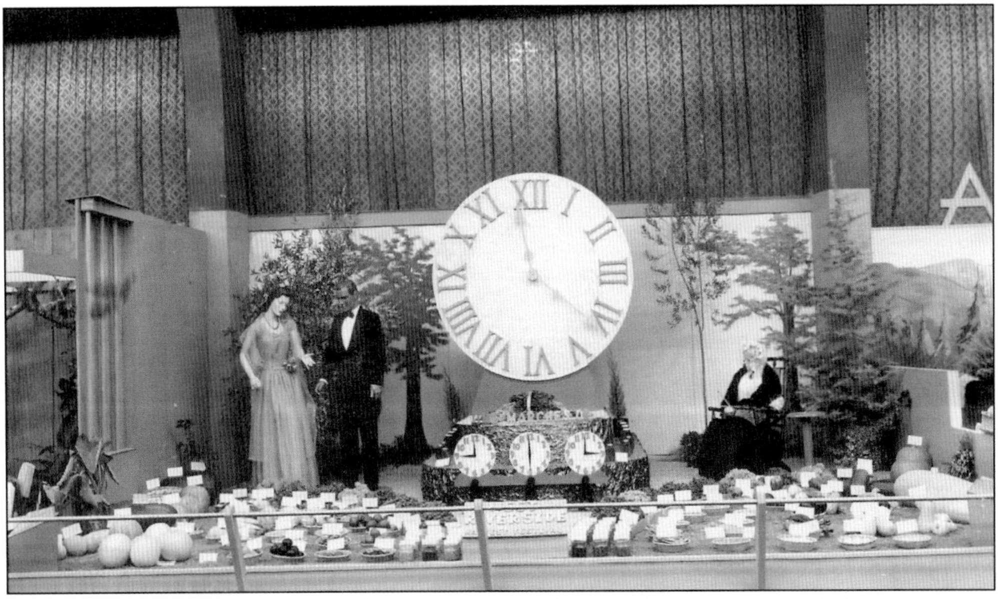

HARVEST FESTIVAL DISPLAY. In addition to staging the annual Harvest Festival, the association produced displays for other fairs and festivals to highlight the Jurupa area. Even after the festival was no longer produced, the festival association continued to produce displays for other fairs in the area. This display was most likely located at the National Orange Show in San Bernardino. (Courtesy Dorothy Thorson Evans.)

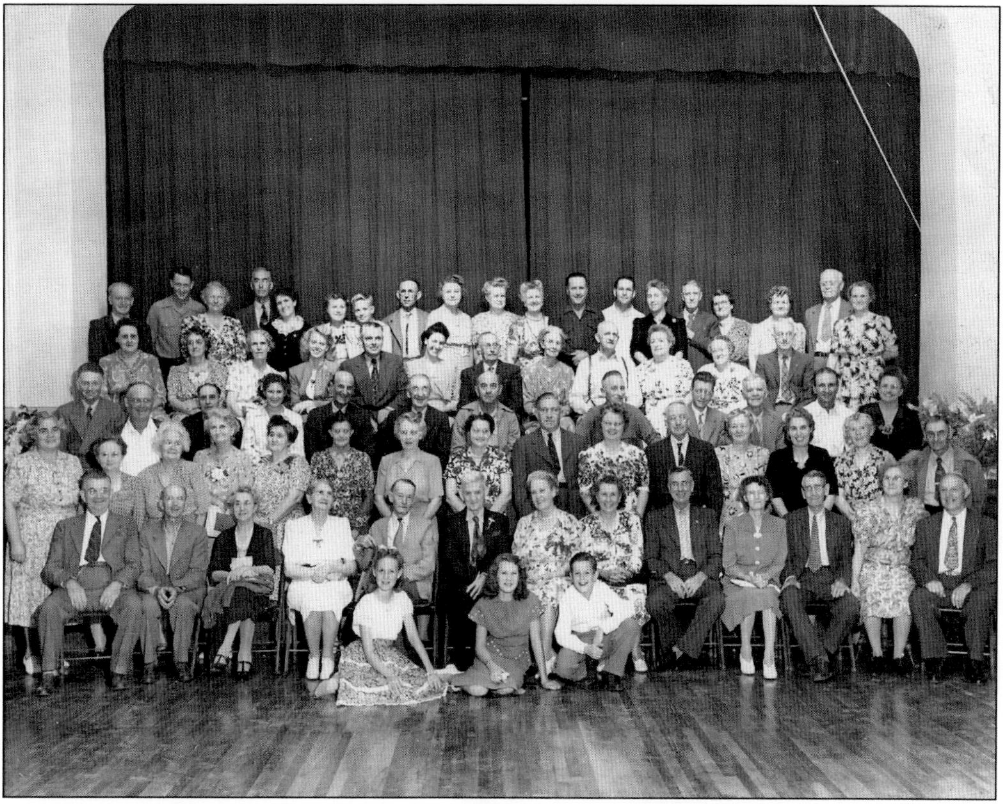

OLD SETTLERS REUNION. First held in 1924 at the new West Riverside School, the Old Settlers Reunion was such a success that an organization was formed to arrange reunions every year. Until the 1980s, reunions continued to be held. This photograph shows a reunion held in the auditorium at West Riverside School in the late 1940s. (Courtesy Engelauf/Flowers families.)

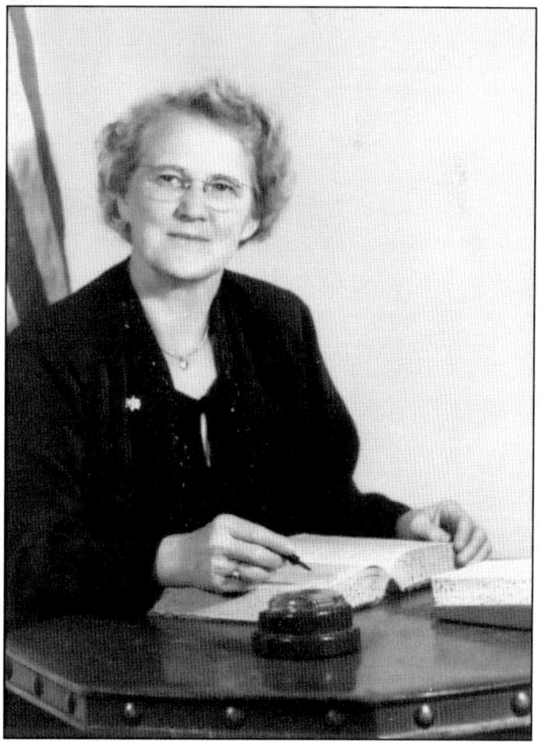

JUDGE MAY STOBBS. Stobbs was the first woman justice in Riverside County. She was appointed to the Jurupa Judicial District to fulfill the unexpired term of her husband, Edward Stobbs, after he passed away in October 1949. She went on to serve 10 years. This 1949 photograph was taken at the time of her appointment. Stobbs Way in Rubidoux was later named for Judge Stobbs. (Courtesy Jurupa Mountains Cultural Center.)

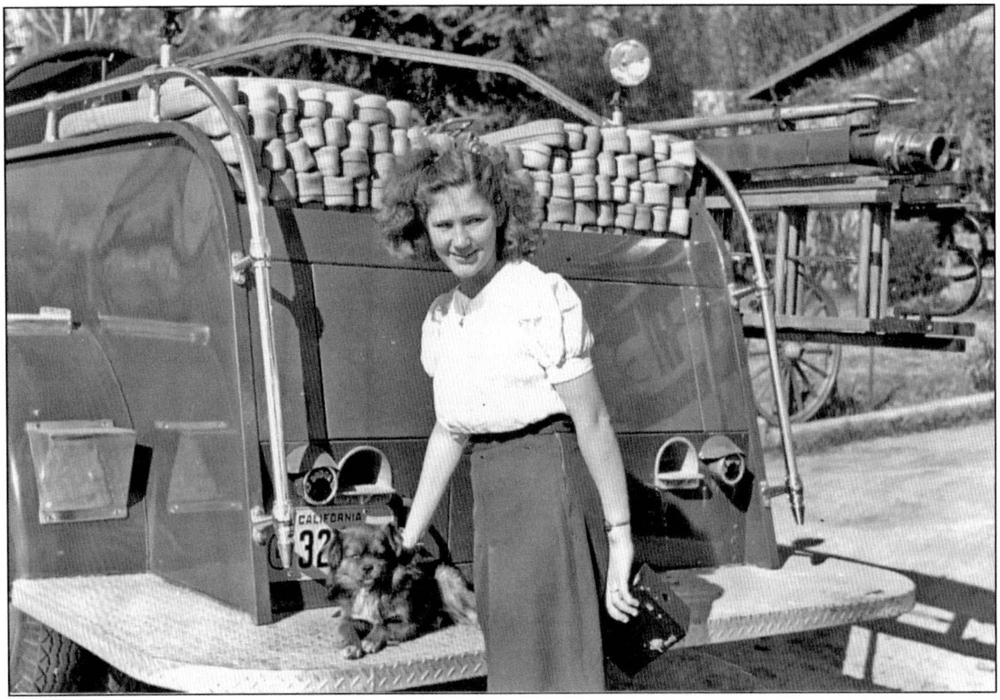

West Riverside Fire Truck. In 1946, the West Riverside Fire Protection District was formed. The first fire station was located at Fort Fremont Street and Mennes Avenue in an old Quonset hut. Eva Engelauf is shown here with her dog Pug and the first fire truck in West Riverside. (Courtesy Engelauf/Flowers families.)

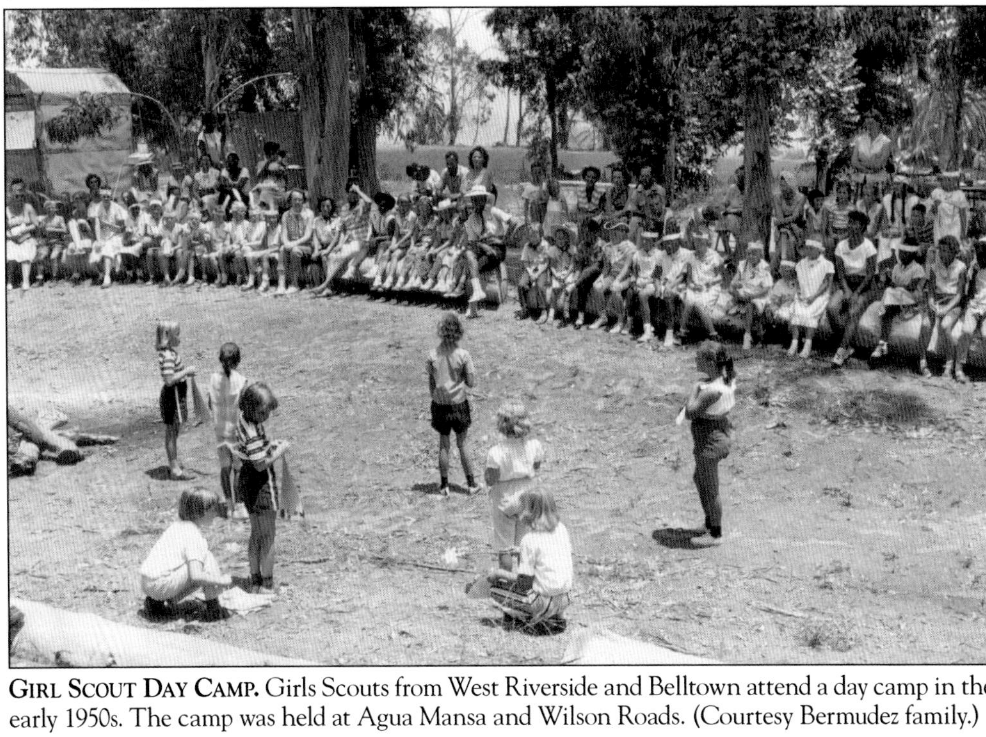

Girl Scout Day Camp. Girls Scouts from West Riverside and Belltown attend a day camp in the early 1950s. The camp was held at Agua Mansa and Wilson Roads. (Courtesy Bermudez family.)

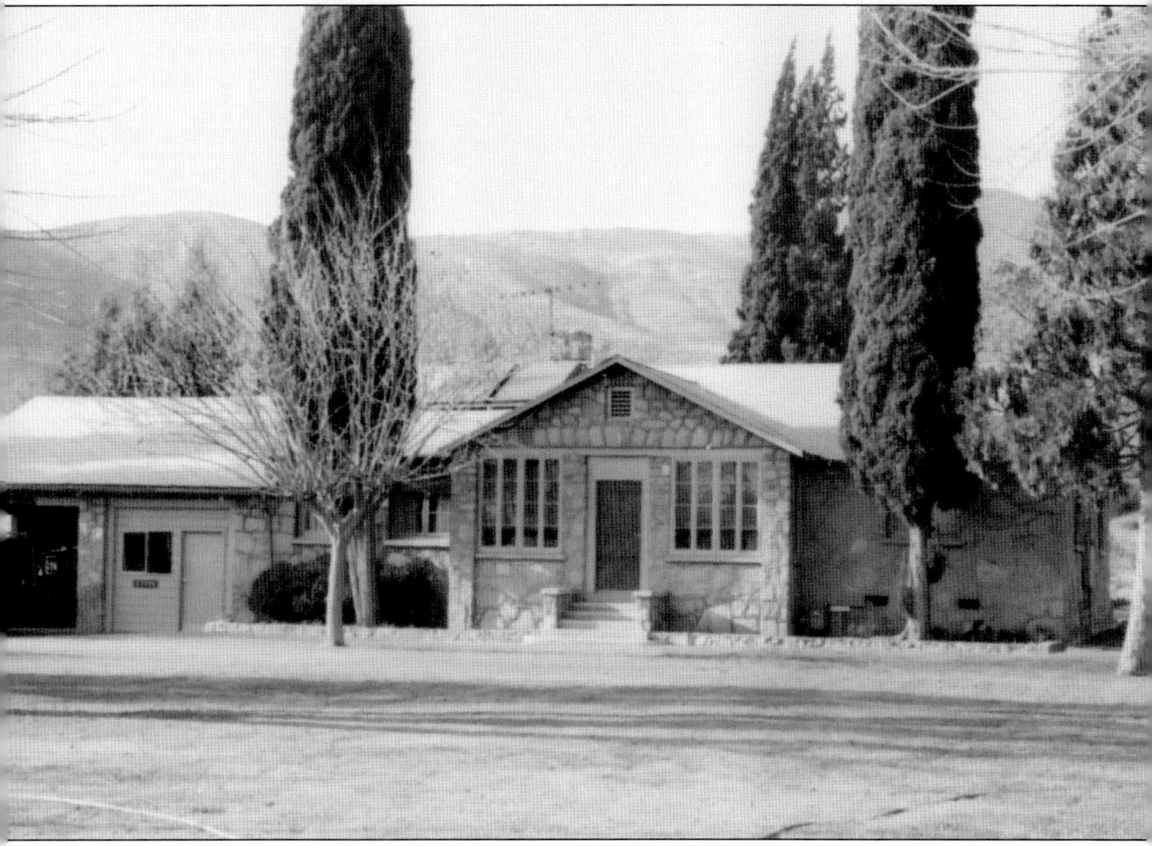

GLEN AVON FIRE STATION. Built in 1934, this California Department of Forestry station has 18-inch deep solid granite exterior walls. The granite is thought to have come from quarries in nearby Rattlesnake Mountain. The station is still located on Mission Boulevard on property donated by the Harvest Festival Association for its construction. Workers who built the station left their names engraved on the vents of the exterior walls. They were Jimmie, Reds, Hawkins, Whitey, and Rus. (Courtesy Riverside County Regional Park and Open-Space District.)

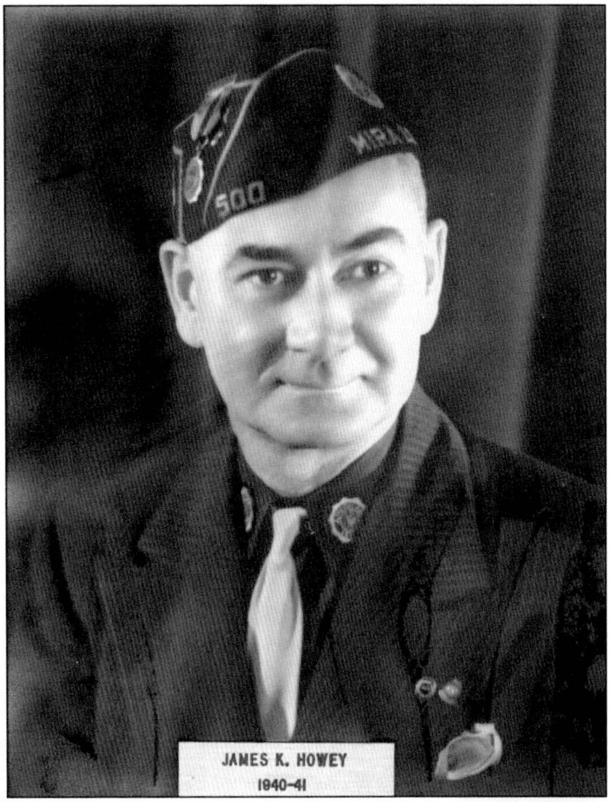

AMERICAN LEGION POST COMMANDER, 1940–1941. In 1938, World War I veterans formed American Legion Mira Loma Post 500. This photograph shows James K. Howey, one of the founding members and one of the earliest post commanders. (Courtesy American Legion Mira Loma Post 500.)

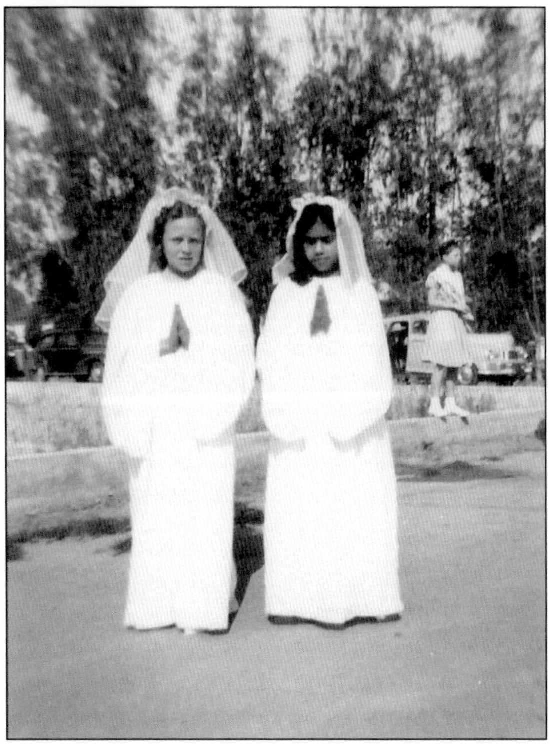

SACRED HEART CHURCH ACOLYTES. In 1945, Sacred Heart Parish was formed. Doreen Fogarty and Ethel Chavez act as acolytes for a first communion service at Sacred Heart Church in the late 1940s. The Jahn family donated property on Mission Boulevard in Glen Avon for the church. (Courtesy Ethel Chavez Sanborn.)

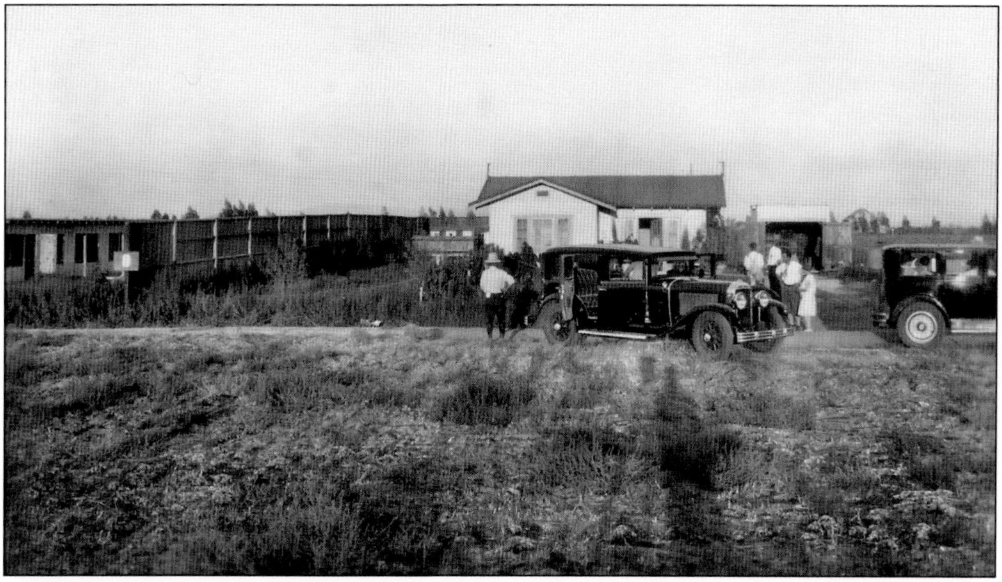

Northcott Farm, September 1928. In 1928, an infamous murder case occurred at the Gordon Northcott farm in the Wineville area—the "Wineville Chicken Coop Murders," named after the chicken coops on the property. Publicity was so widespread that the residents of Wineville decided in 1931 to change their community's name to Mira Loma. Only Wineville Road is left to remind us of the community's former name. (Courtesy Riverside Metropolitan Museum.)

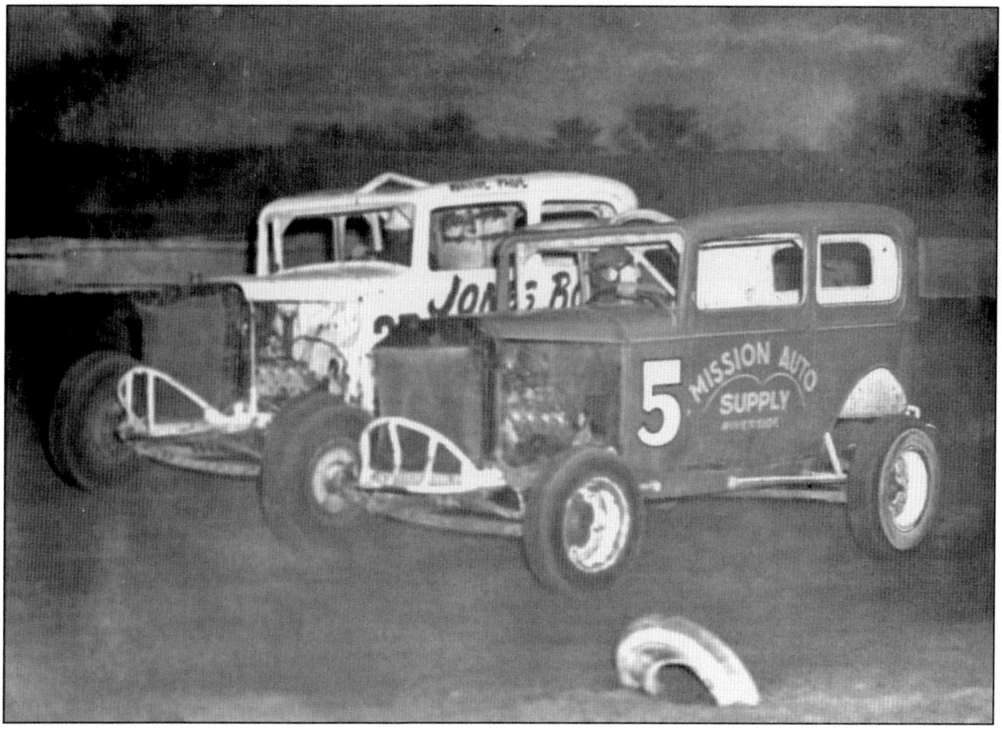

Jalopy Racing. On December 16, 1956, Jurupa residents Wayne Paige (in white car) and Vallie Engelauf race their jalopies at the orange show in San Bernardino. Several Jurupa residents participated in jalopy races around this time. (Courtesy Engelauf/Flowers families.)

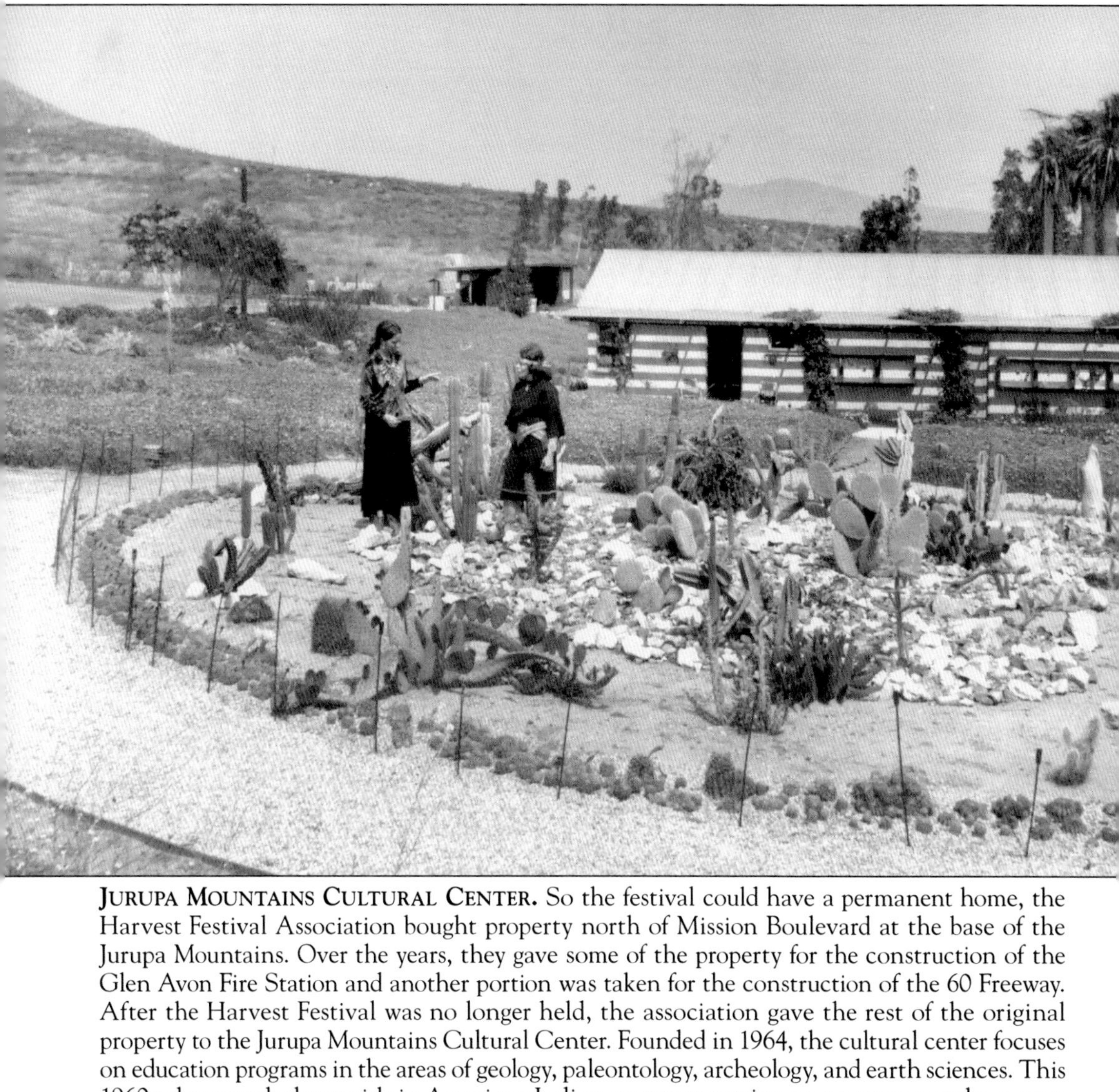

JURUPA MOUNTAINS CULTURAL CENTER. So the festival could have a permanent home, the Harvest Festival Association bought property north of Mission Boulevard at the base of the Jurupa Mountains. Over the years, they gave some of the property for the construction of the Glen Avon Fire Station and another portion was taken for the construction of the 60 Freeway. After the Harvest Festival was no longer held, the association gave the rest of the original property to the Jurupa Mountains Cultural Center. Founded in 1964, the cultural center focuses on education programs in the areas of geology, paleontology, archeology, and earth sciences. This 1960s photograph shows girls in American Indian costumes putting on a program at the center. (Courtesy Jurupa Mountains Cultural Center.)

Five

BUSINESS LIFE

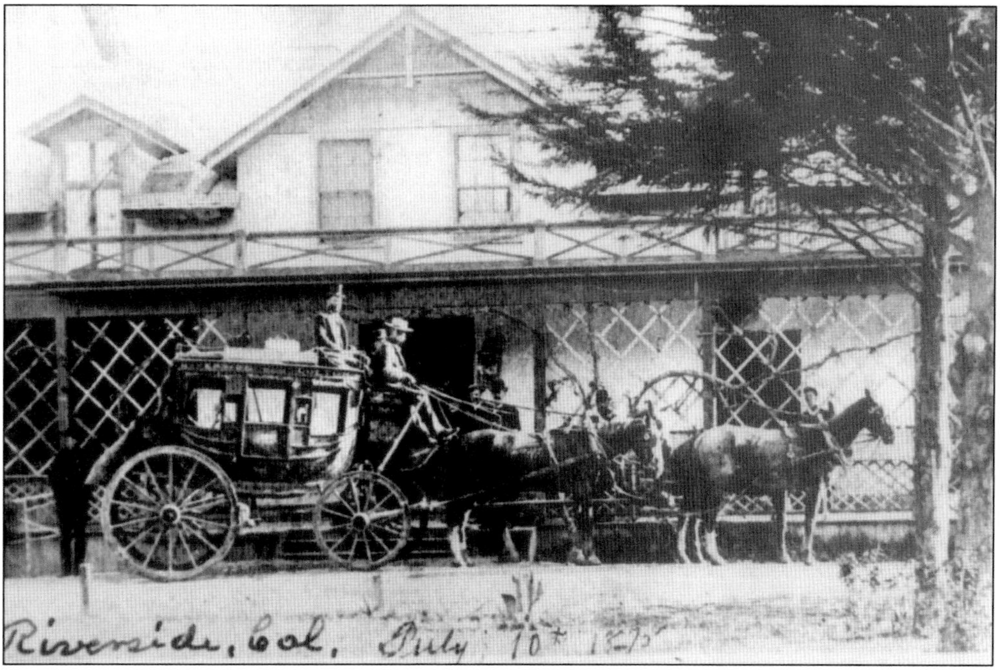

LOCAL STAGE LINE. In 1869, a rail line was completed from Los Angeles to Spadra, located in what is now the Pomona area. This was the closest that rail service had gotten to the inland area. A stagecoach line was started, with West Riverside resident Heber Parks as its first driver. The stage left Spadra and stopped at Rincon (now Corona), Riverside, and San Bernardino. The next day it turned around and went back. The fare was $3.00. (Courtesy Clara Thorne.)

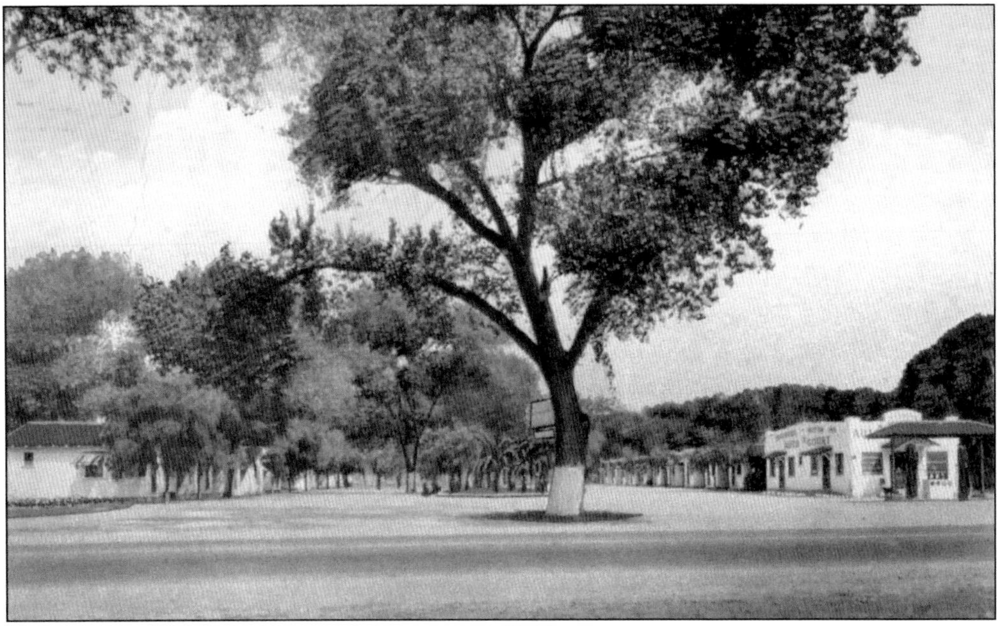

RIVERSIDE MOTOR INN. The back of the postcard for this auto court, *c.* 1920s, says, "Riverside Motor Inn is one mile west of Riverside, Calif., on main road from Los Angeles to San Diego. Contains strictly modern cabins with store in addition gas station. It is 'Just Like Home' and visited yearly by same tourists; shady grounds and picturesque surroundings make it enjoyable. G. C. Anderson is the proprietor . . . Located at Foot of Famous Mt. Rubidoux." (Courtesy Steve Lech.)

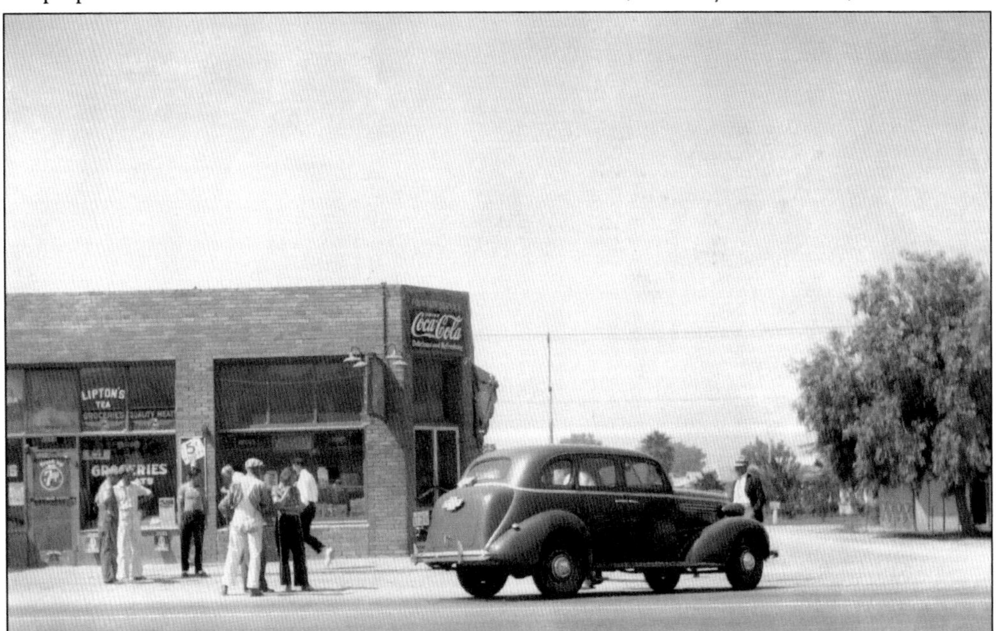

PHILIAN'S MARKET. The building at the corner of Mission Boulevard and Mennes Avenue was originally Philian's Market, built in the late 1920s or early 1930s. This business marked the end of the Rubidoux business district as Mission Boulevard approached the Santa Ana River. This building is still located in Rubidoux and still houses a market. (Courtesy Jurupa Mountains Cultural Center.)

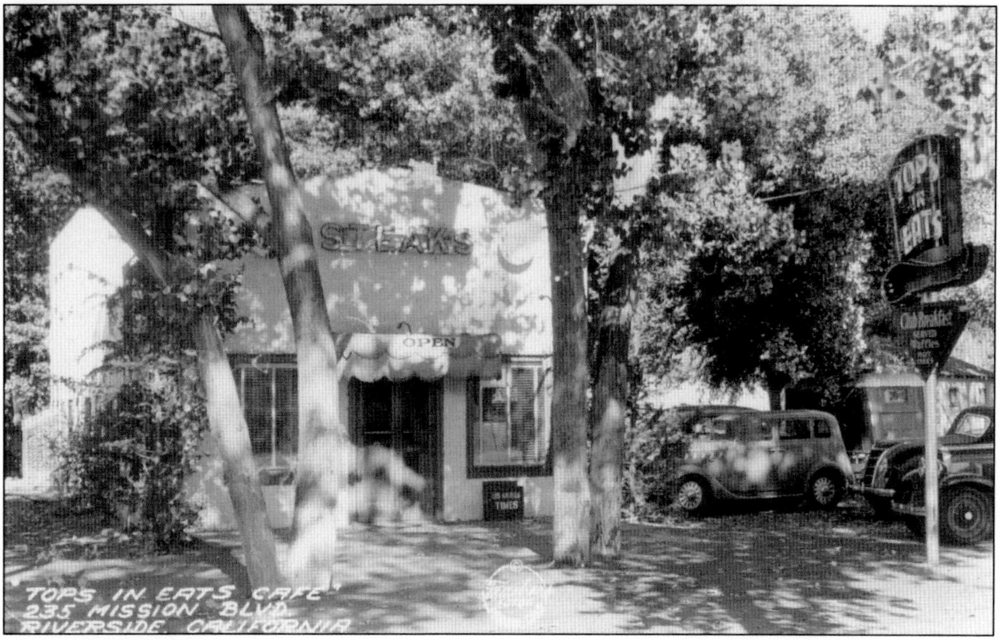

Tops In Eats Cafe. This cafe, located on Mission Boulevard near the Santa Ana River, is an example of a business catering to the motoring public in the 1930s. (Courtesy Frasher's Fotos, Pomona.)

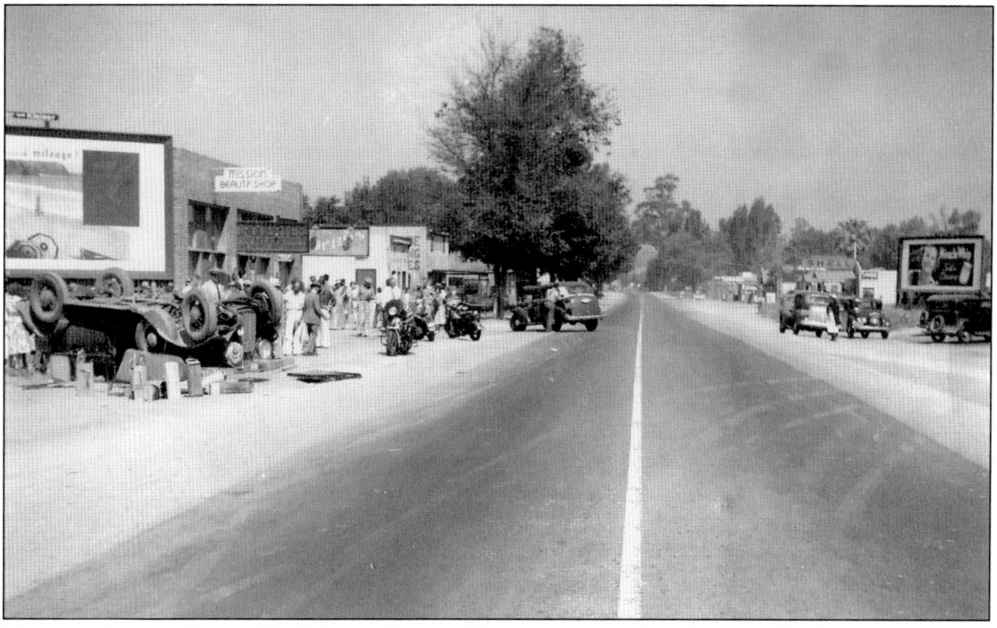

Mission Beauty Shop. The Mission Beauty Shop appears in this photograph of an auto accident on Mission Boulevard. This photograph, probably taken as part of the investigation into the accident, came to the Jurupa Mountains Cultural Center from Judge May Stobbs. (Courtesy Jurupa Mountains Cultural Center.)

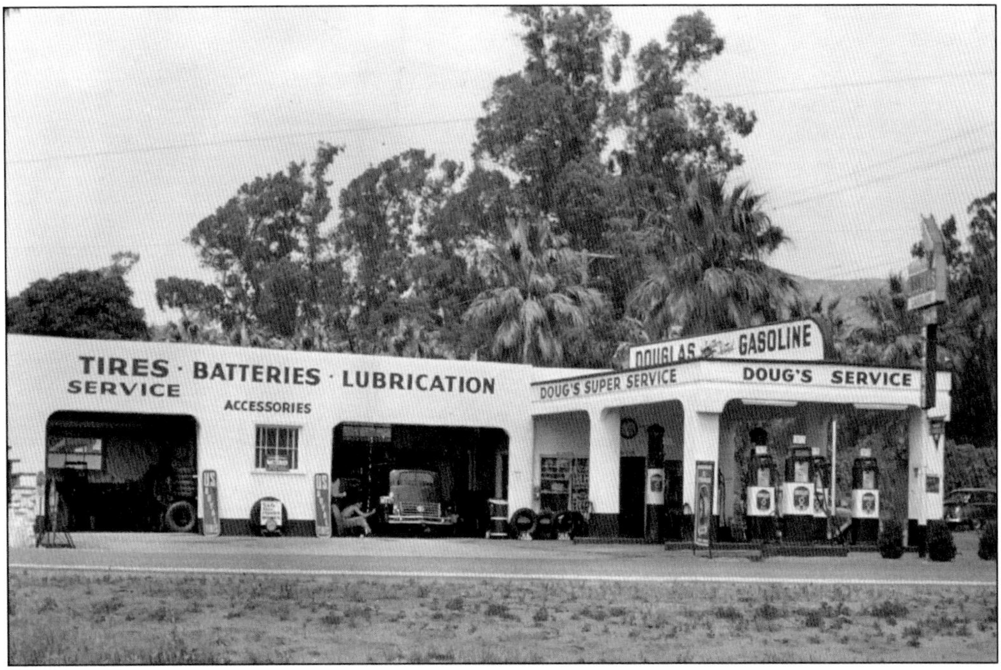

DOUG'S SERVICE STATION. In 1940 or 1941, James Douglas "Doug" Walker started this service station, seen here in 1943, on the corner of Mission Boulevard and Pacific Avenue. He later sold it and started a new service station on the corner of Jurupa Road and Fairbanks Avenue. Both service station buildings are still standing. (Courtesy Anita Walker Blount.)

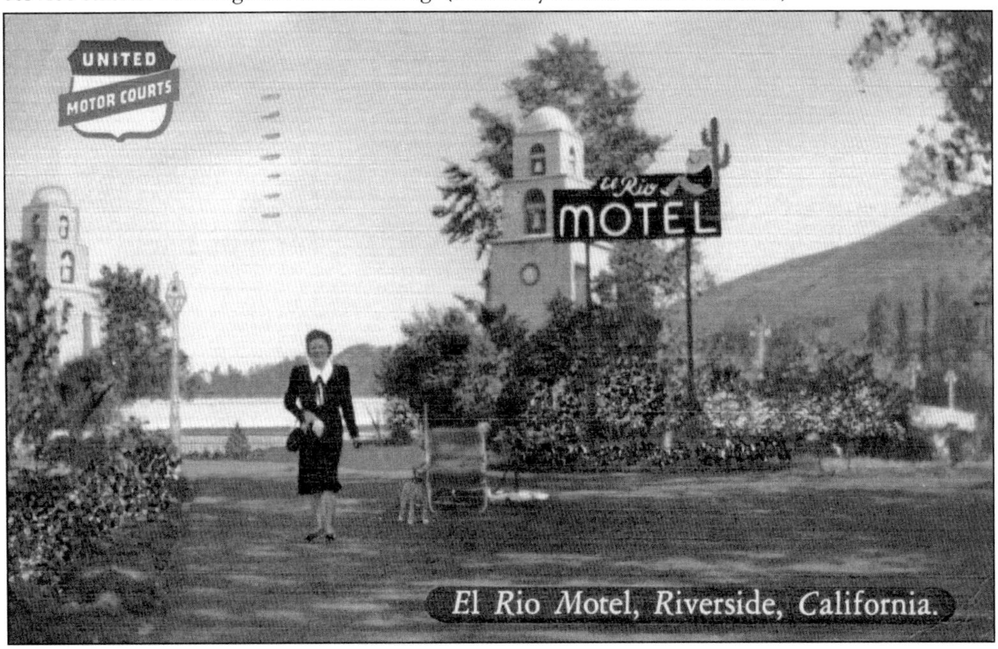

EL RIO MOTEL. This motel was located on the south side of Mission Boulevard, at the end of the Santa Ana River Bridge. (Note the bridge in the right portion of the postcard.) The postcard says this was a "high grade motel" with 20 rooms, all with bathrooms and garages. It was established by Floyd Redman around 1946 and closed sometime in the mid-1950s. (Courtesy Steve Lech.)

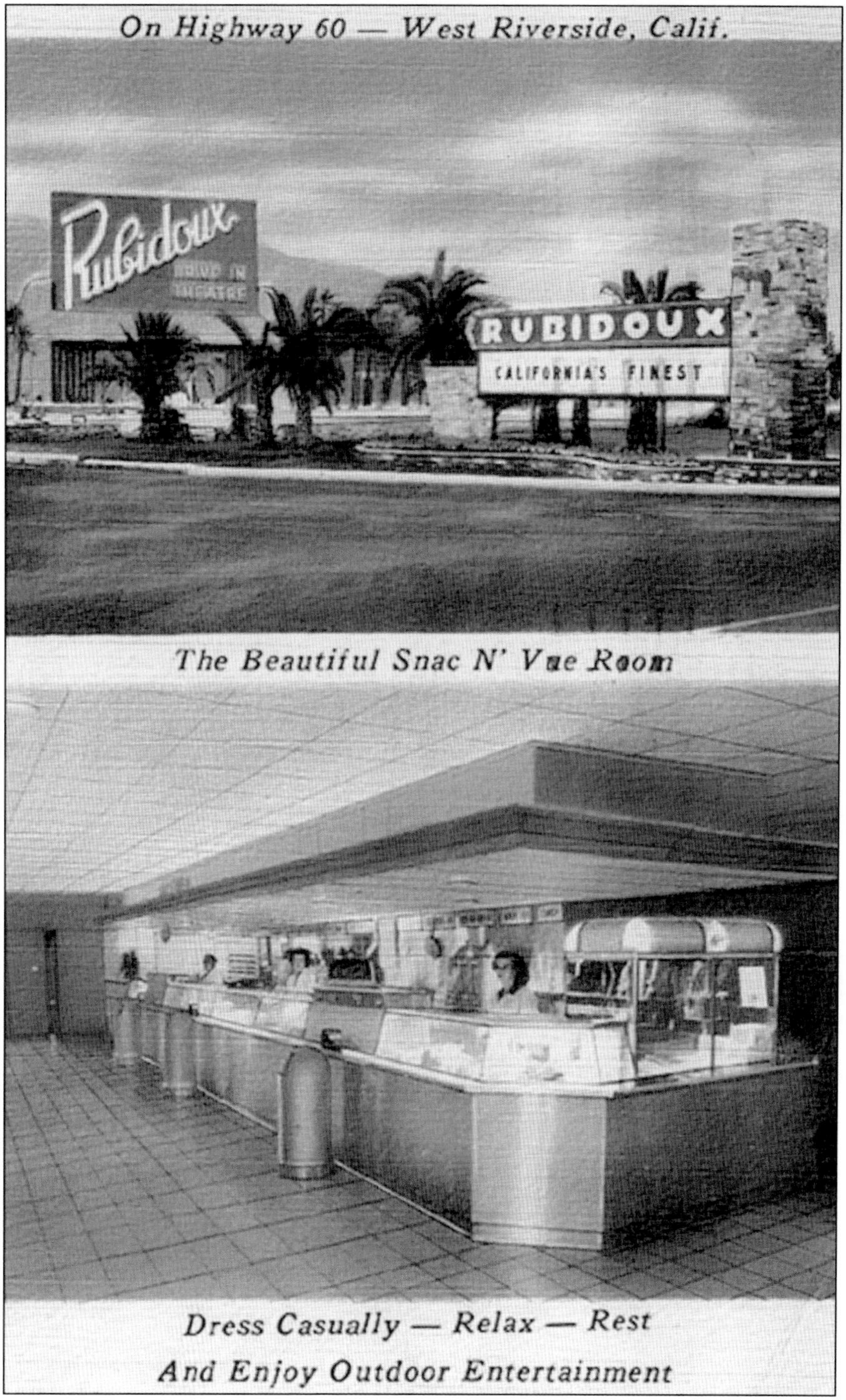

RUBIDOUX DRIVE-IN. Built in 1948 at the beginning of the drive-in theater boom in California, Jurupa's own drive-in theater was located at the corner of Mission Boulevard and Opal Street. It will soon be the last in Riverside County, as the only other drive-in is slated for development. This postcard of the drive-in is postmarked 1952. (Courtesy Steve Lech.)

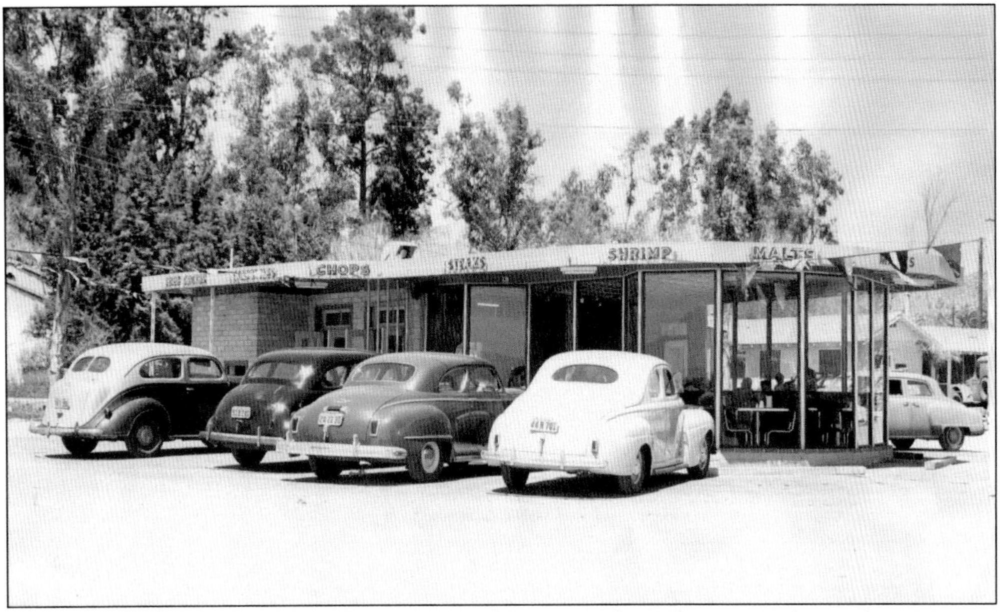

RAINBOW DRIVE-IN. This drive-in, popular for its root beer floats, was located on Mission Boulevard between Riverview Drive and Avalon Street, now the site of the new Rubidoux Fire Station. This photograph was taken in June 1948. (Courtesy Riverside Metropolitan Museum.)

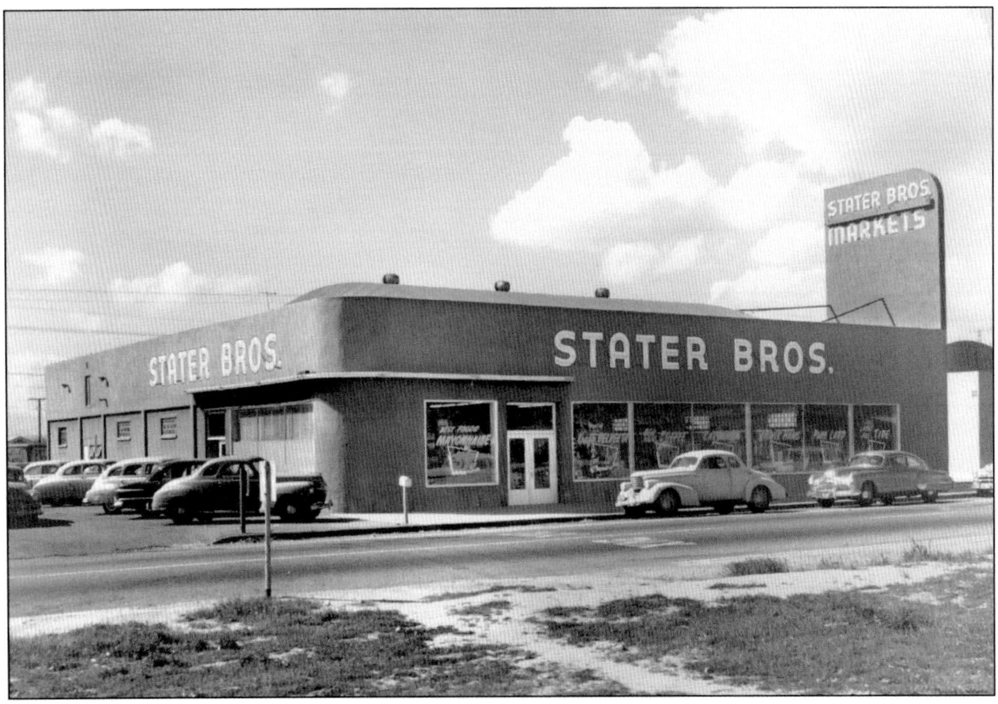

STATER BROTHERS MARKET. Stater Brothers opened their first "super" market, the sixth market in their chain, at the corner of Mission Boulevard and Pontiac Street in Rubidoux. It was "super" because it had 12,500 square feet, fluorescent lighting, an air-cooling system, and an intercom system that played music. (Courtesy Stater Brothers.)

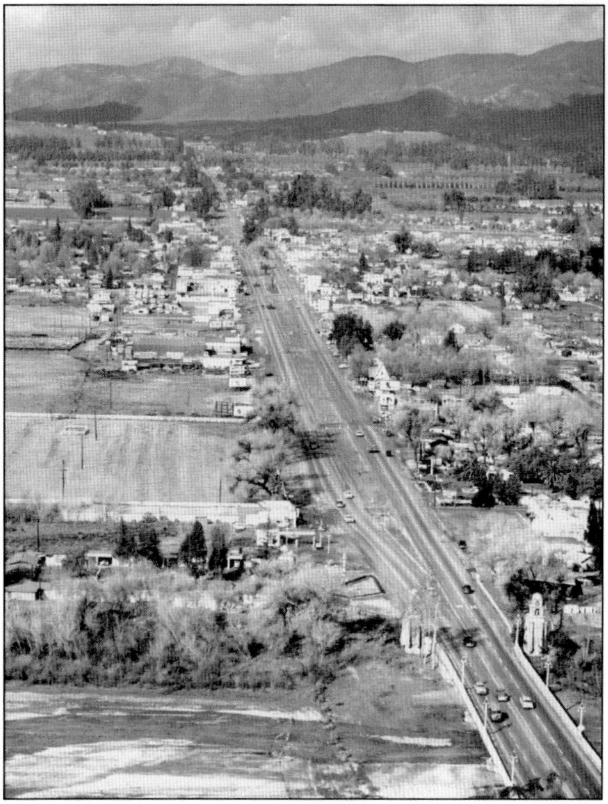

West Riverside, 1955. Taken in October, this photograph is looking west down Mission Boulevard. (Courtesy Riverside Metropolitan Museum.)

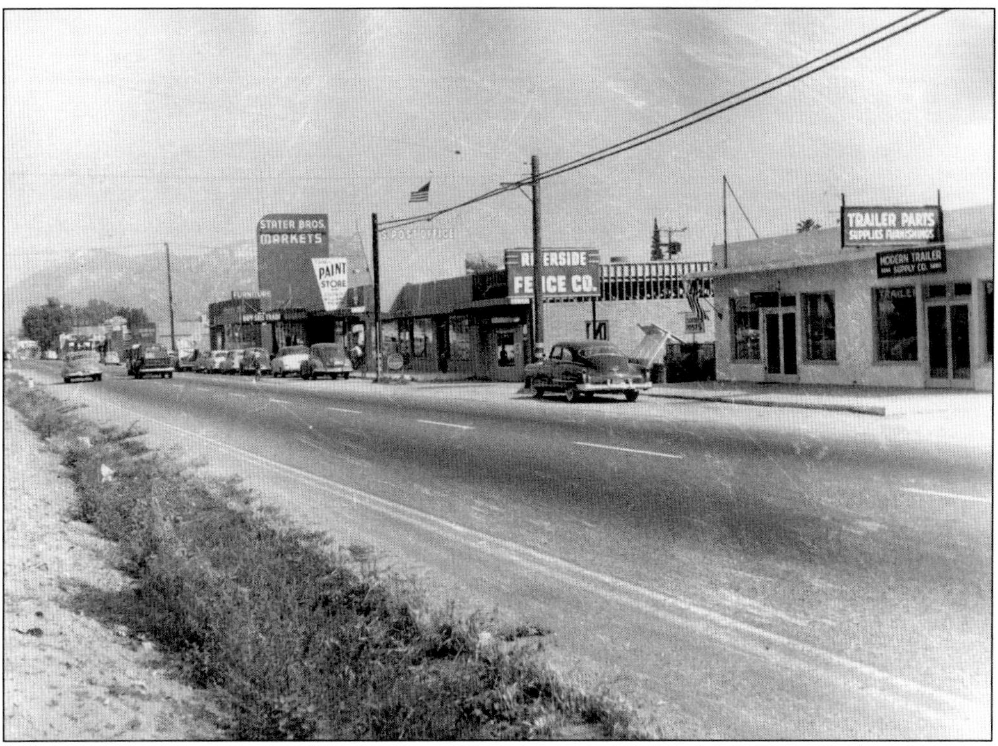

Downtown Rubidoux. The caption on this photograph reads, "A entire block of new buildings pushes its way into the old business district of Rubidoux (West Riverside)." It shows the west side of the block of Mission Boulevard bounded by Avalon and Pontiac Streets around 1958. Note the original Stater Brothers Market. (Courtesy Jurupa Mountains Cultural Center.)

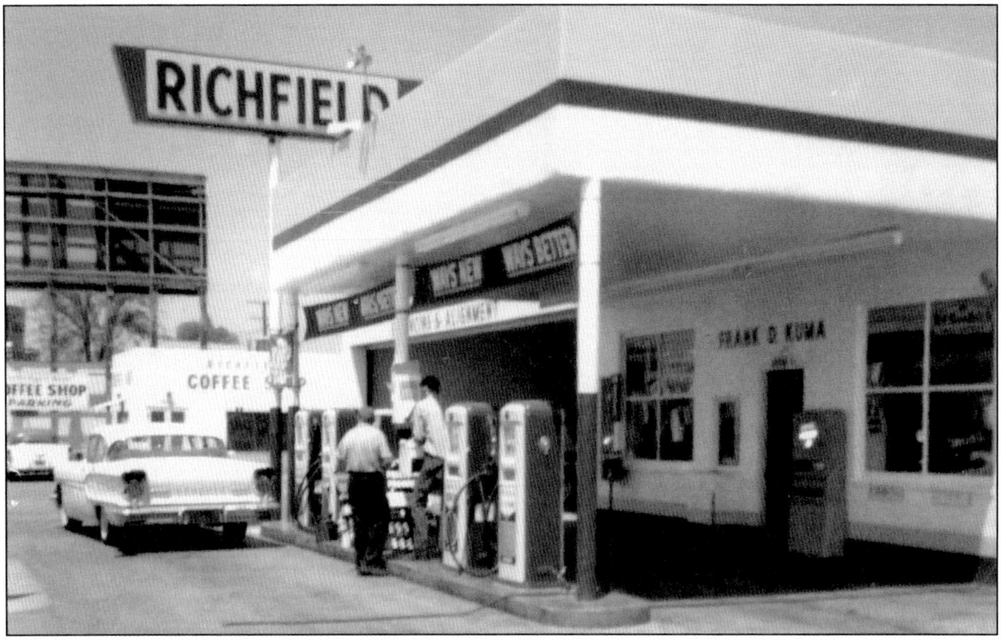

RICHFIELD STATION. This early 1960s photograph shows the Richfield Gas Station and some adjacent businesses in downtown Rubidoux. The station was located at the corner of Mission Boulevard and Wallace Street. Frank and Emma Jane Kuma, who purchased it in 1958 from Owen and Fern Smith, owned it at the time. The building and property are now a tire store. (Courtesy Frank and Emma Jane Kuma.)

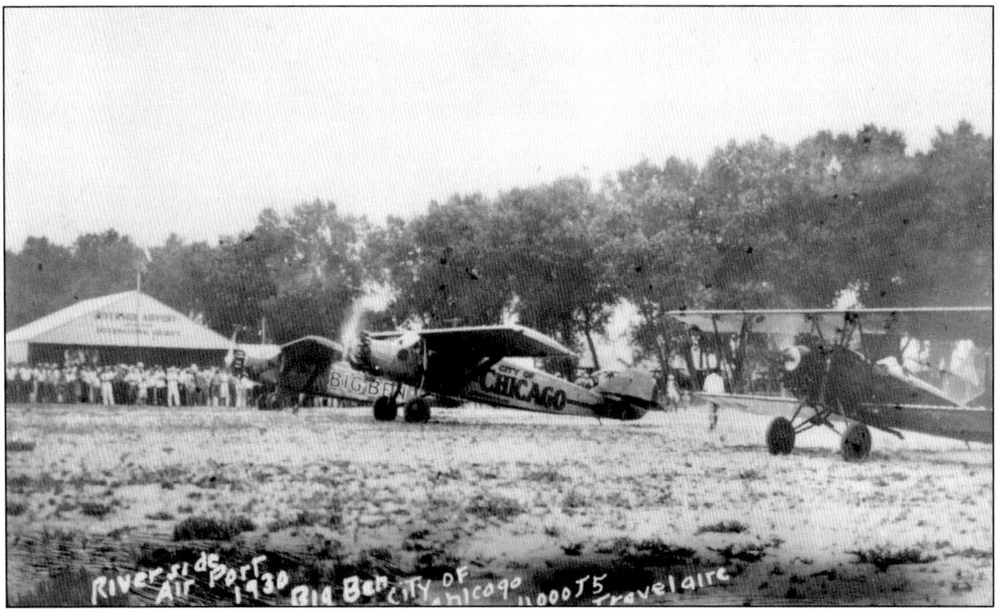

RIVERSIDE AIRPORT. The City of Riverside's first airport was actually located in Jurupa. It was situated along Mission Boulevard next to the Santa Ana River. Roman Warren, aviation pioneer and future county supervisor, was the primary force behind the establishment of the airport, begun in the 1920s. Most of the landing field was washed away in the 1938 flood, spelling the end of Riverside's airport in Jurupa. (Courtesy Riverside County Library System, Louis Robidoux Library.)

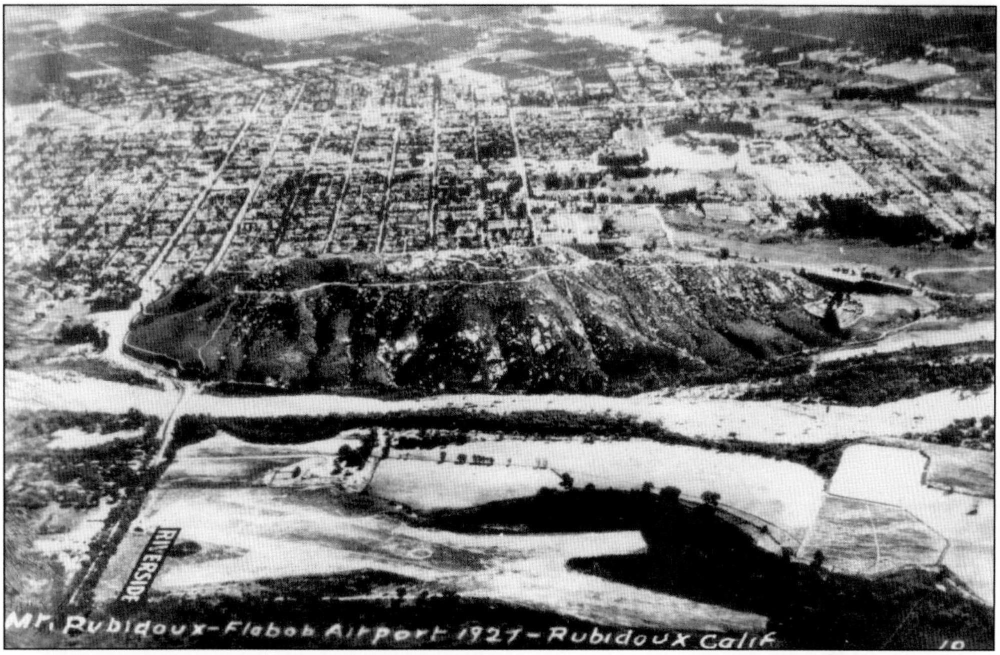

RIVERSIDE AIRPORT. This photograph of the Riverside airport was taken after 1932, as that was the year the large sign spelling out "Riverside" in white rock was installed. (Courtesy Riverside County Library System, Louis Robidoux Library.)

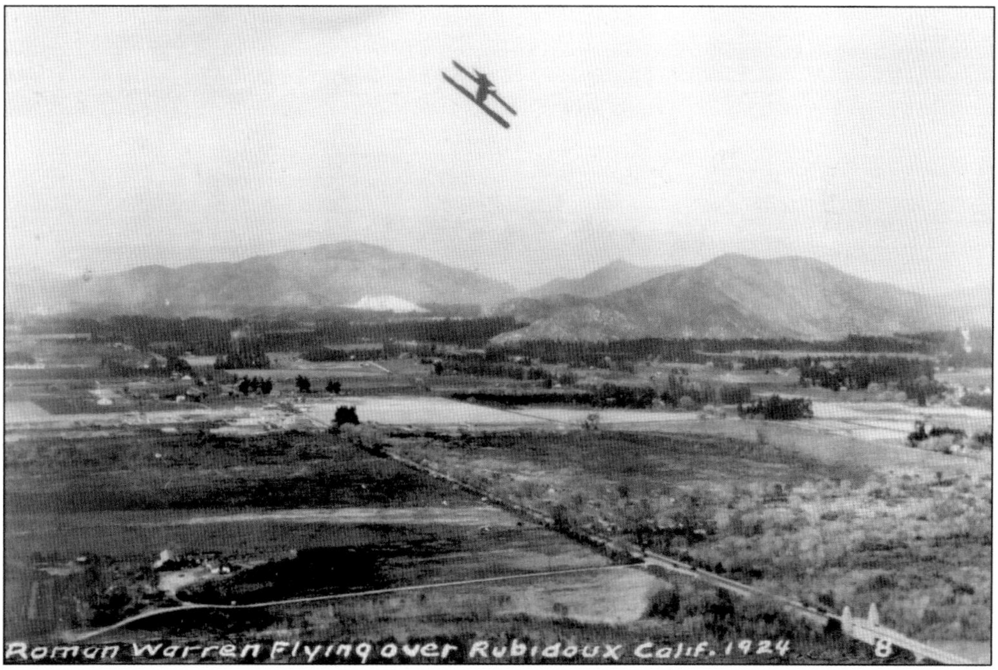

FLYING OVER WEST RIVERSIDE. Famed aviator Roman Warren is shown flying over West Riverside. The bridge over the Santa Ana River is located in the lower right corner. Rattlesnake Mountain is in the middle right of the photograph. (Courtesy Flabob Airport.)

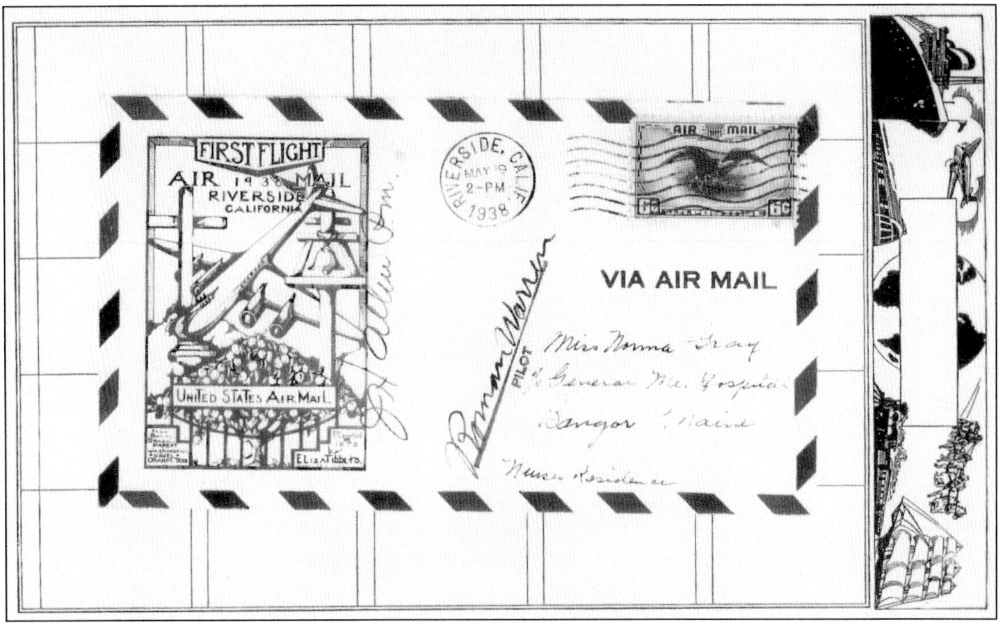

FIRST AIRMAIL FLIGHT. In 1930, Roman Warren accomplished the first airmail flight within Riverside County. He did so at his own expense and in his own airplane. Special envelopes were prepared, and Warren signed over 4,000 of them. Another pilot flew the mail from Blythe to Indio. Warren flew from Indio to Glendale with stops in Palm Springs and Riverside. The Riverside stop was at the airport in Jurupa. (Courtesy Flabob Airport.)

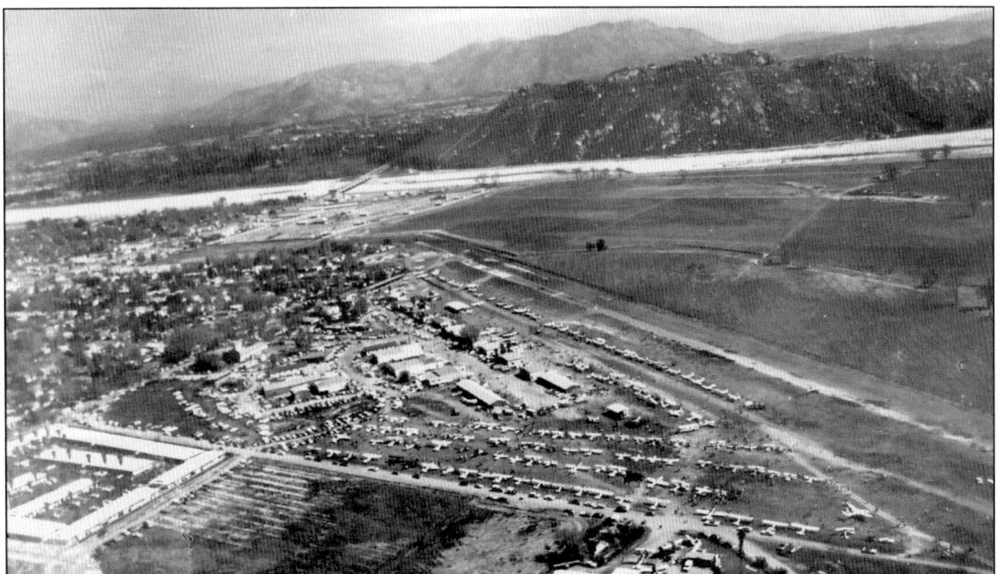

FLABOB AIRPORT. In 1945, Flavio Madariaga and Bob Bogan became partners and bought what was left of the old Riverside Airport. They named their new enterprise using parts of their first names—Flabob. Their airport was smaller and located farther from Mission Boulevard, but it had the same advantages the old airport had—it was close to the Los Angeles area and easy to locate from the air because of close proximity to Mount Rubidoux and the Santa Ana River. (Courtesy Riverside County Library System, Louis Robidoux Library.)

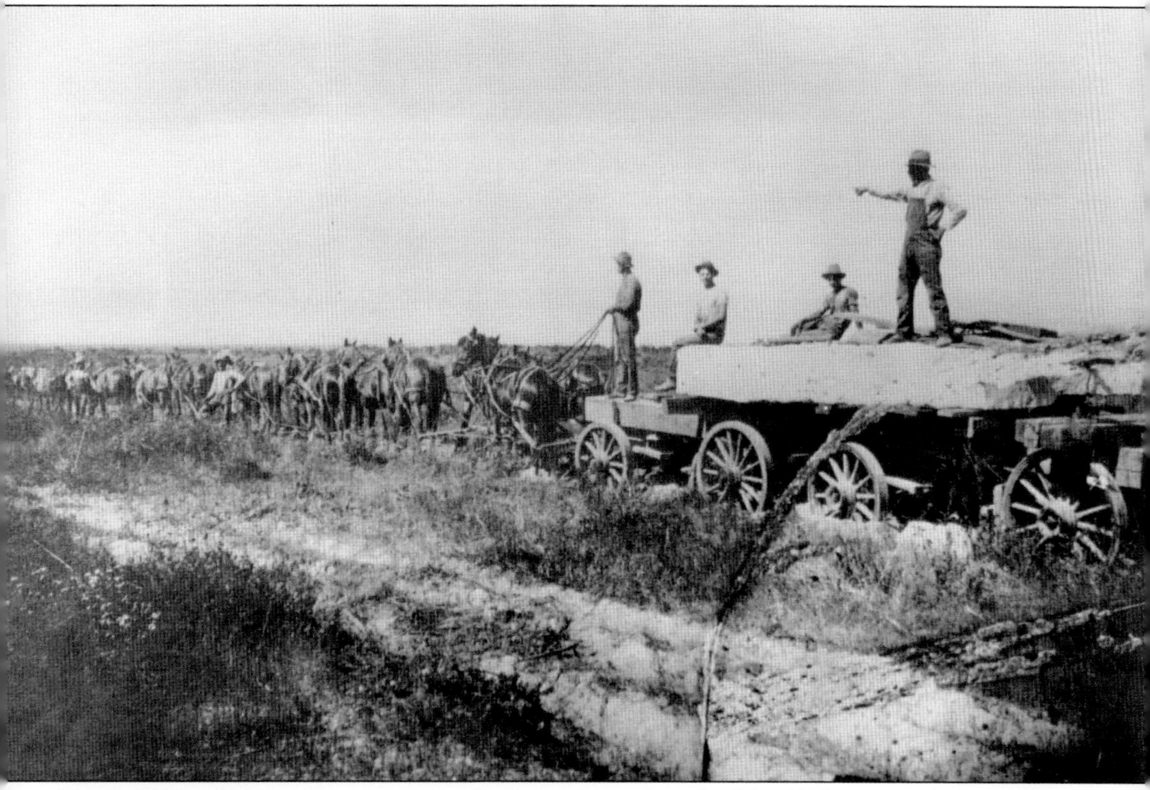

QUARRYING IN PYRITE CANYON. Pyrite Canyon is located north of the 60 Freeway and west of the Jurupa Mountains Cultural Center. It stretches deep into the Jurupa Mountains and its abundant granite deposits. The Bly brothers opened a quarry in Pyrite Canyon in 1904, and a railroad spur line was built from Pedley to their quarry. The quarry provided a fine quality of granite cut as "dimension stone" as well as a large quantity of riprap. This quarry supplied the riprap for the Long Beach breakwater and stone for San Pedro Harbor. This photograph shows a particularly large dimension stone being hauled on two wagons by a team of 20 mules and horses. Francisco Silva is standing on top of the large stone. The Silva family moved to the Pyrite Canyon area before 1900 and homesteaded there. In 1900, Mr. Silva received the title to the land he homesteaded. (Courtesy Riverside Metropolitan Museum.)

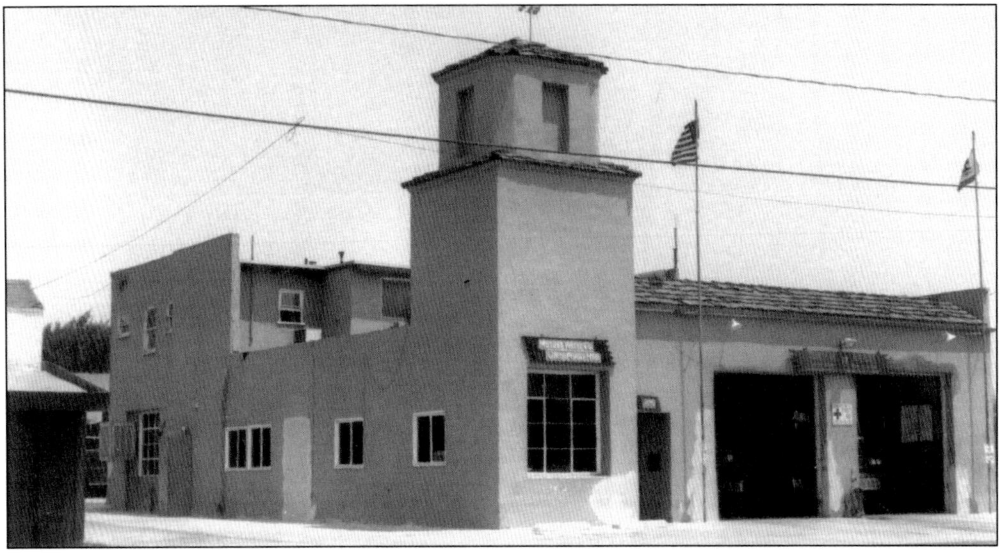

MUTUAL WATER COMPANY OF GLEN AVON HEIGHTS. As the population grew in Glen Avon, particularly after 1900, more and more land was planted in crops that required irrigation. To provide a more reliable source of water to the growing community, the Mutual Water Company of Glen Avon Heights was formed in 1922. Shares in the company were sold with land for about $7 per share. In 1997, it became part of the Jurupa Community Services District. This photograph was taken in 1983. The building now houses a private business. (Courtesy Riverside County Regional Park and Open-Space District.)

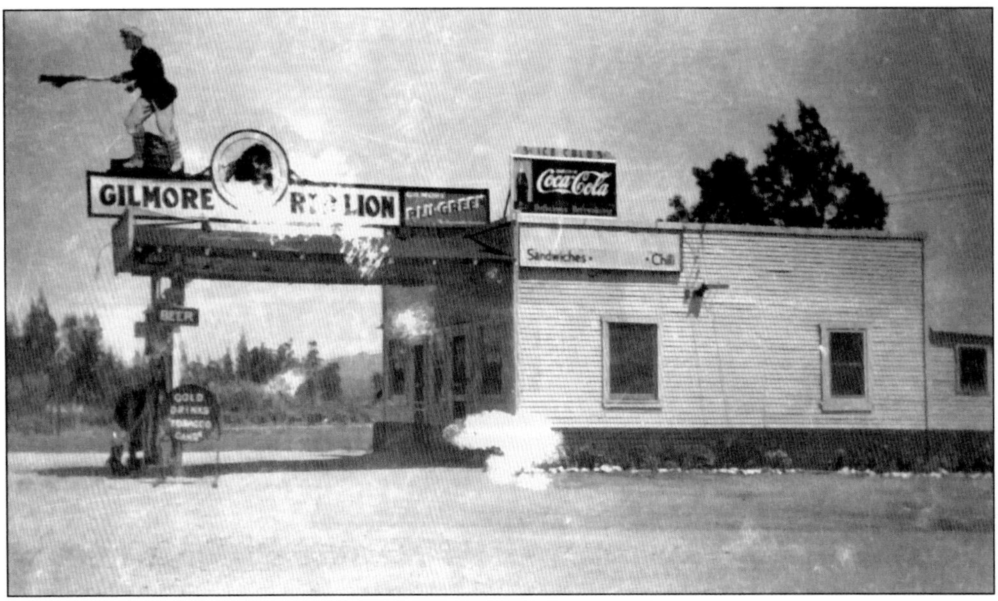

GLEN AVON GAS STATION. This 1938 photograph shows a combination gas station, grocery store, and lunch counter that was located on the southeast corner of Mission Boulevard and Lindsay Street in Glen Avon. As shown on the sign, the station sold Gilmore Red Lion gasoline. Lawrence St. Marie ran this business for just one year—he and his family had to weather the 1938 flood here. For two weeks, they had to go to Ontario for supplies because the route into Riverside was cut off. (Courtesy Bill St. Marie.)

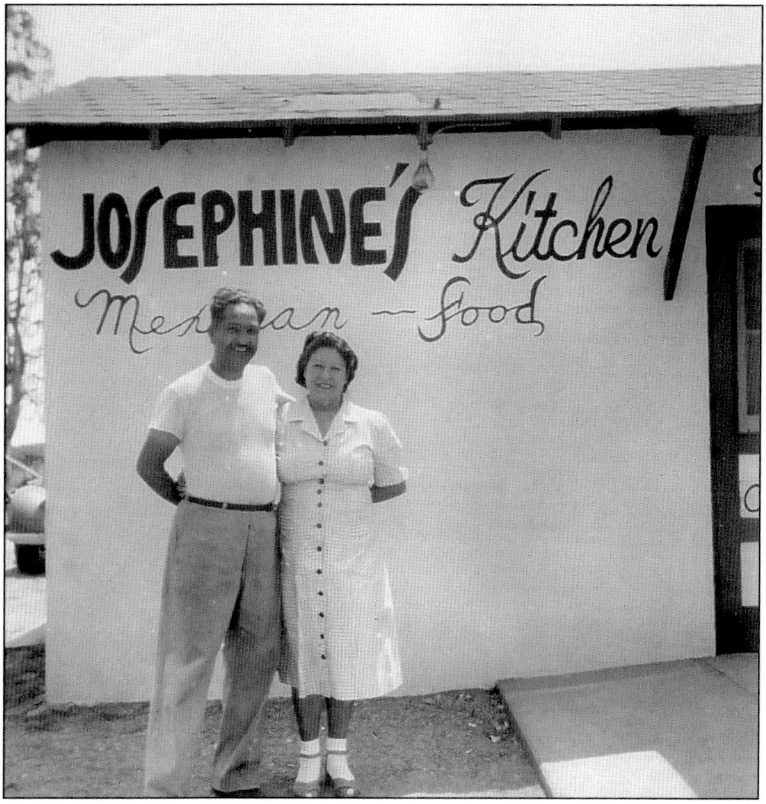

JOSEPHINE'S KITCHEN. This Mexican restaurant, owned by Ben and Josephine Chavez from 1946 to 1964, was located in Glen Avon on Mission Boulevard across from Sacred Heart Church. This photograph shows the Chavezes outside the restaurant. (Courtesy Ethel Chavez Sanborn.)

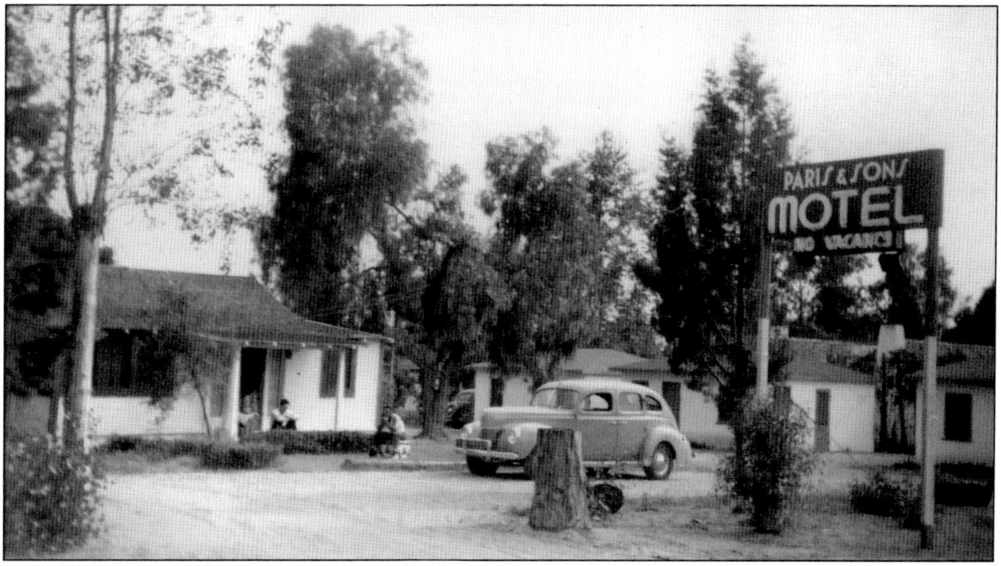

PARIS AND SONS MOTEL, 1948. In 1946 or 1947, C. L. Paris Sr. built this motel. The hoped for overnight traffic along Highway 60 did not materialized so the motel soon became apartments. These apartments are still located on Ben Nevis Boulevard between Kenneth and Hunter Streets in Glen Avon. (Courtesy Cates family.)

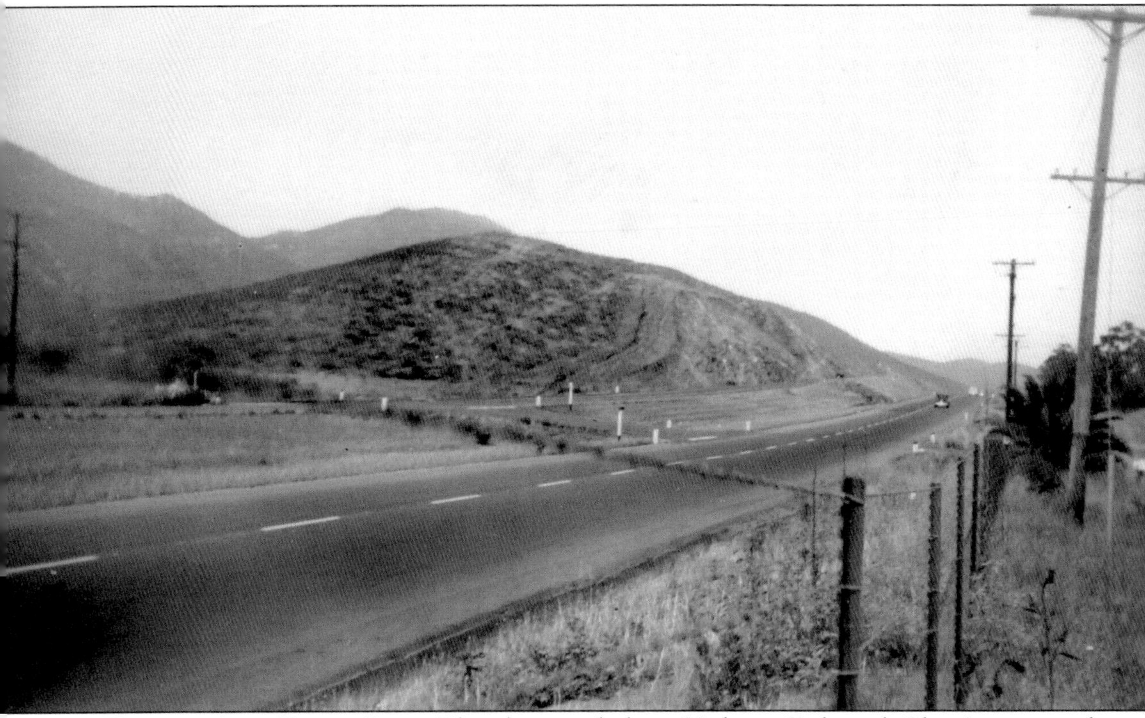

HIGHWAY 60 AT PEDLEY ROAD. This photograph shows Highway 60 through Glen Avon around 1948. The two-lane road was later replaced with the much wider 60 Freeway. When a race was happening at Riverside International Raceway, neighborhood children would watch the traffic go by on its way from the Los Angeles area to the races. It was their chance to see new and expensive cars that they might never see in Glen Avon. The children thought it was great fun to pick out their dream cars as they watched the traffic go by. (Courtesy Cates family.)

CIRCLE INN CAFE. Jack, Jean, and Cliff Paris Jr. are in front of the Circle Inn Cafe at Mission Boulevard and Lindsay Street in Glen Avon. Their parents, C. L. and Lola (Bobbie) Paris, owned the cafe from 1936 to 1940. (Courtesy Cates family.)

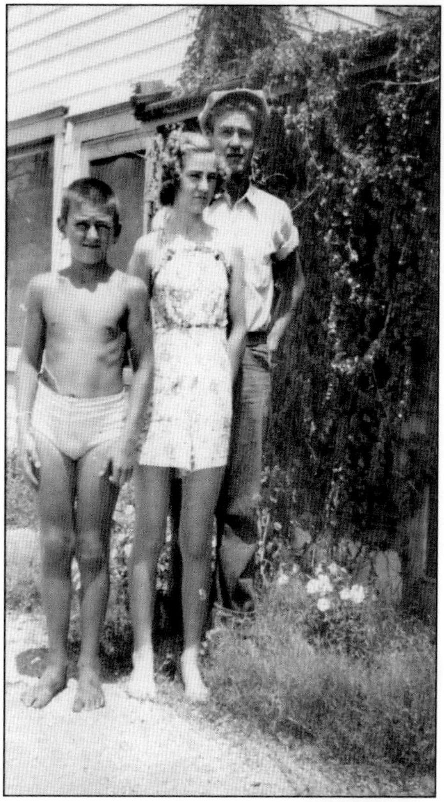

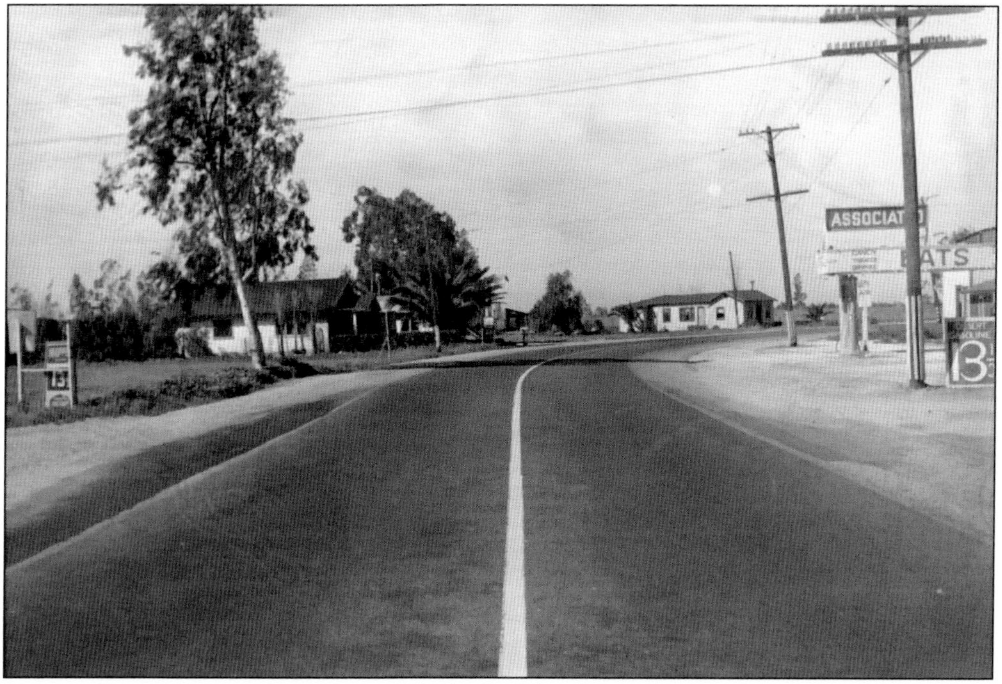

MISSION BOULEVARD IN GLEN AVON. The back of the photograph says this is Mission Boulevard, 1949, in Glen Avon near the Circle Inn. (Courtesy Jurupa Mountains Cultural Center.)

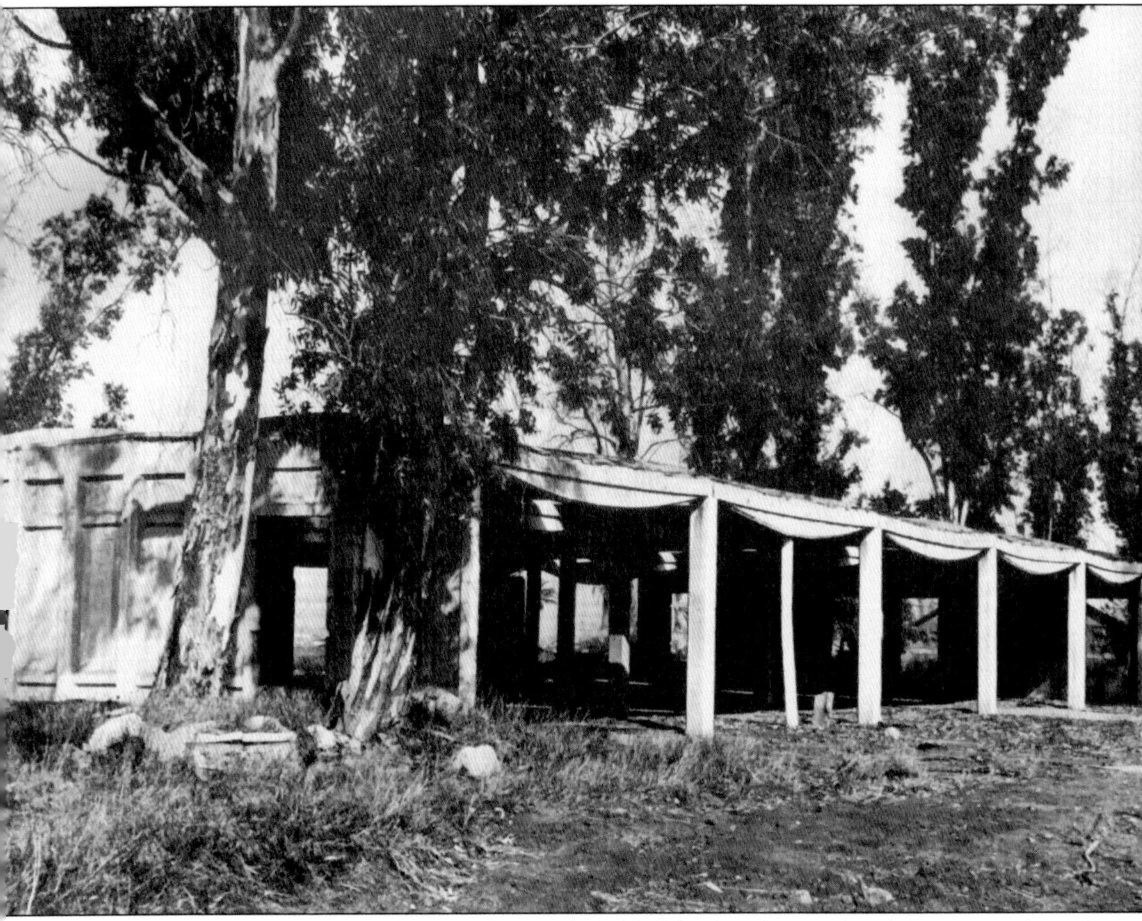

PEDLEY PACKINGHOUSE. William Pedley, on behalf of the San Jacinto Land Company, planted hundreds of acres of citrus in the Pedley area. To accommodate the crop, Pedley built a packinghouse in 1905, along the newly laid railroad tracks near the river. He built the packinghouse using a then innovative technique. He prefabricated much of the building by pouring cement into molds on the ground and then "tilting" the pieces up into place. (Courtesy Riverside Municipal Museum.)

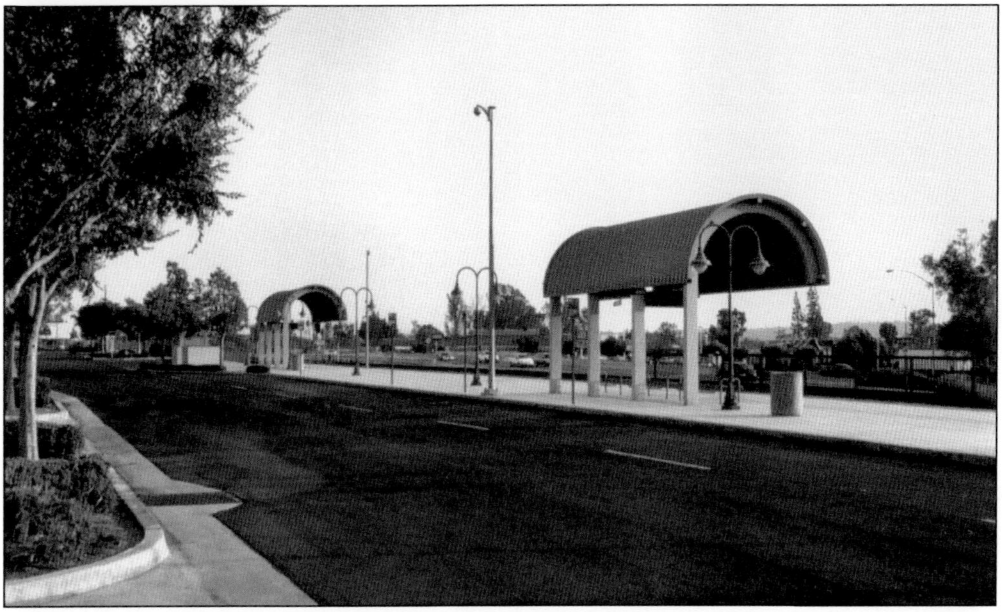

SITE OF PEDLEY STATION. On the site of the present-day Metrolink Station was the original Pedley Train Station. Built when the railroad came through (about 1904) and named for William Pedley, it burned down in 1920 and was never rebuilt. (Courtesy author.)

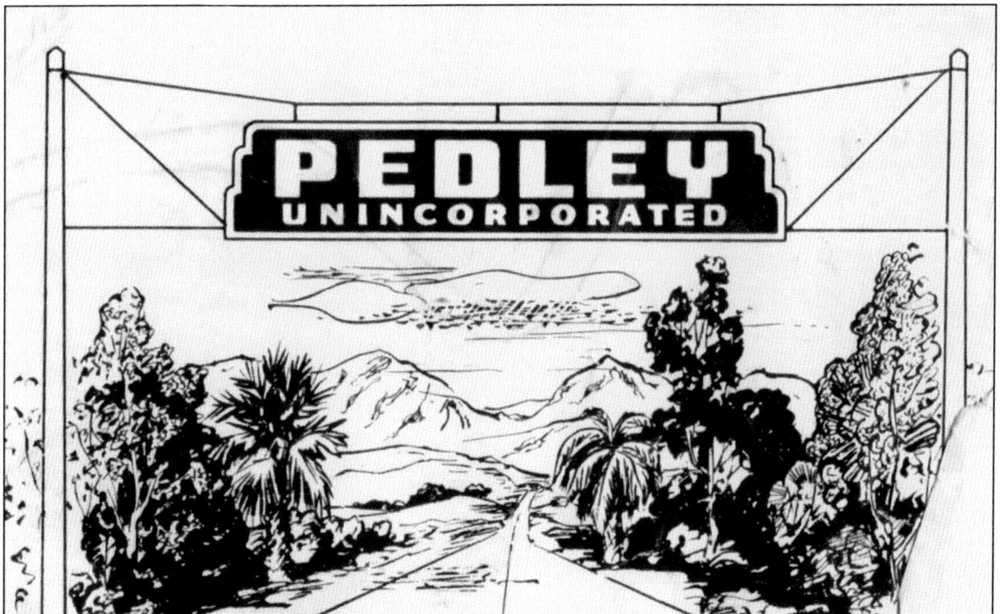

PEDLEY SIGN. Prior to 1946, Pedley was a community with very little in the way of business and shopping. That began to change in the late 1940s when several businesses were established along Limonite Avenue on either side of the railroad tracks. (Van Buren Boulevard did not extend to Pedley at that time.) Around 1950, the businessmen of Pedley chipped in $600 to buy a neon sign that said "Pedley, Unincorporated." It was hung over Limonite Avenue. This is a drawing of that sign that appeared on the cover of the map of Pedley published by the Pedley Chamber of Commerce in the early 1950s. (Courtesy Julie and Del Coats.)

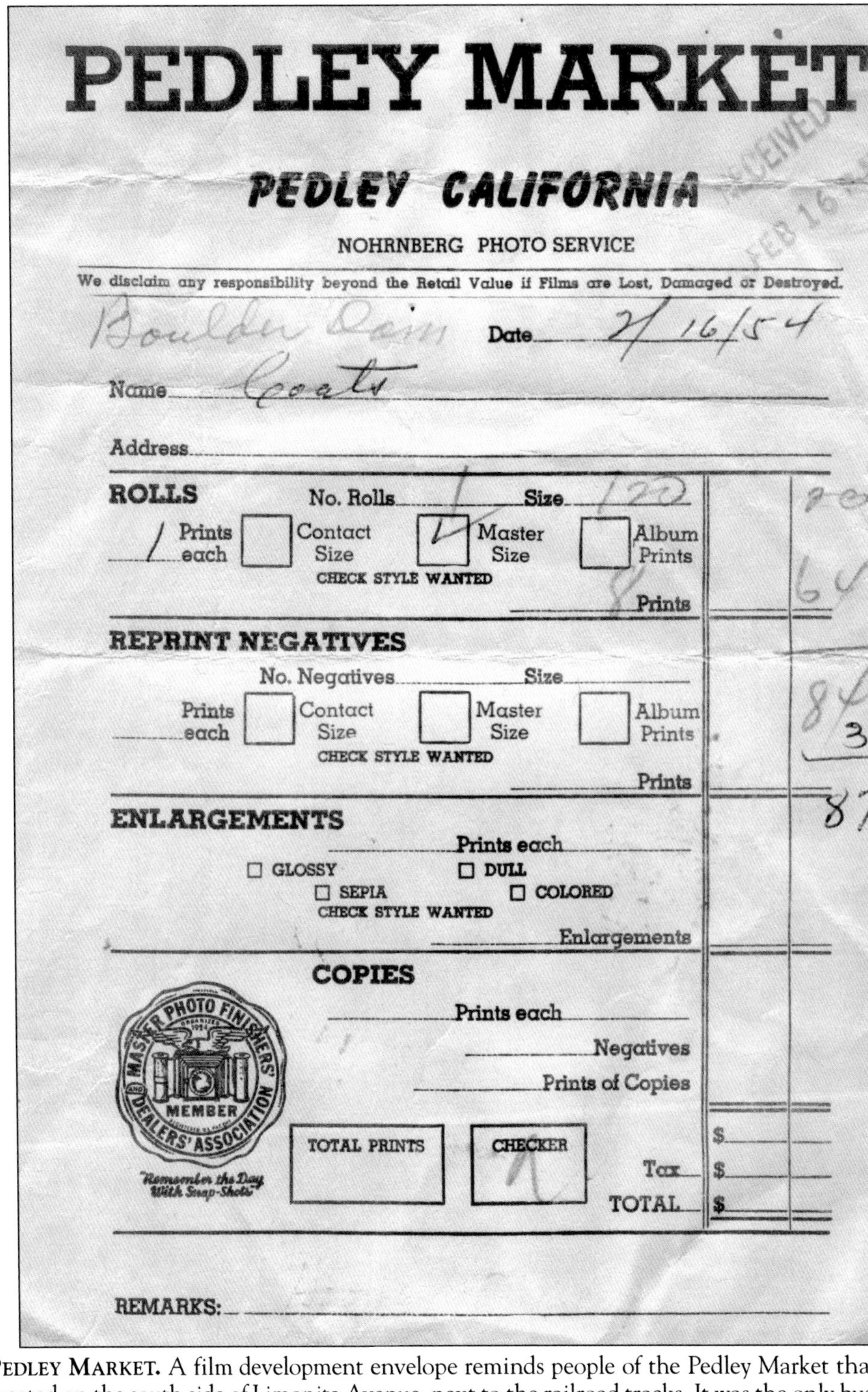

PEDLEY MARKET

PEDLEY CALIFORNIA

NOHRNBERG PHOTO SERVICE

We disclaim any responsibility beyond the Retail Value if Films are Lost, Damaged or Destroyed.

Boulder Dam Date 2/16/54

Name Coats

Address

ROLLS No. Rolls 1 Size 120

1 Prints each | Contact Size | Master Size | Album Prints

CHECK STYLE WANTED

8 Prints

REPRINT NEGATIVES

No. Negatives Size

Prints each | Contact Size | Master Size | Album Prints

CHECK STYLE WANTED

Prints

ENLARGEMENTS

Prints each

GLOSSY DULL SEPIA COLORED

CHECK STYLE WANTED

Enlargements

COPIES

Prints each

Negatives

Prints of Copies

MASTER PHOTO FINISHERS' AND DEALERS' ASSOCIATION MEMBER

"Remember the Day With Snap-Shots"

TOTAL PRINTS

CHECKER

$

Tax $

TOTAL $

REMARKS:

PEDLEY MARKET. A film development envelope reminds people of the Pedley Market that was located on the south side of Limonite Avenue, next to the railroad tracks. It was the only business in Pedley before the building boom of the late 1940s. This envelope dates from 1954. (Courtesy Julie and Del Coats.)

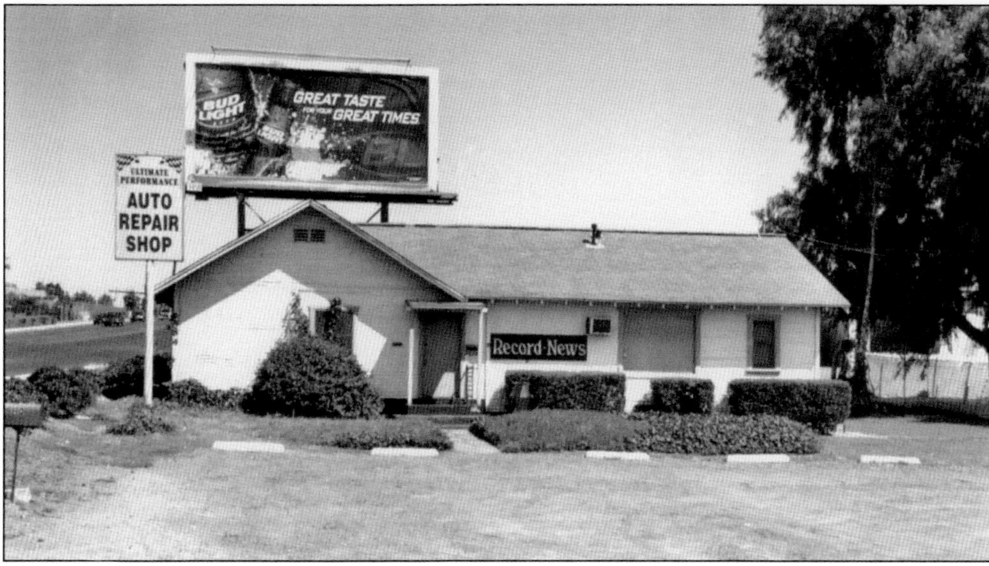

Tom Clay's Water Company Office. Lawyer Tom Clay was brought to Riverside in 1929 by Jurupa landowner and sub divider William Sparr (Sparrland) to help Sparr avoid foreclosure. Clay took over the $200,000 mortgage himself, beginning a decades-long association with Jurupa. He bought up additional property and began ranching his "1001 Ranch." This building started life in 1929 as a house and was converted to the Jurupa Heights Water Company office in 1947. Clay later sold off his holdings, including the land for what became Jurupa Hills and Indian Hills. (Courtesy author.)

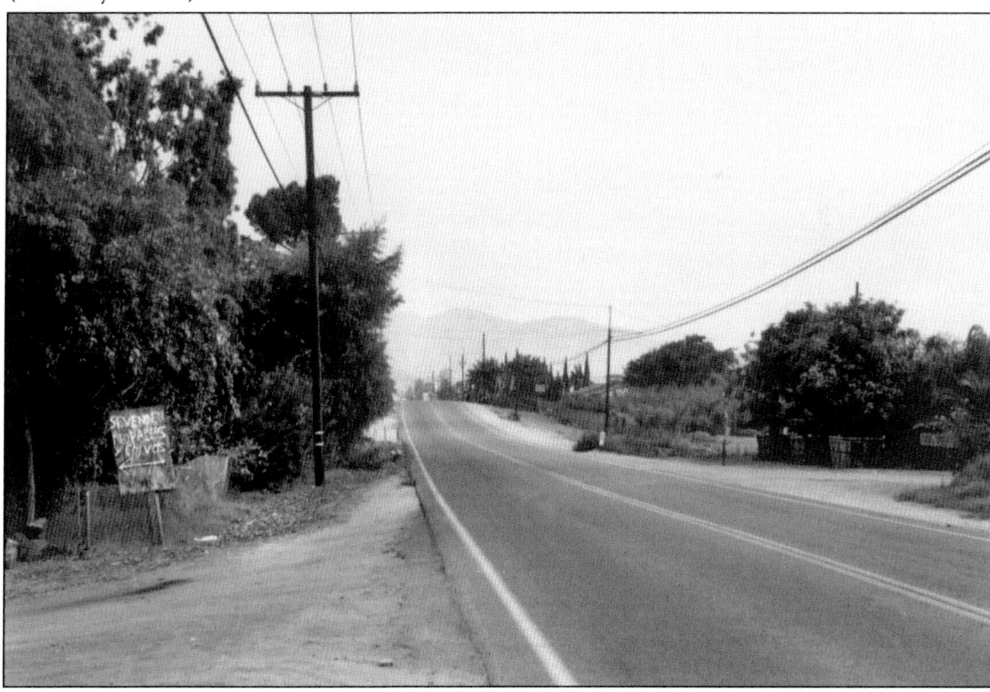

Pedley Road. Pedley Road looks much today like it did 50 years ago. It was one of the earliest paved roads in Jurupa, possibly as early as 1928. This view of Pedley Road looks north. (Courtesy author.)

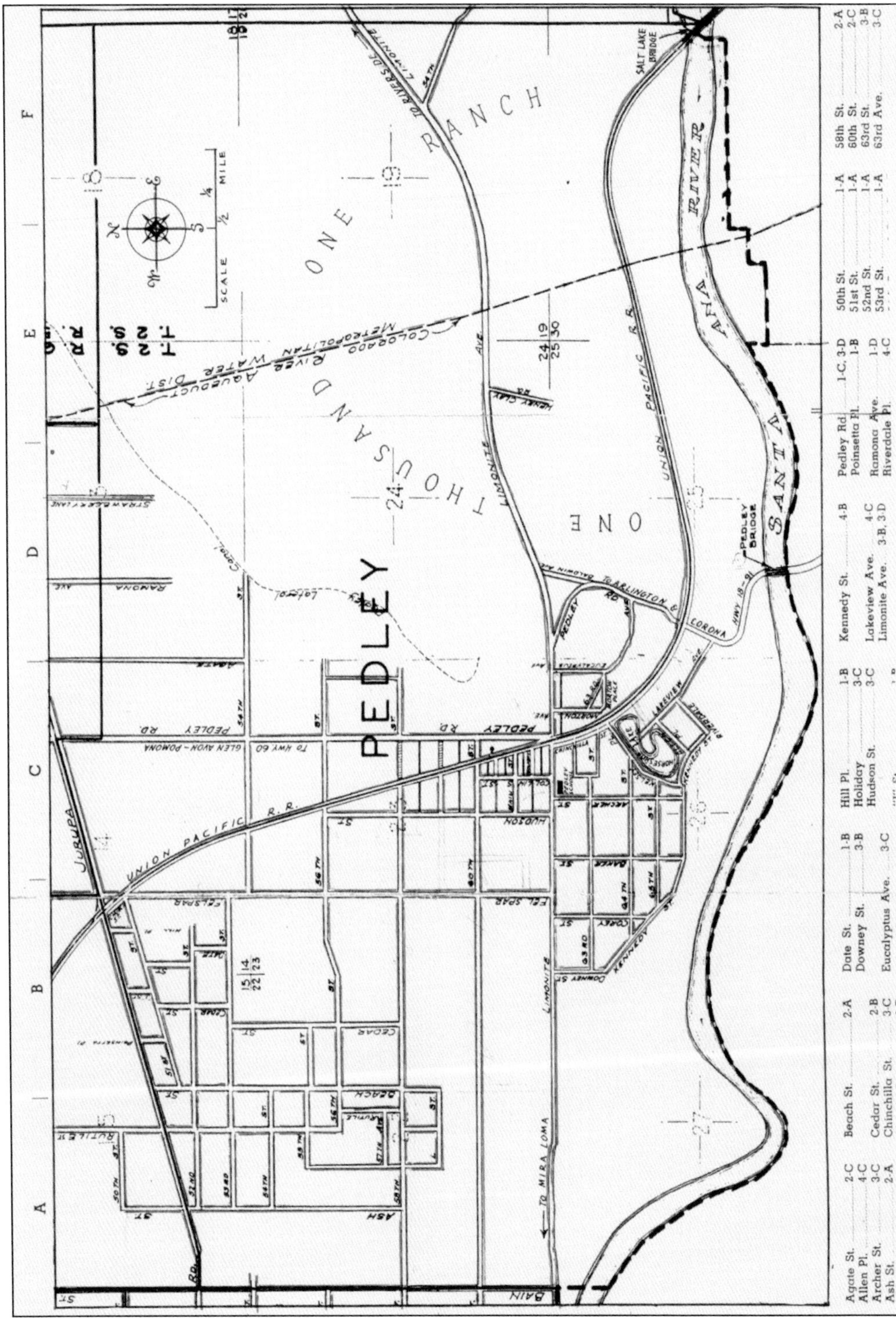

MAP OF PEDLEY. This map, which probably dates from the early 1950s, shows Pedley before the development of Indian Hills. To the lower right of the map is Tom Clay's 1001 Ranch. (Courtesy Julie and Del Coats.)

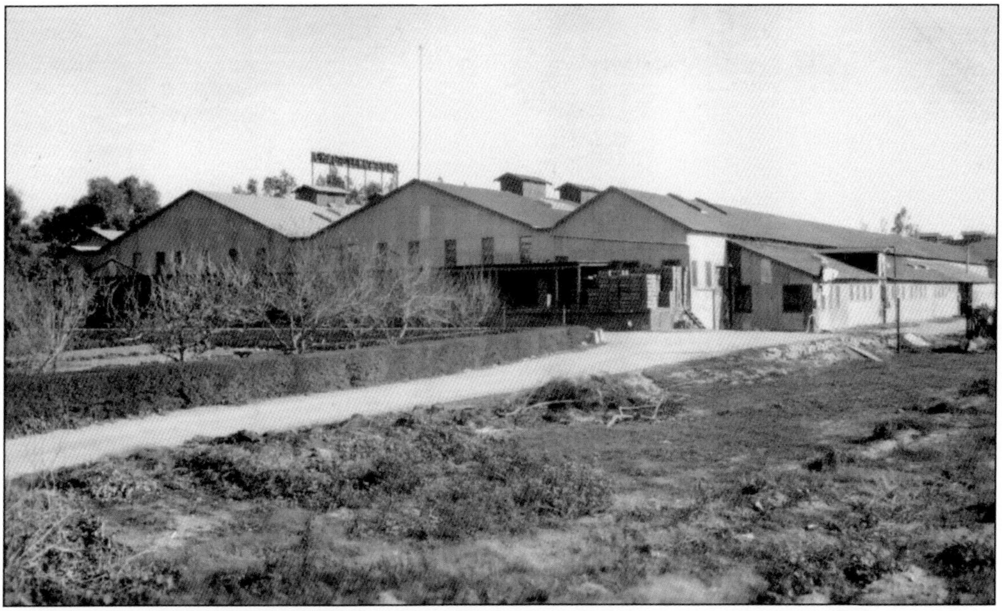

STEARNS CANNERY. Charles Stearns started the Riverside Vineyard Company and built a winery on the east side of Etiwanda Avenue, a mile north of today's 60 Freeway, near the Riverside–San Bernardino County line. It later became a cannery for fruits, primarily apricots. (Courtesy Riverside Metropolitan Museum.)

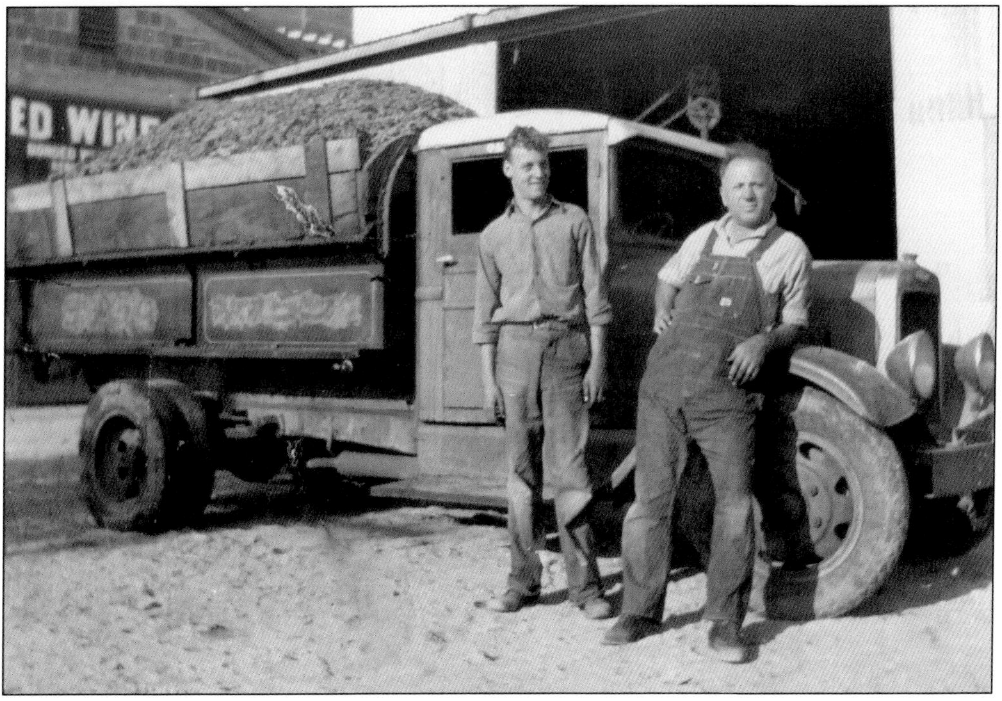

MARIETTA WINERY. In 1935, the Marietta family constructed their winery at the northeast corner of Bellgrave Avenue and Wineville Road. They had 65 acres of vineyards. Standing next to the truck full of grapes is Charlie Marietta, right, with his nephew Frank. The original house is still on the property, but the winery closed in 1959. (Courtesy Chuck Marietta.)

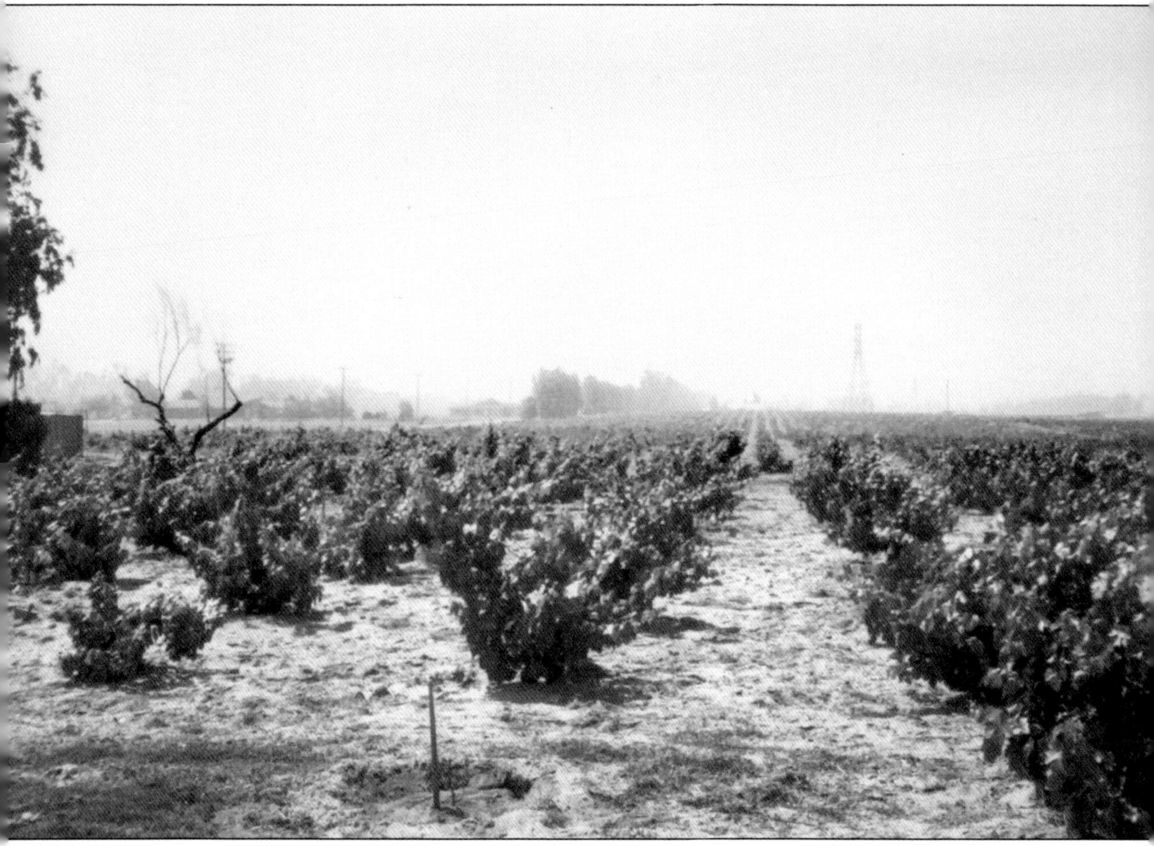

GALLEANO GRAPE VINEYARD. The extreme northwest portion of Jurupa is part of the larger Cucamonga Valley grape-growing area, an area that became well known for its wine production. In 1927, Dominico and Lucia Galleano, Italian immigrants, purchased the 160-acre Cantu ranch in Wineville, including a vineyard. The Galleanos began making wine in their basement. After the repeal of Prohibition in 1933, the winery opened as a commercial business. Along with the other wineries in the Cucamonga Valley, the Galleano Winery grew and thrived. It is the only winery in the area still owned by its founding family and operating at its original site. The winery complex on Wineville Road is on the National Register of Historic Places. (Courtesy Galleano family.)

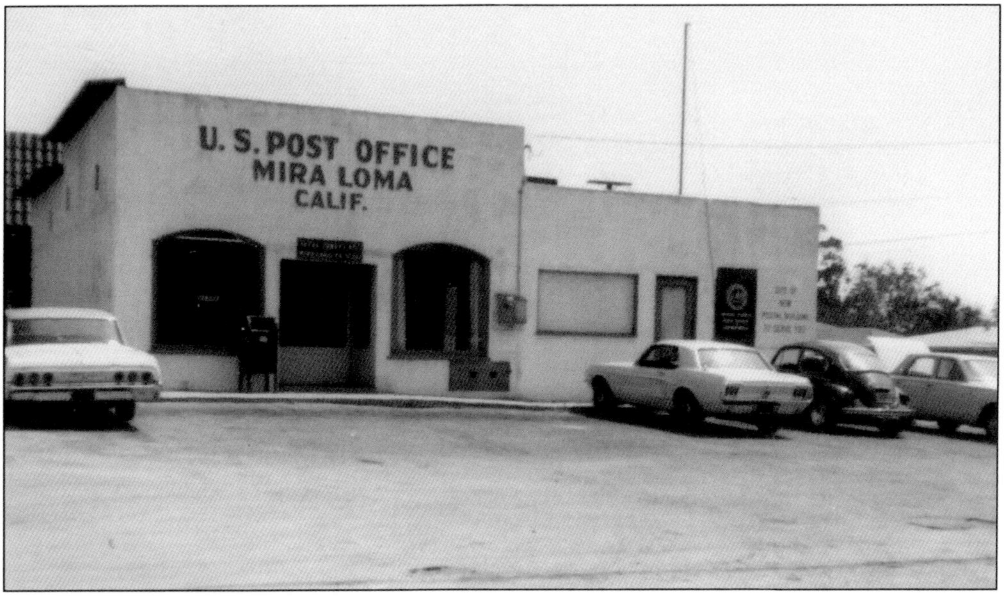

MIRA LOMA POST OFFICE. Until this post office was built in the mid-1940s at the corner of Martin Street and Jurupa Road, the Mira Loma Post Office had been in someone's home or store. The small building on the right was the post office, and Margaret Blair had one of her stores in the larger building. Later the post office took over the larger building as well. In the 1970s, an even larger office was needed. The current post office was built on the same site, facing Jurupa Road, and the old post office was torn down. (Courtesy Phillip and Arletta Klock collection.)

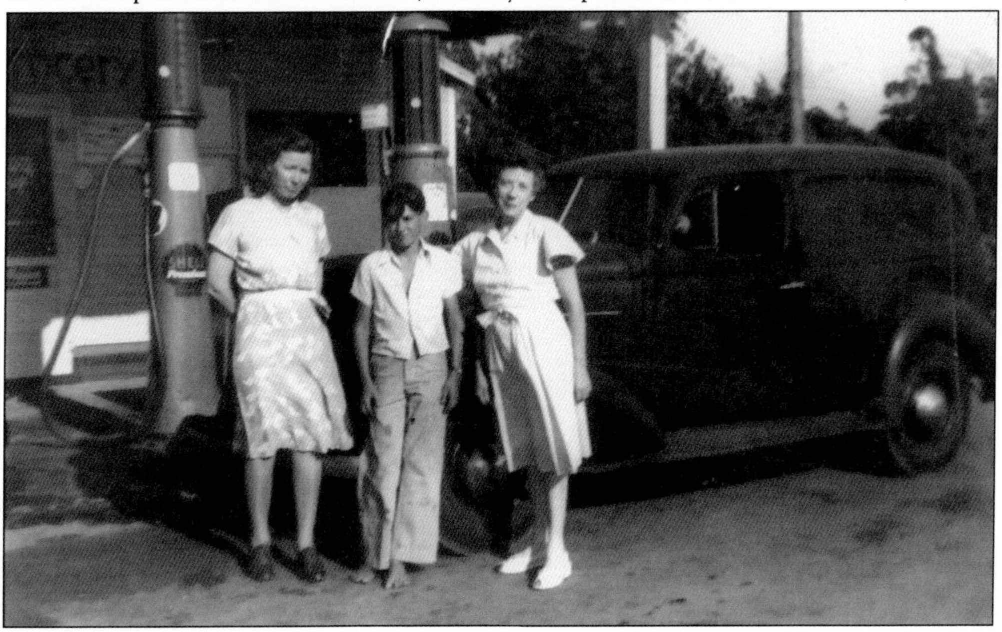

MARGARET BLAIR'S MARKET, 1946. At one time or another, Margaret Blair owned at least three different markets in Mira Loma. This market was located at Etiwanda Avenue and Jurupa Road. In addition to the market, it had gas pumps out front. Shown in front of the market are unidentified, Dewey Spencer, and Margaret Blair. Dewey was 13 years old and had recently gone to work at the market. (Courtesy Helen Abacherli Spencer.)

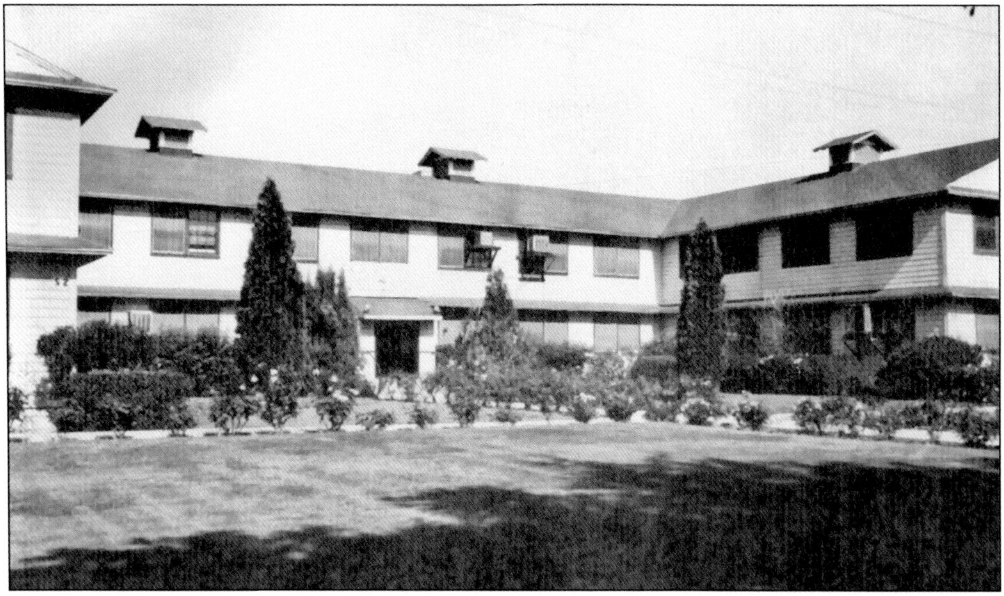

Mira Loma Quartermaster Depot. In 1942, the farm fields at Etiwanda Avenue and U.S. Highway 60 were replaced by the Mira Loma Quartermaster Depot of the U.S. Army. From there, supplies were sent all over the Pacific theater. It was scheduled for closing in 1949 until the Korean War broke out. It was transferred to the air force in 1955 and became home to a number of air force activities. It was later privatized and is now known as the Mira Loma Space Center, which is located at 3401 Etiwanda Avenue. (Courtesy Riverside Municipal Museum.)

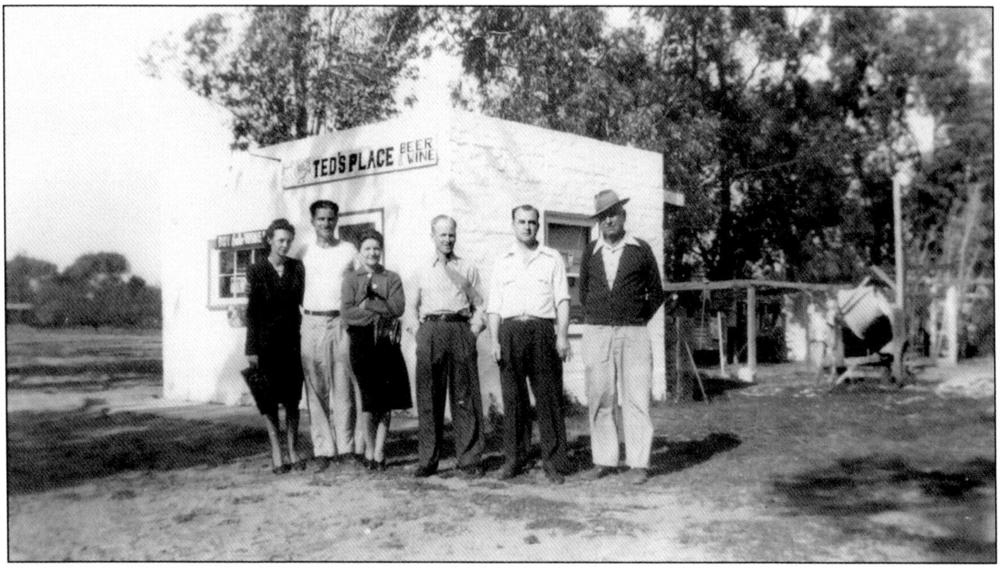

Ted's Place. In 1948, Ted and Rose Parma started this small market. Its name, however, made people think the business was a bar so in the mid-1950s, Rose insisted on a name change to Parma's Market. The market was located at 5348 Troth Street on the Parma family property. It closed in the 1960s. Pictured, from left to right, are Mabel Parma, Ted Parma, Rosalie and Carl Swanson, Bill Parma, and Luis Parma. Luis, Ted's father, came to the Mira Loma area from Mexico to manage the Cantu Ranch. That property later became part of the Galleano Winery property. (Courtesy Grace Parma Sollecito.)

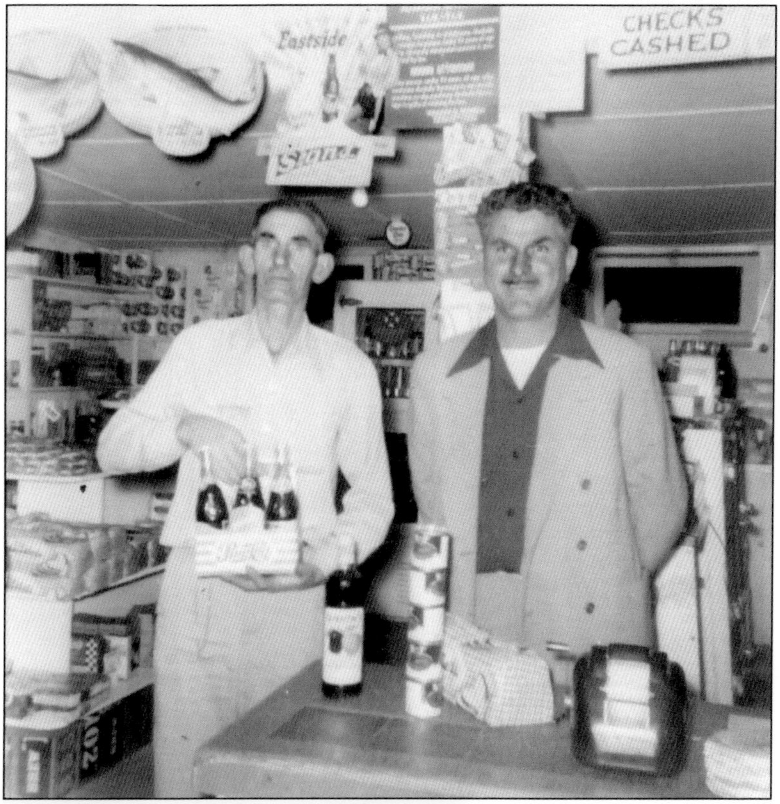

INSIDE TED'S PLACE. Glen Galvas and Ted Parma are shown inside the Parma family market about 1954. (Courtesy Grace Parma Sollecito.)

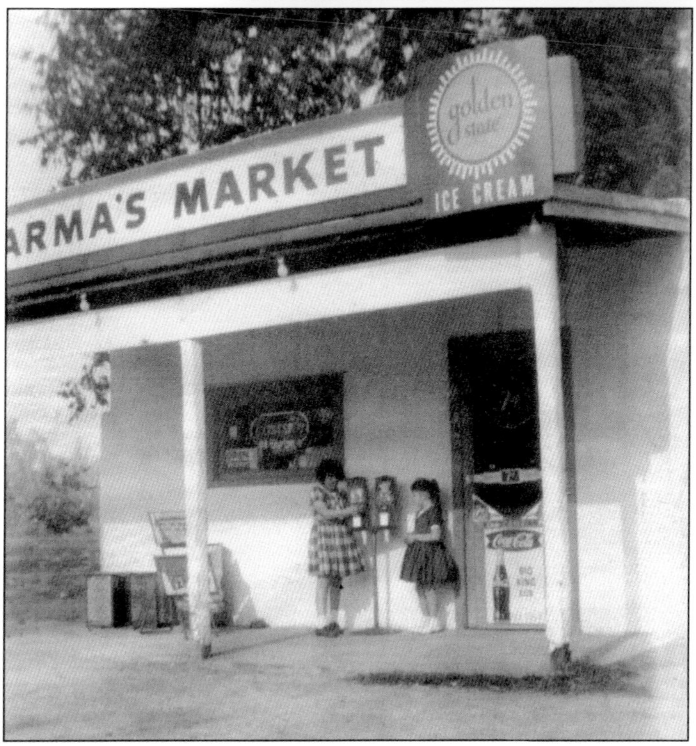

PARMA'S MARKET. In 1959, Linda Parma and a friend are shown outside Parma's Market. (Courtesy Grace Parma Sollecito.)

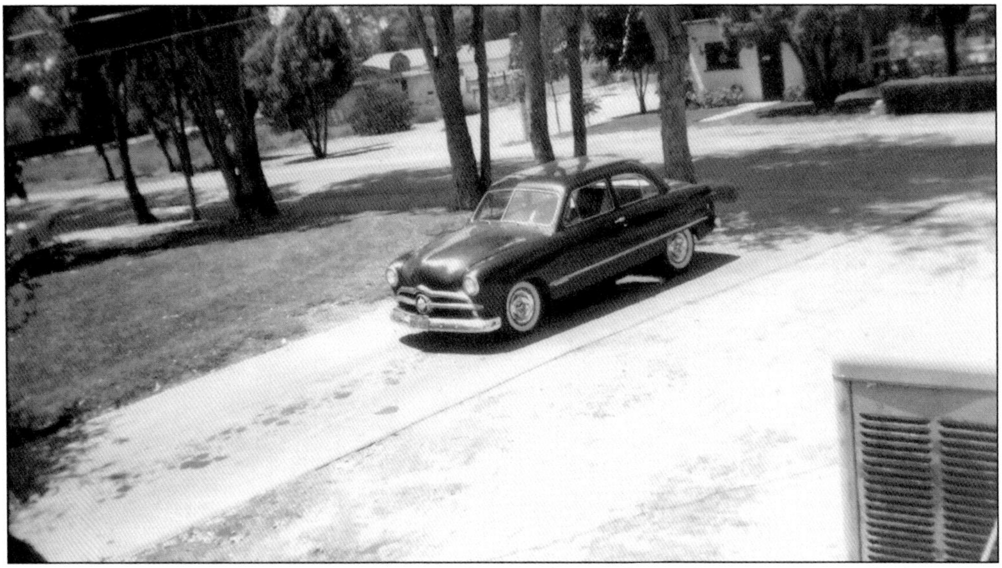

BESSER'S SHOE STORE. This 1960 photograph was taken in front of Parma's Market looking west across Troth Street. The building across the street was Besser's Shoe Store. (Courtesy Grace Parma Sollecito.)

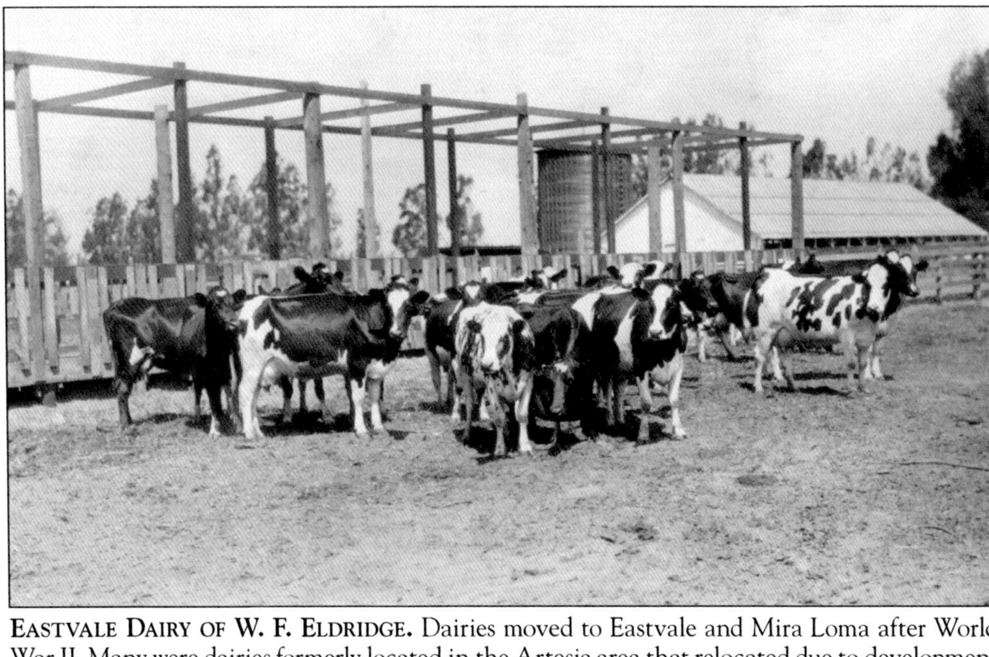

EASTVALE DAIRY OF W. F. ELDRIDGE. Dairies moved to Eastvale and Mira Loma after World War II. Many were dairies formerly located in the Artesia area that relocated due to development pressures. This story is repeating itself as these same dairies are now being replaced by housing developments. (Courtesy Riverside Metropolitan Museum.)

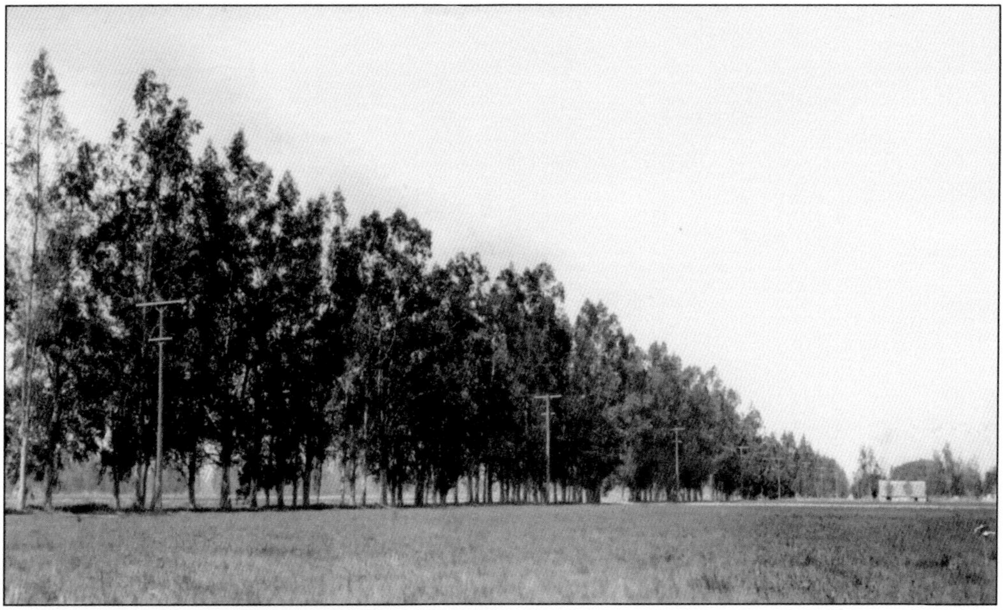

CLOVERDALE ROAD, EASTVALE. After Limonite Avenue crosses Hamner Avenue, it becomes Cloverdale Road. This photograph shows Cloverdale Road when it was still rural and Mira Loma was home to agricultural uses. Now this area is full of businesses and homes. (Courtesy Riverside Metropolitan Museum.)

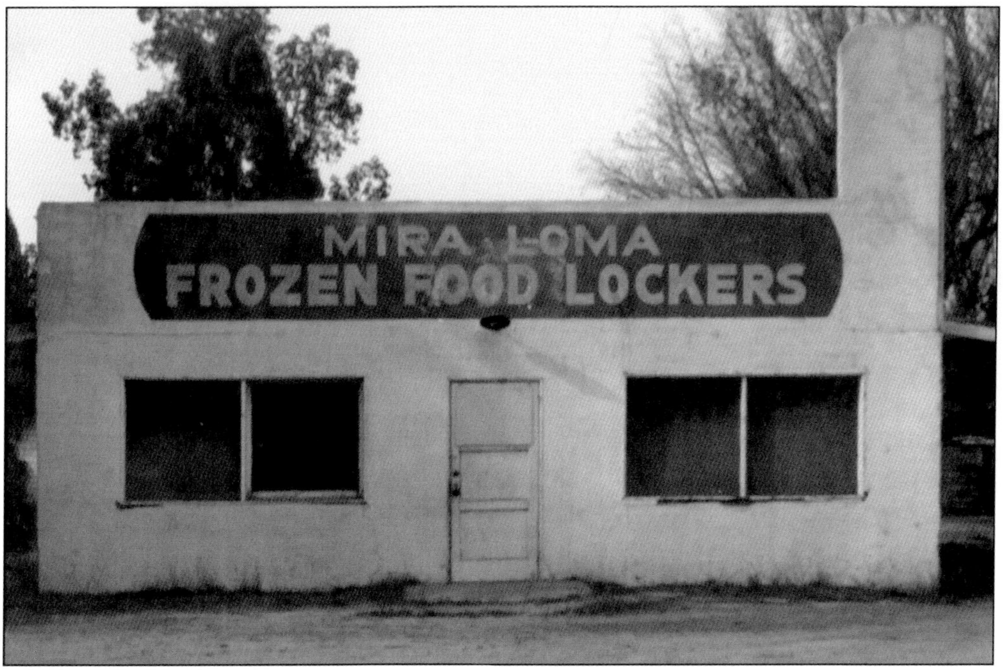

MIRA LOMA FROZEN FOOD LOCKER. In a rural area, the frozen food locker business was an important one. Many people raised their own animals for meat and brought their animals to the Mira Loma Frozen Food Locker for butchering and wrapping. The locker could store the meat in their freezer as well, if a home freezer was not available. The Mira Loma Frozen Food Locker was located on Troth Street, south of Fifty-sixth Street. (Courtesy Dorothy Brown.)

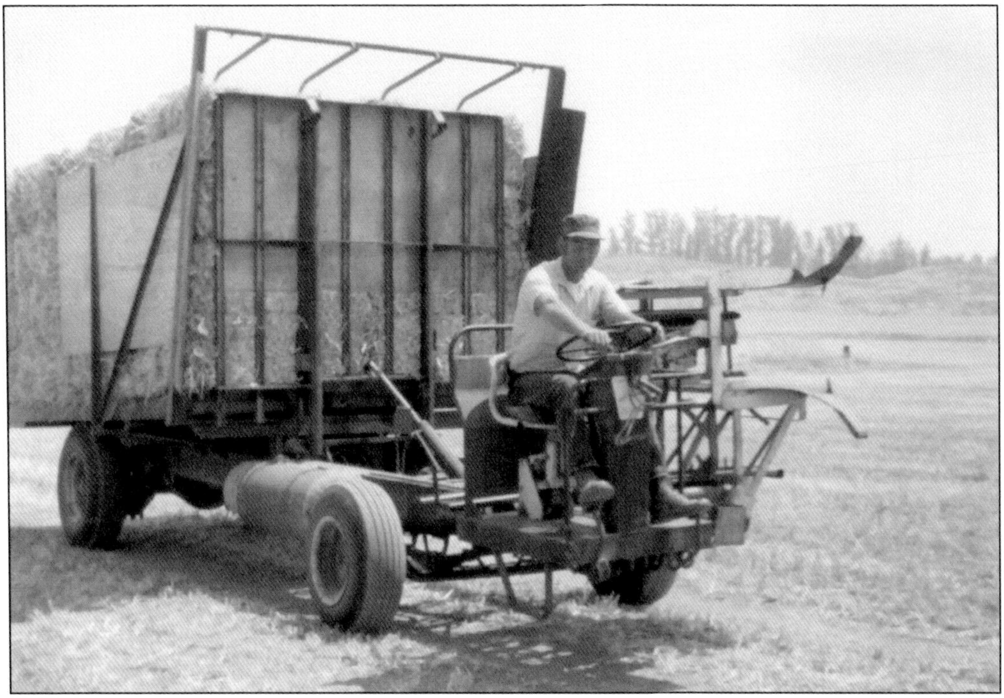

BALING HAY. Until the 1990s, agriculture was the main business in the Mira Loma and Eastvale areas. Here Dewey Spencer is shown baling hay on property at Etiwanda and Limonite Avenues about 1972. (Courtesy Helen Abacherli Spencer.)

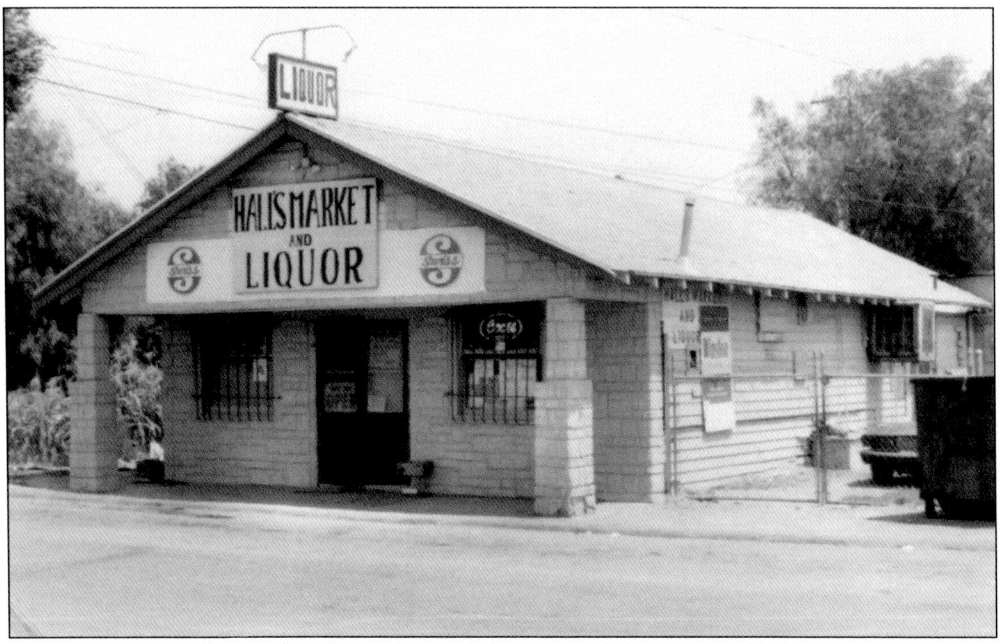

HALL'S MARKET. Originally a bungalow-style home on Hall Street in Belltown c. 1926, it was later converted to a market. The market became important to the residents of Belltown who didn't have any other stores close by. The market is still in business today. (Courtesy Riverside County Regional Park and Open-Space District.)

Six

Home Life

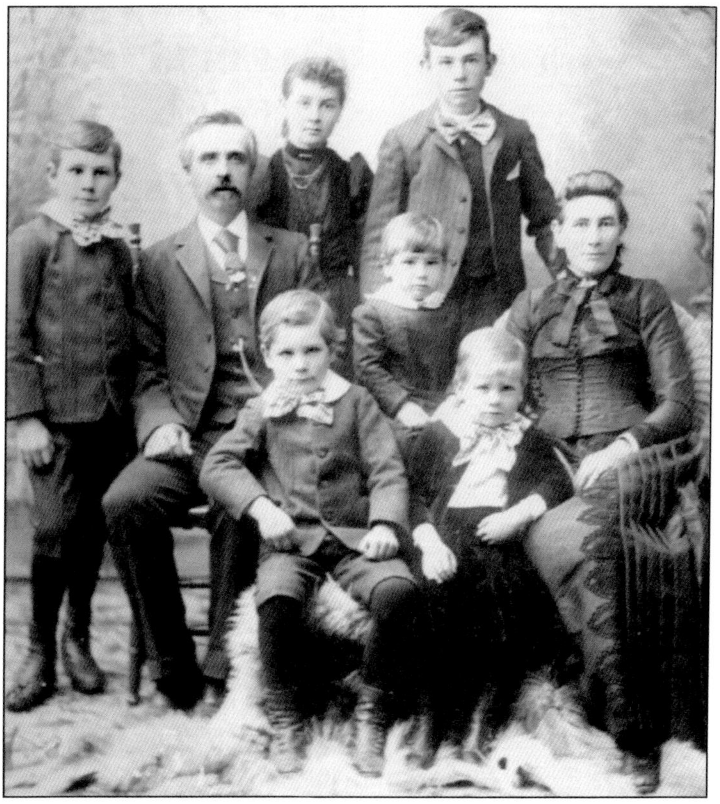

Heber Parks Family, 1891. By 1891, the Parks family had six children. Pictured, from left to right, are (first row) Albert and Russell, (second row) Elmo, Heber, Arch, and Ida; (third row) Gertrude and George. The family added two more children in the next three years: Miran was born in 1892 and Lydia in 1894. (Courtesy Ida Parks Condit family.)

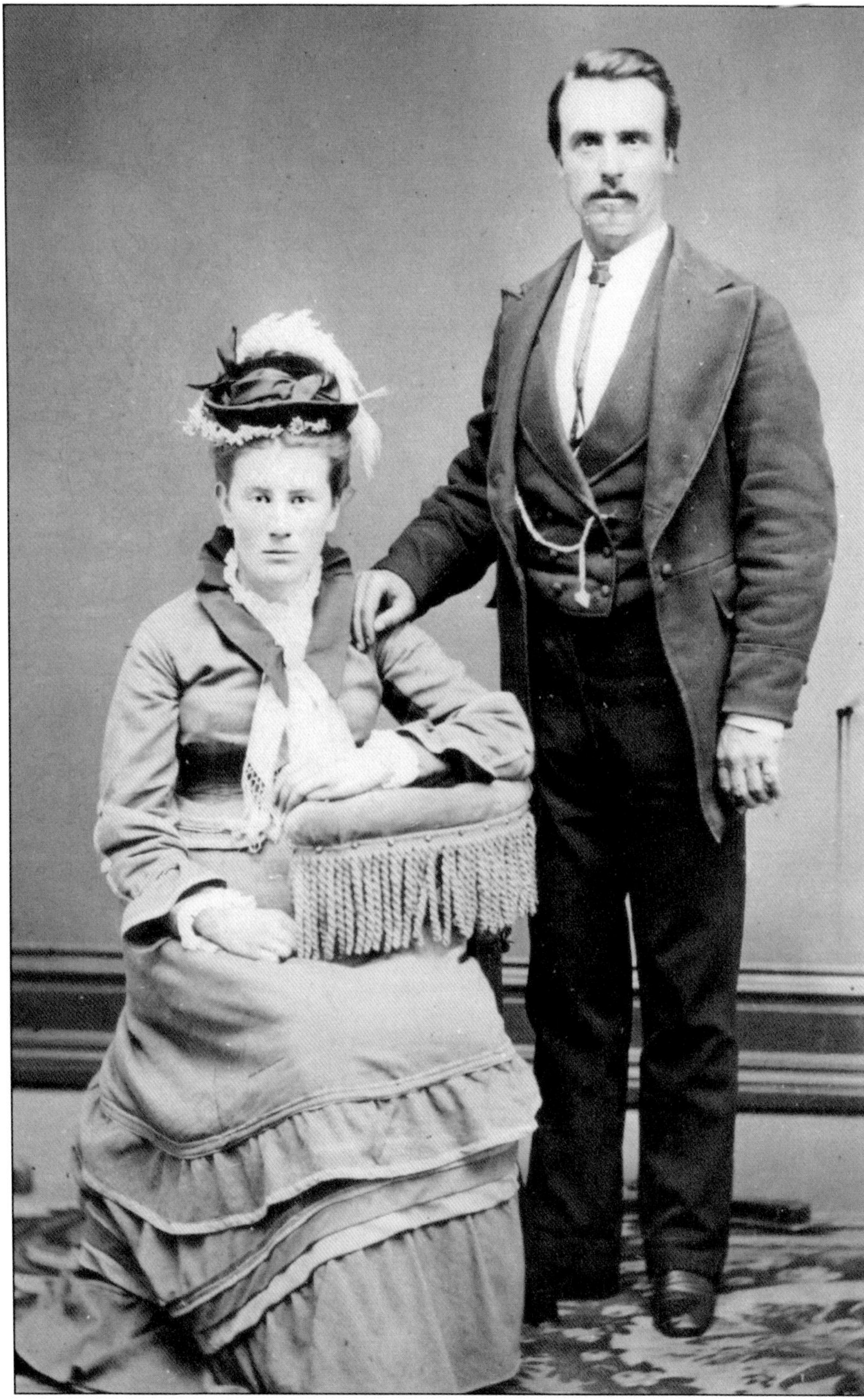

HEBER AND IDA PARKS. This is the wedding photograph of early settler Arthur Parks' oldest son. On May 19, 1875, Heber and Ida were married. Like his father, Heber was involved in the local community. He was elected to the school board several times, was a registrar of voters, and was inspector on the election board for many years. (Courtesy Helen Lair.)

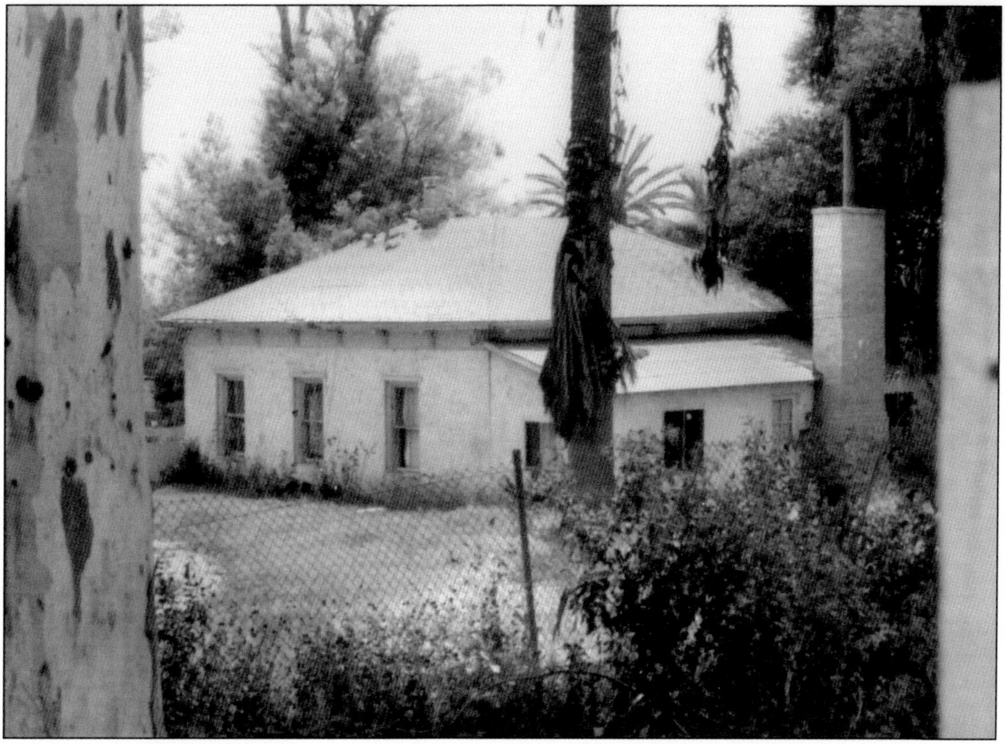

Jose Jensen Home. In 1887, Cornelius Jensen's son Jose married Valencia Case, a West Riverside School teacher who had boarded with the Jensens. Jose built an adobe home that stood at the corner of Riverview Road and Forty-second Street until it burned in 1983. (Courtesy Riverside County Regional Park and Open-Space District.)

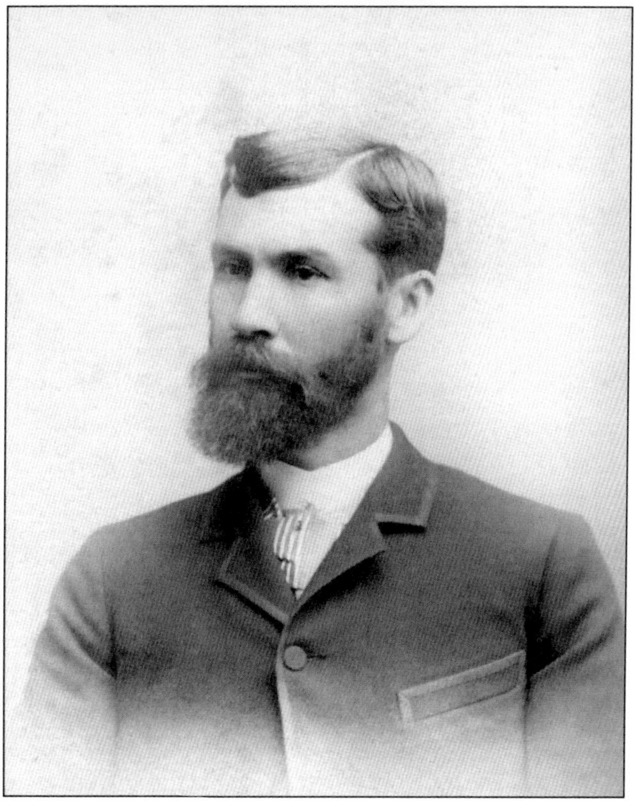

Jose Jensen. Jose was Cornelius and Mercedes Jensen's oldest son. (Courtesy Jensen family.)

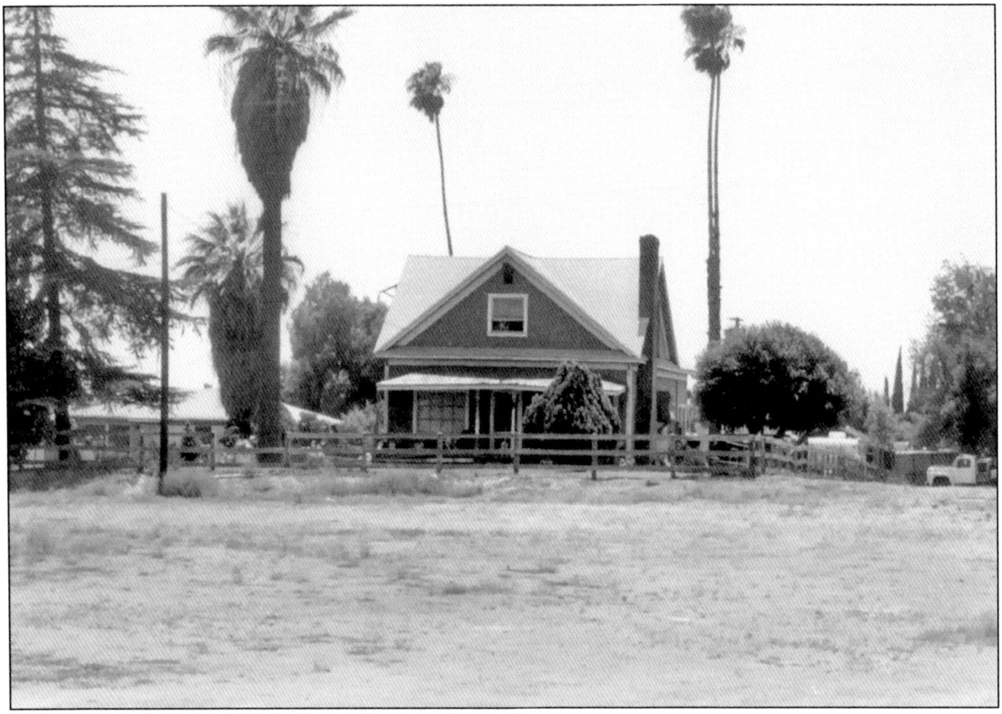

HENRY JENSEN HOME. Henry Jensen built a wood-framed home in 1890 on a portion of his parents ranch. He and his wife, Elizabeth, raised chickens, both for meat and eggs. Their house still stands on Forty-second Street, north of Riverview Drive. (Courtesy author.)

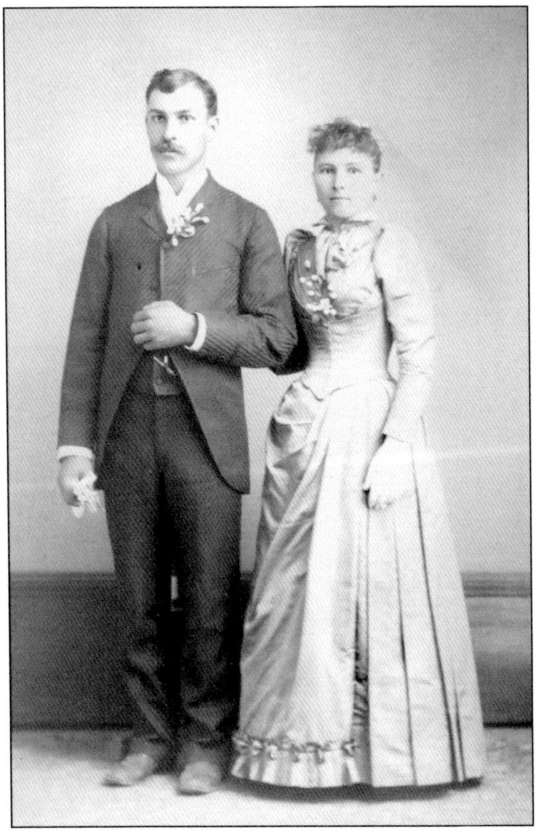

HENRY AND ELIZABETH JENSEN. Henry Jensen married Elizabeth Graser in August 1891. Henry was the seventh child of Cornelius and Mercedes Jensen. (Courtesy Jensen family.)

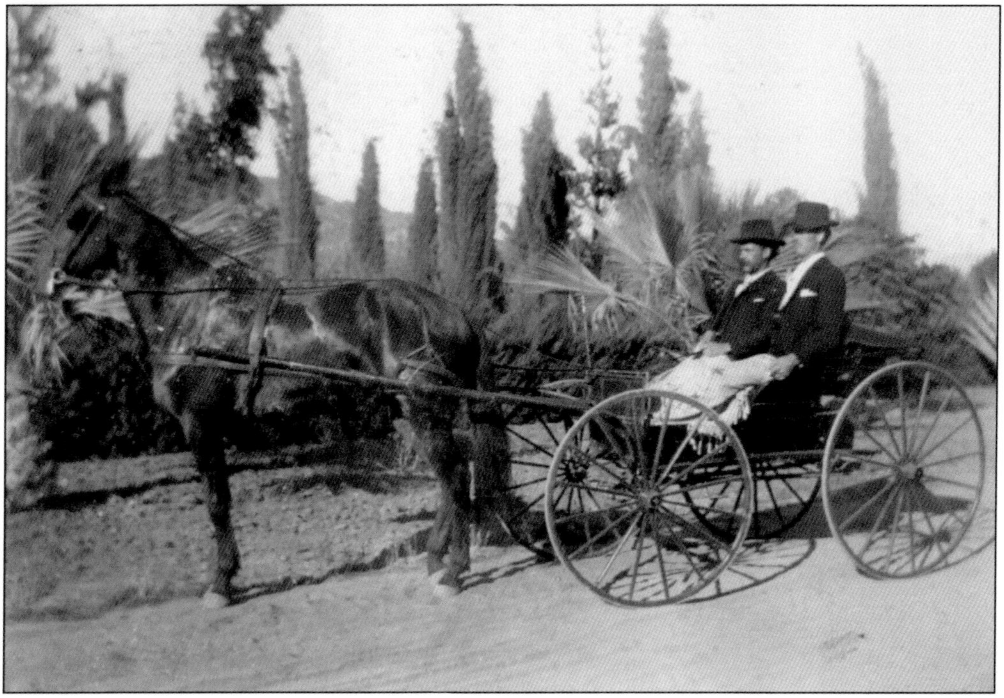

BUGGY ON MISSION BOULEVARD. IN 1899, John Jensen and an unidentified man are shown in a buggy on Mission Boulevard near Pacific Avenue. (Courtesy Jensen family.)

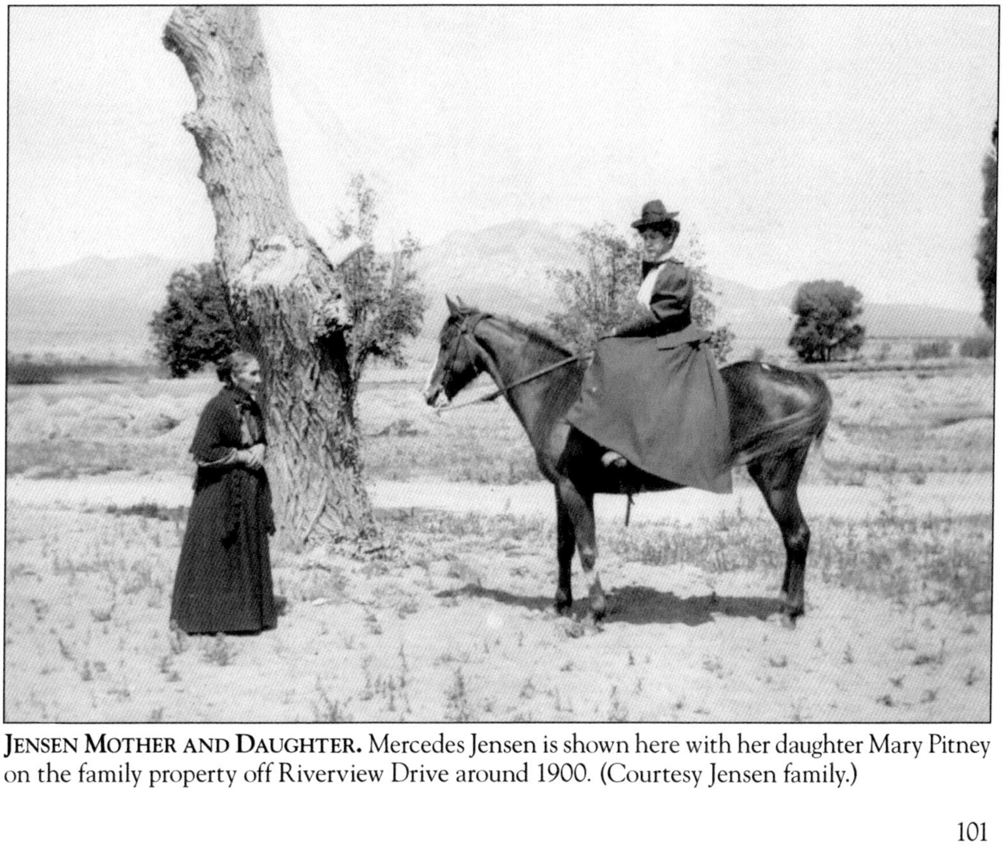

JENSEN MOTHER AND DAUGHTER. Mercedes Jensen is shown here with her daughter Mary Pitney on the family property off Riverview Drive around 1900. (Courtesy Jensen family.)

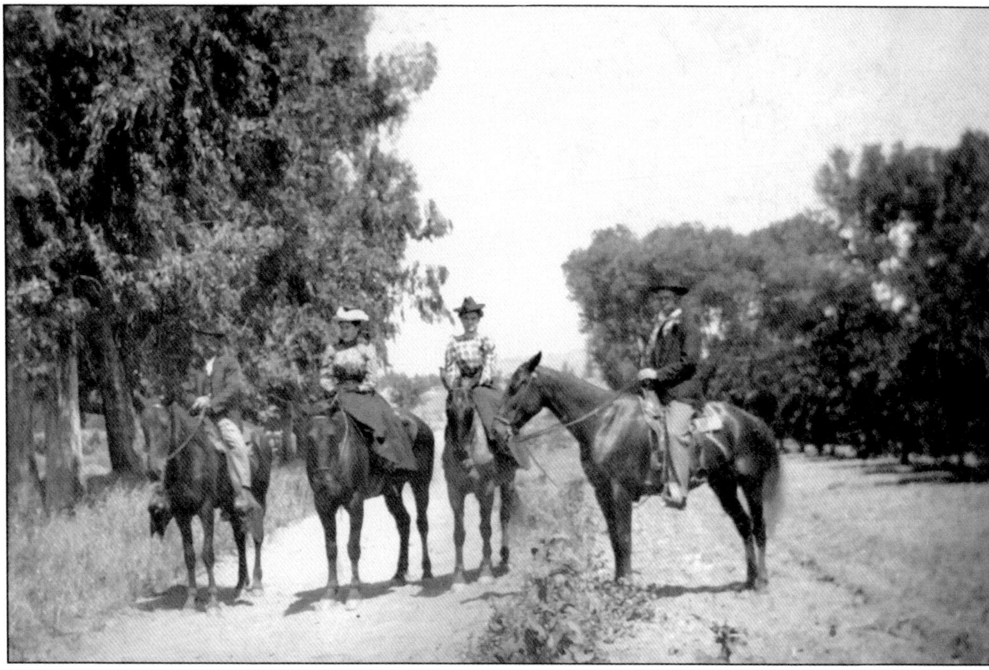

HORSEBACK RIDERS. Here members of the Jensen family are shown on the Jensen ranch enjoying a horseback ride. (Courtesy Jensen family.)

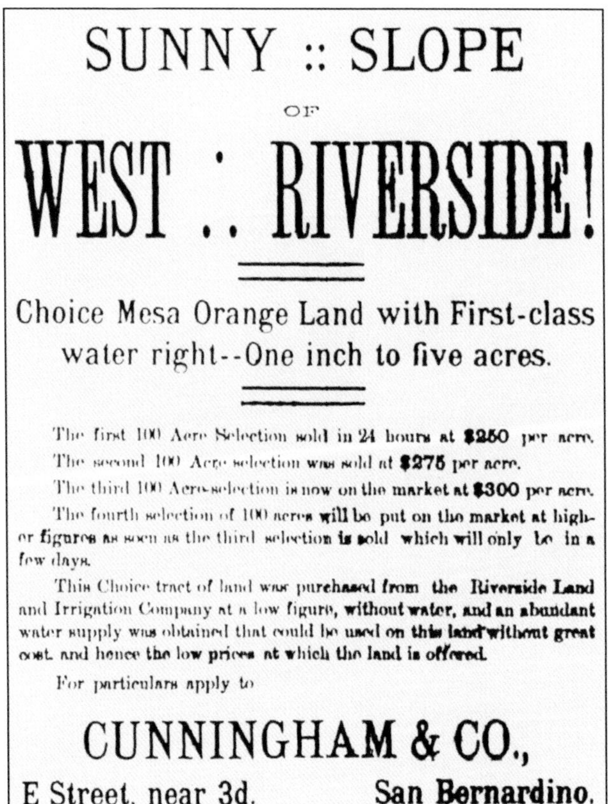

SUNNY :: SLOPE

OF

WEST .. RIVERSIDE!

Choice Mesa Orange Land with First-class water right--One inch to five acres.

The first 100 Acre Selection sold in 24 hours at **$250** per acre.

The second 100 Acre selection was sold at **$275** per acre.

The third 100 Acre selection is now on the **market at $300** per acre.

The fourth selection of 100 acres **will be** put on the **market at** higher **figures** as soon as the third selection **is** sold **which will only** be **in a** few days.

This Choice tract of land was **purchased from the Riverside Land** and Irrigation Company at a low figure, **without water, and an abundant** water supply was obtained that could be **used on this land without great** cost, and hence **the** low **prices** at **which the land is offered.**

For particulars apply to

CUNNINGHAM & CO.,

E Street, near 3d. **San Bernardino.**

SUNNY SLOPE TRACT ADVERTISEMENT. On January 21, 1888, an advertisement appeared in the *Riverside Press and Horticulturalist*, a newspaper in the City of Riverside. It advertised the Sunny Slope development in West Riverside for sale. The developer, R. F. Cunningham, had purchased part of the Jurupa Rancho in 1887, developed a water system, and then put the land on the market in 1888. This area, located north of the 60 Freeway in the vicinity of Valley Way, is still known as Sunnyslope (now spelled as one word). Its location between West Riverside and Glen Avon, both easily reachable on Mission Boulevard, would have made its own commercial center unnecessary. (Courtesy Steve Lech.)

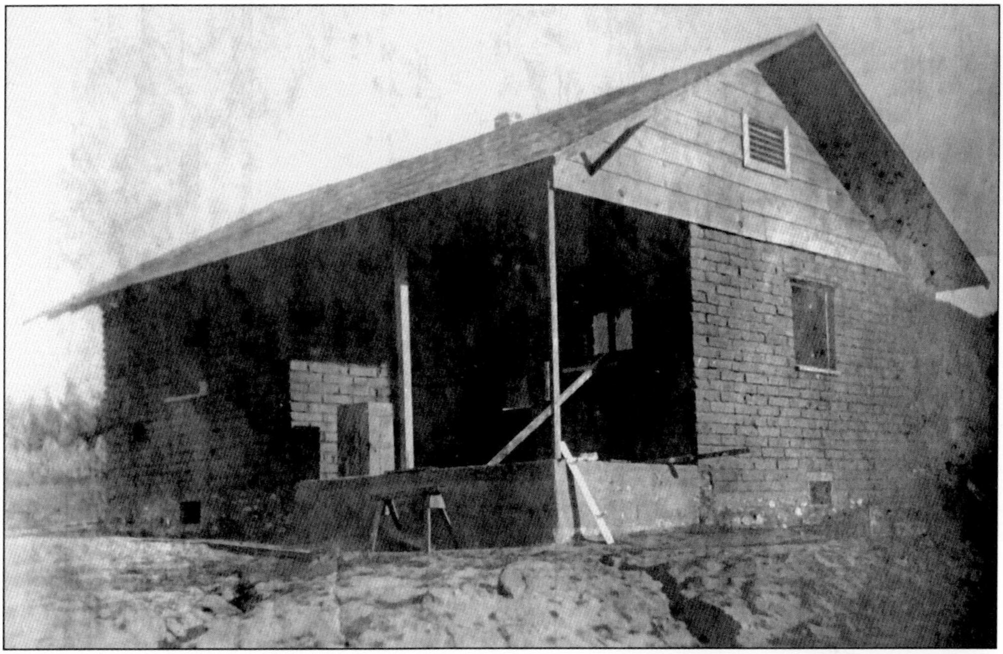

Unfinished Home of George Parks. The oldest son of Heber and Ida Parks built this adobe home in 1905 on what is now Thirty-sixth Street. He and his new wife, Mary, lived with George's parents for almost a year while they built their home. (Courtesy Riverside County Regional Park and Open-Space District.)

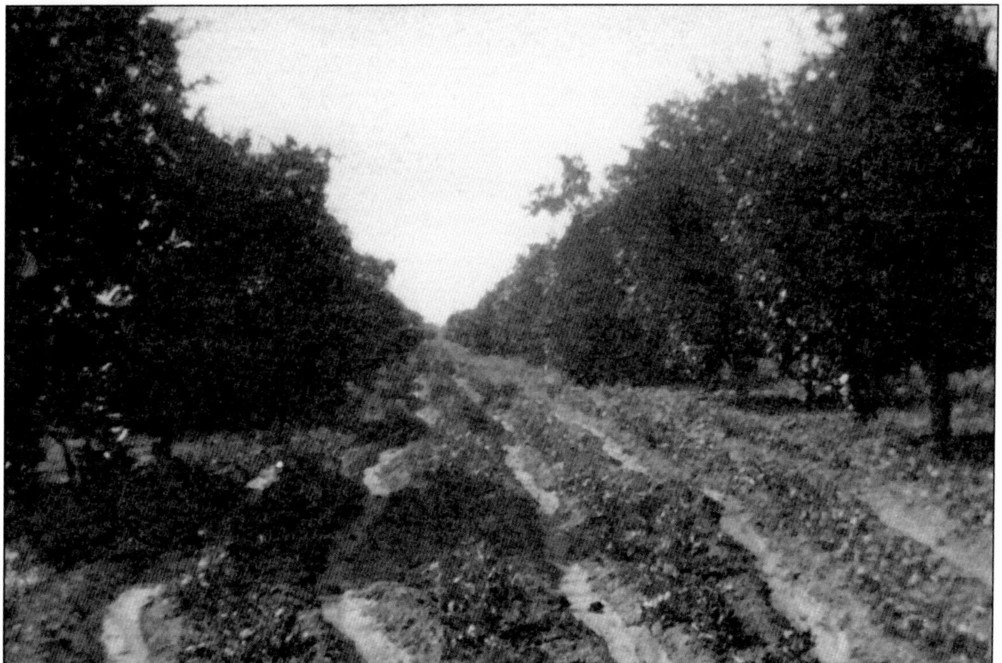

Parks Orange Grove. Most residents of Jurupa raised some sort of crop on their property. Some just raised plants and animals for their own use. Others raised crops for sale. This is Heber Parks's orange grove in 1905. (Courtesy Riverside County Regional Park and Open-Space District.)

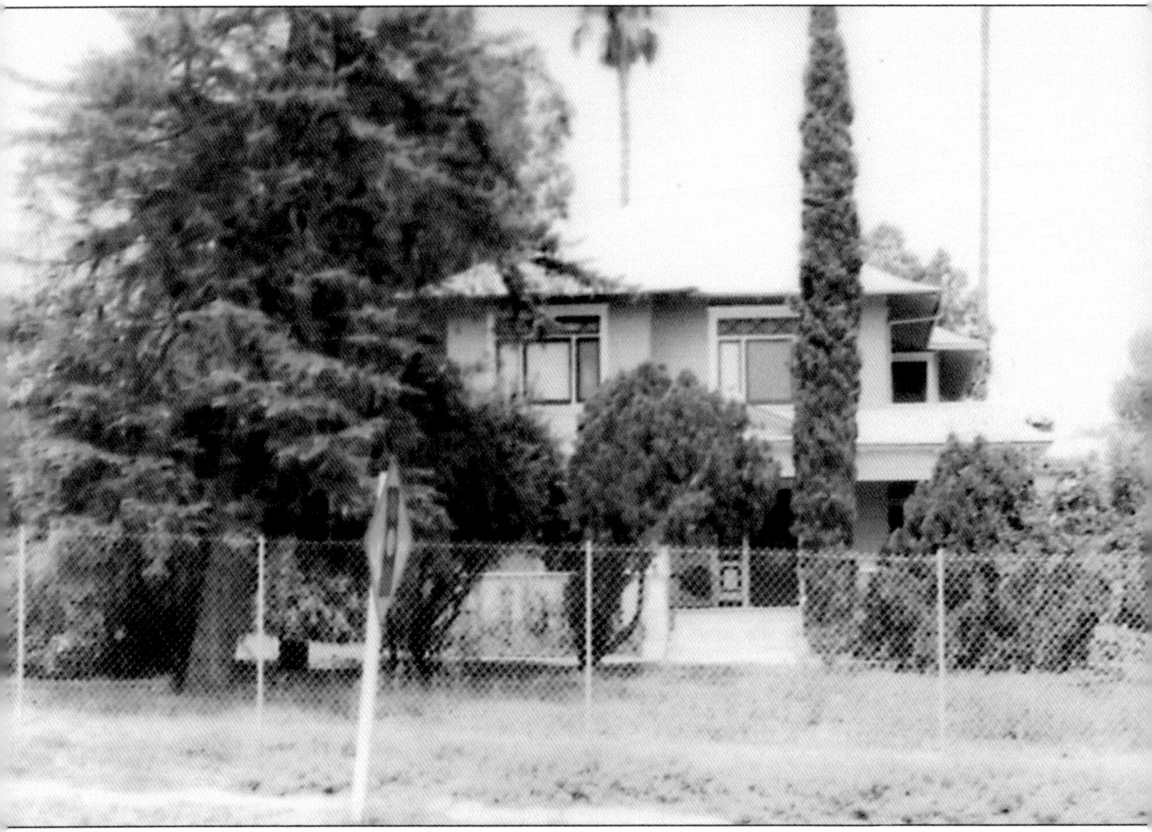

MISSION BOULEVARD HOME. G. Stanley Wilson is said to have built this home at 5841 Mission Boulevard in 1905. Wilson is famous for being the architect of the Mission Inn Rotunda. The home has been preserved as part of the Mission Palms Apartments, a senior apartment complex. (Courtesy Riverside County Regional Park and Open-Space District.)

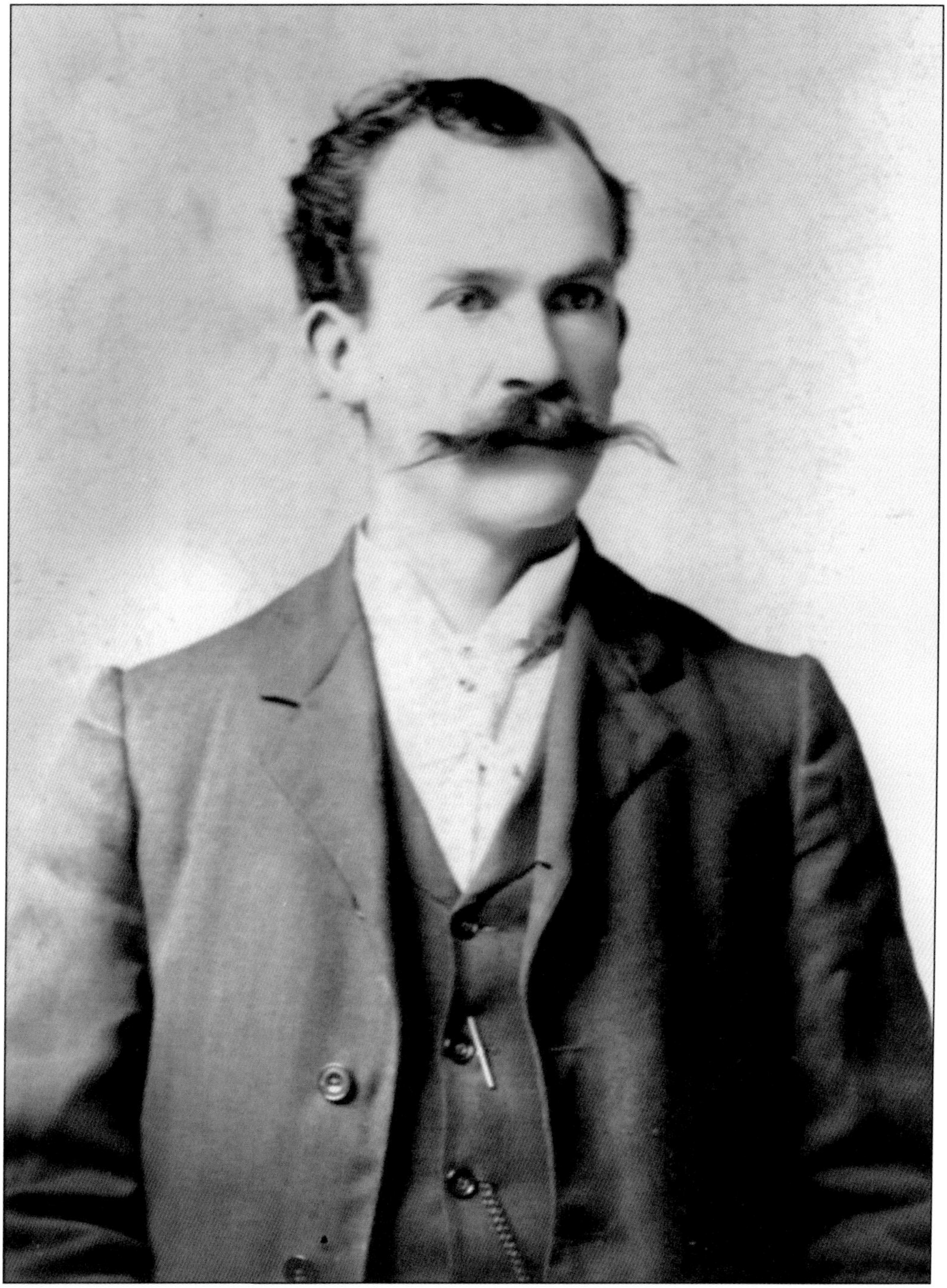

JOHN JENSEN. In 1900, John Jensen, the ninth child of Cornelius and Mercedes Jensen, married Emily Crowder. He built a wood-framed house on what is now Forty-second Street. During Jensen's lifetime, Forty-second Street didn't exist in that area; a dirt driveway from Riverview Drive accessed John's home. Later when apartments were proposed for that property, John's home was moved to the Jensen-Alvarado Historic Ranch and Museum where it serves as the caretaker's home. (Courtesy Jensen family.)

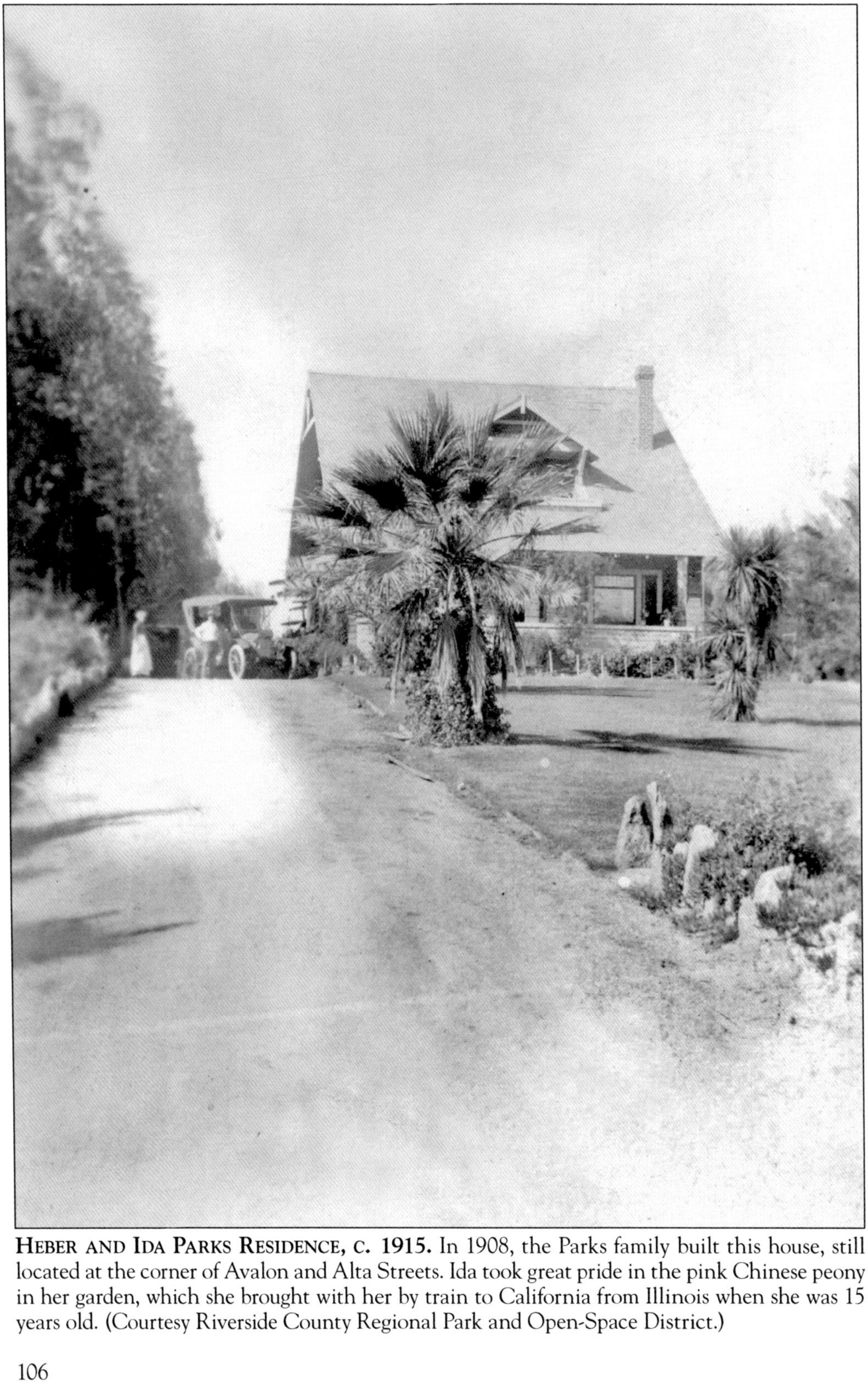

HEBER AND IDA PARKS RESIDENCE, C. 1915. In 1908, the Parks family built this house, still located at the corner of Avalon and Alta Streets. Ida took great pride in the pink Chinese peony in her garden, which she brought with her by train to California from Illinois when she was 15 years old. (Courtesy Riverside County Regional Park and Open-Space District.)

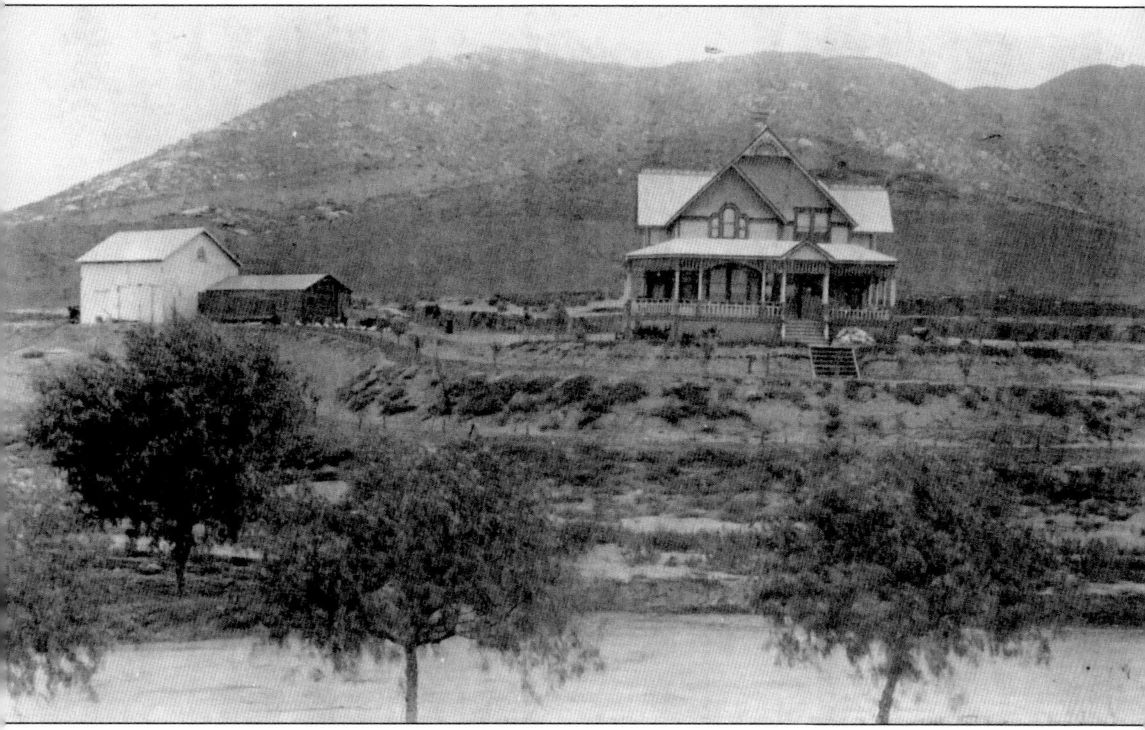

WITTE HOME. Built in 1898 for a cost of $3,000, this 4,400 square foot home is clearly a mansion compared to most of the other homes in Jurupa at that time. It is located on Mission Boulevard at the base of Pyrite Canyon in the Glen Avon area. It is not known who built the home, but Arthur and Grace Witte owned it from about 1905 to the 1940s. The Wittes were farmers who raised alfalfa, produced eggs, and had groves of fruit trees—typical crops for that era in Jurupa. At the front of the photograph is Mission Boulevard, still a dirt road, lined with young pepper trees. (Courtesy Linda Spinney.)

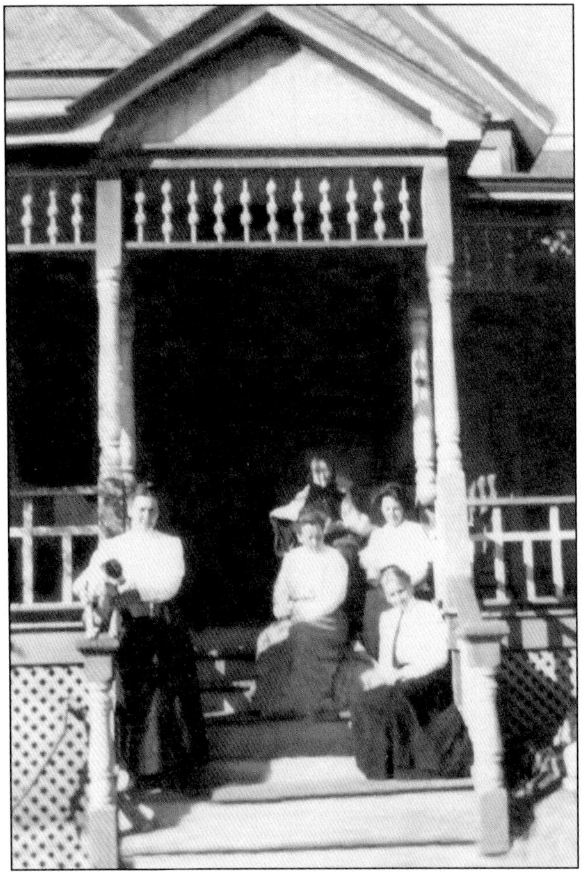

Porch of the Witte Home. The ladies on the porch, from left to right, are (first row) ? McCurdy; (second row) A. B. Houston, Grace Roberts Witte, and ? Osborne; (third row) Rebecca Roberts, Grace Witte's mother. (Courtesy Linda Spinney.)

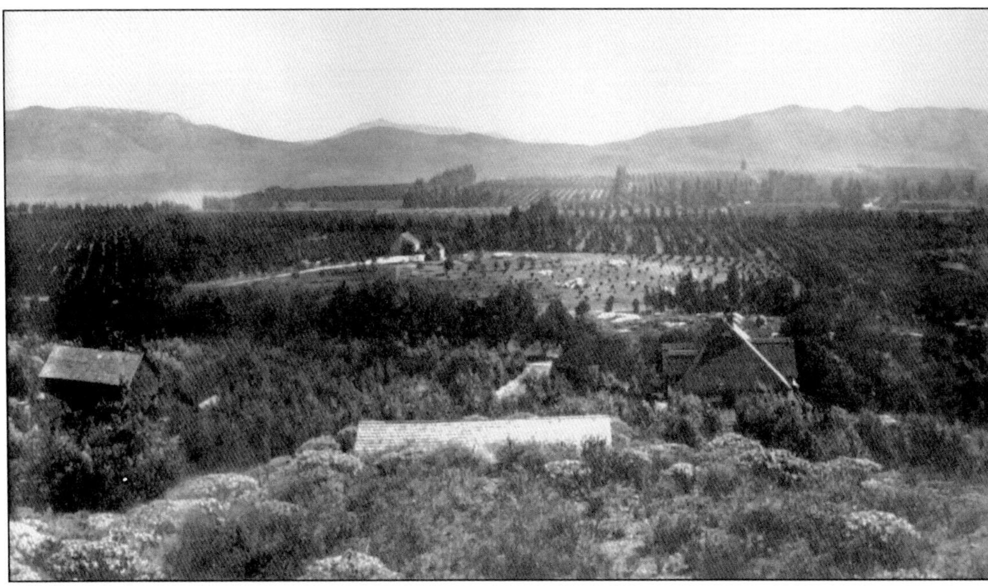

View of Glen Avon. This view was taken from the hill behind the Witte home, looking south. The small white house in the distance is the Johnson House, still located on Galena Street near Jurupa Road. (Courtesy Linda Spinney.)

ARCH PARKS FAMILY. Archie Gusdorf Parks was the sixth child of Heber and Ida Parks. He didn't like his name and went by Arch for most of his life. On August 20, 1911, he married Mary Stark. This photograph shows their family in 1924, with daughters Margaret, left, and Clara. (Courtesy Richard Nyman.)

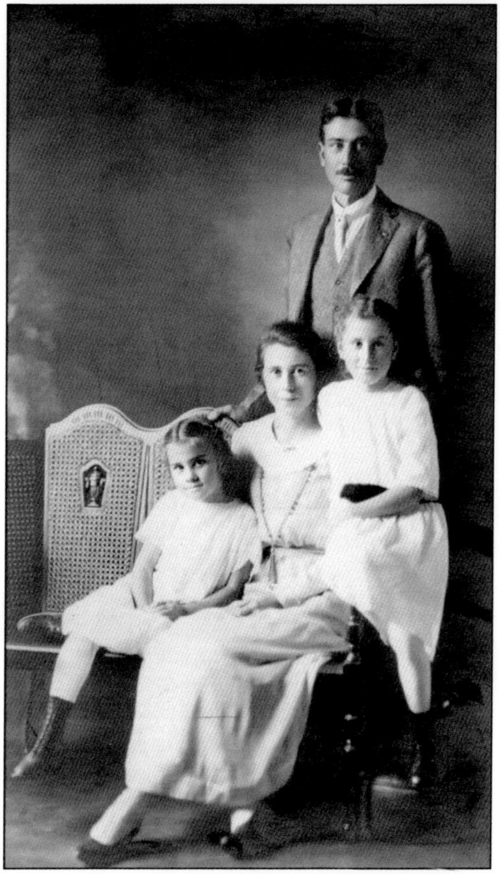

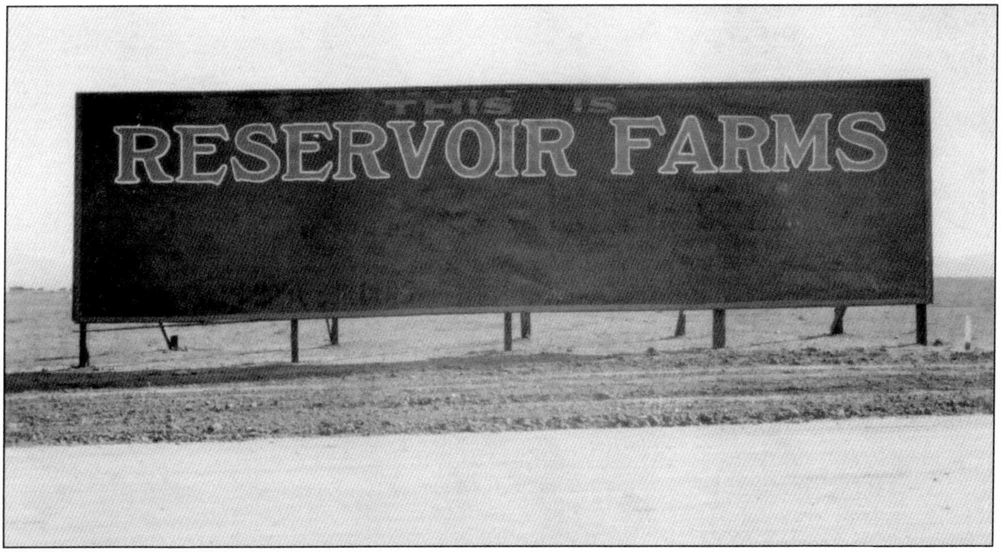

RESERVOIR FARMS. This photograph advertises the 1925 Reservoir Farms subdivision in Mira Loma. It was bounded by Bellgrave Avenue, Bain Street, Fifty-fourth Street, and Etiwanda Avenue. It had 157 lots, including 82 lots that were about five acres in size, with smaller lots along Etiwanda Avenue and Fifty-fourth Street. (Courtesy Riverside Metropolitan Museum.)

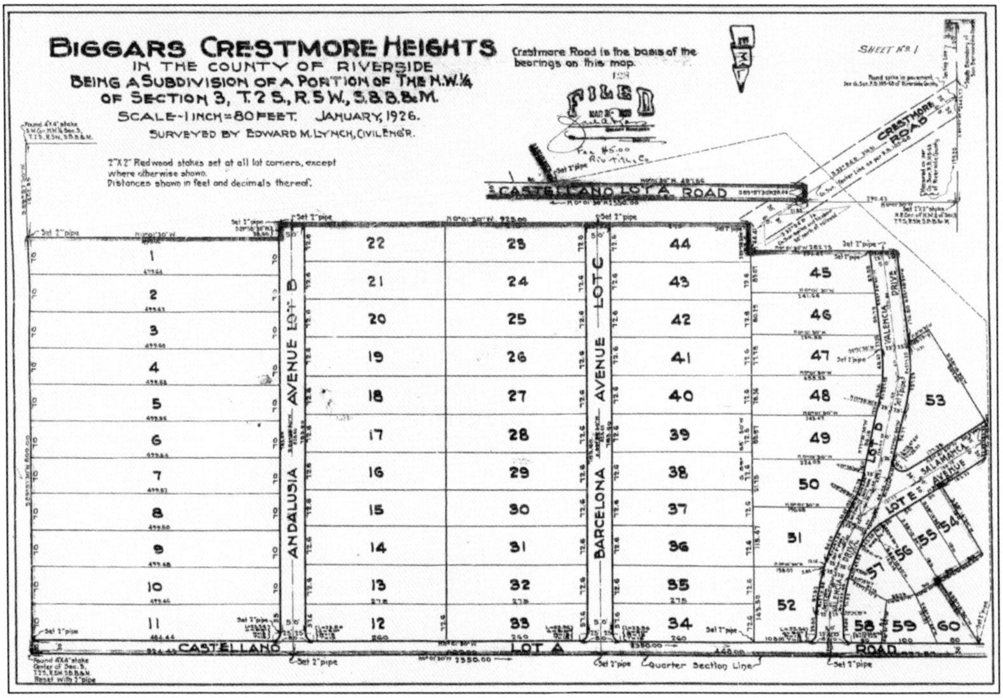

CRESTMORE HEIGHTS. In 1926, Irvine and May Keith Biggar filed a subdivision map for Biggar's Crestmore Heights, located just south of the Riverside–San Bernardino County line and west of today's Rubidoux Boulevard. Just north of this subdivision, in San Bernardino County, was the 1907 subdivision of the City of Crestmore, which is where the Biggars got the idea for the name. (Courtesy author.)

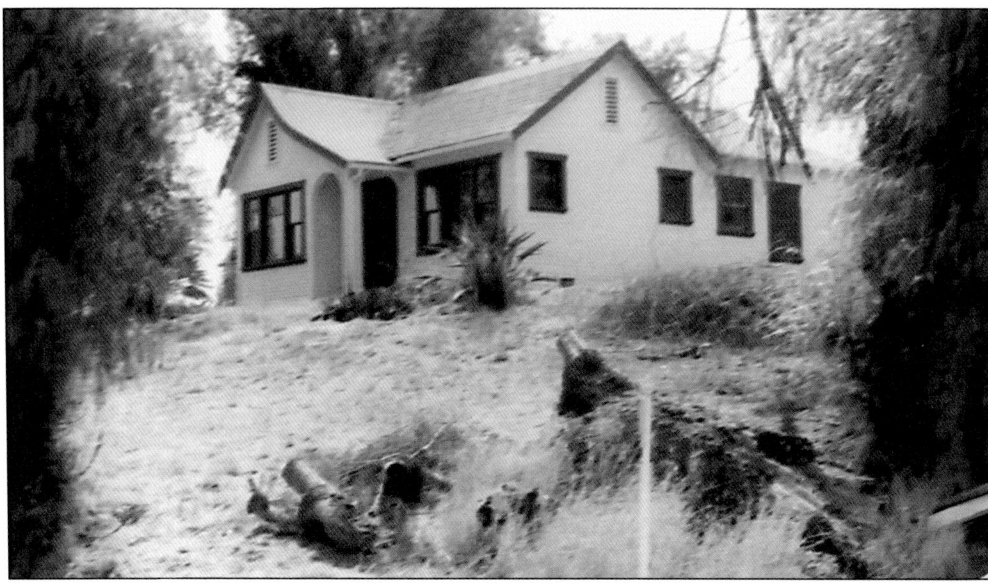

CRESTMORE HEIGHTS HOME. This home, located on Rouner Street in Crestmore Heights (now simply referred to as Crestmore), is an example of one of the earliest homes built in this subdivision. This neighborhood has examples of homes from every decade since the land was first subdivided in 1926. (Courtesy Riverside County Regional Park and Open-Space District.)

ENGELAUF HOME. In the mid-1920s, William and Marcia Engelauf moved into a house on Wallace Street in West Riverside. This 1926 photograph shows Marcia with her two sons George and baby Vallie in front of the Wallace Street home. (Courtesy Engelauf/Flowers families.)

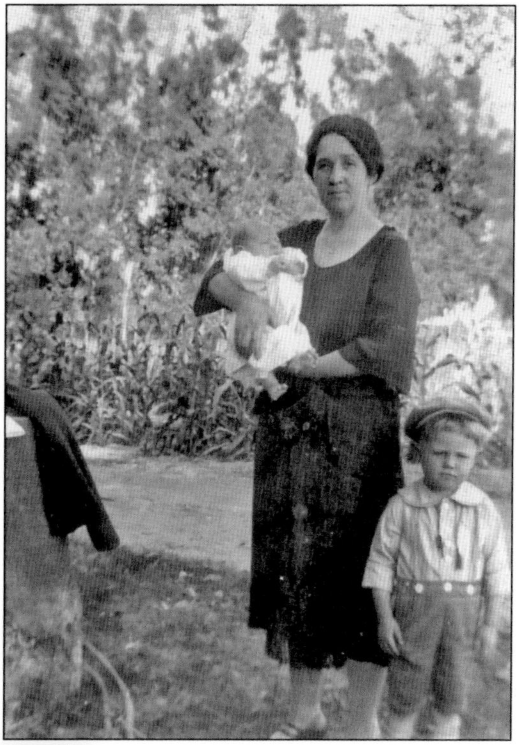

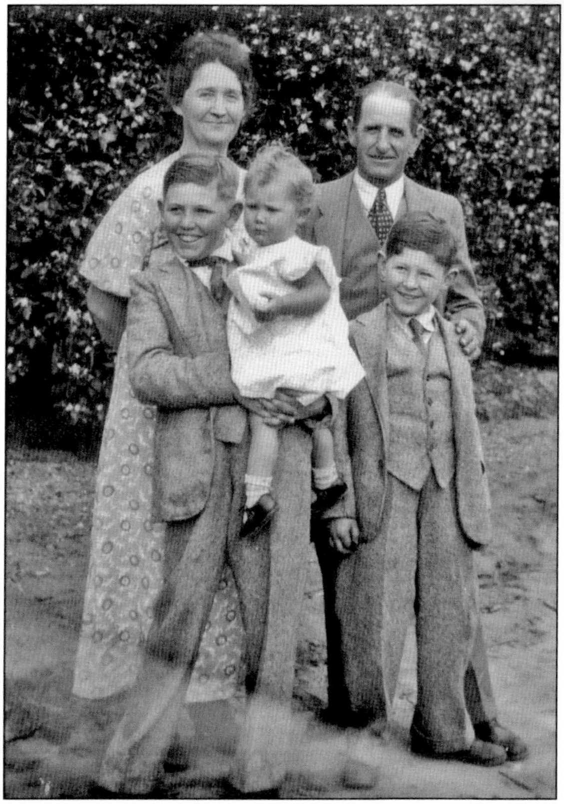

ENGELAUF FAMILY. The Engelauf family moved from Wallace Street to Wilson Street (now Thirty-fourth Street) in West Riverside. Pictured in 1933 in their yard, from left to right, are Marcia; George, who is holding Eva; William; and Vallie. (Courtesy Engelauf/Flowers families.)

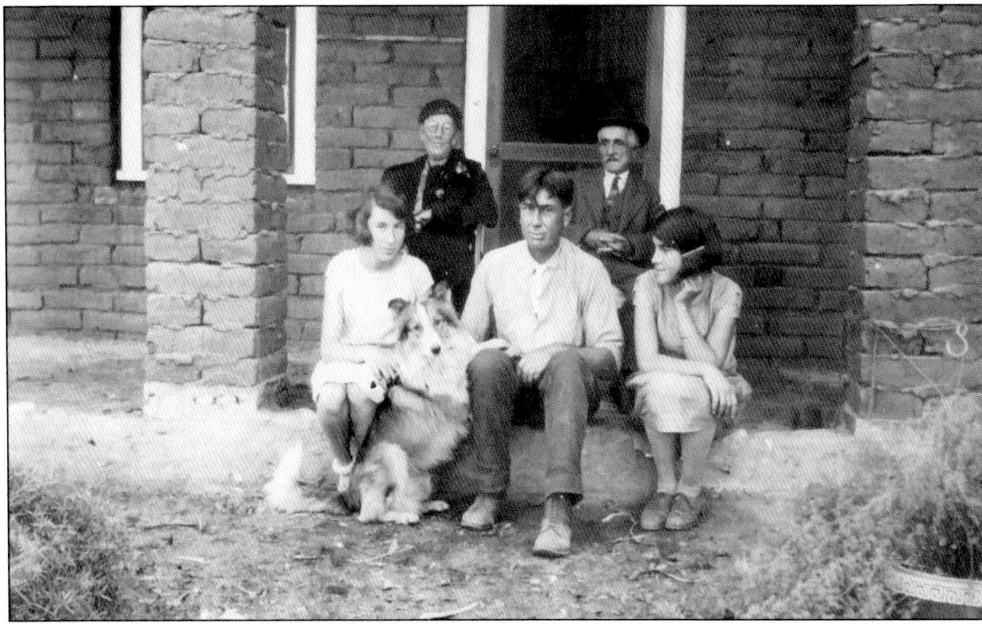

ARCH PARKS HOME. Arch and Mary Parks built an adobe home on Thirty-fourth Street in West Riverside, now Rubidoux. This 1927 photograph shows the Parks family on the porch of their home. Pictured are (first row) Arch Parks in the middle with his two daughters Clara and Margaret; (second row) Ida and Heber Parks. (Courtesy Richard Nyman.)

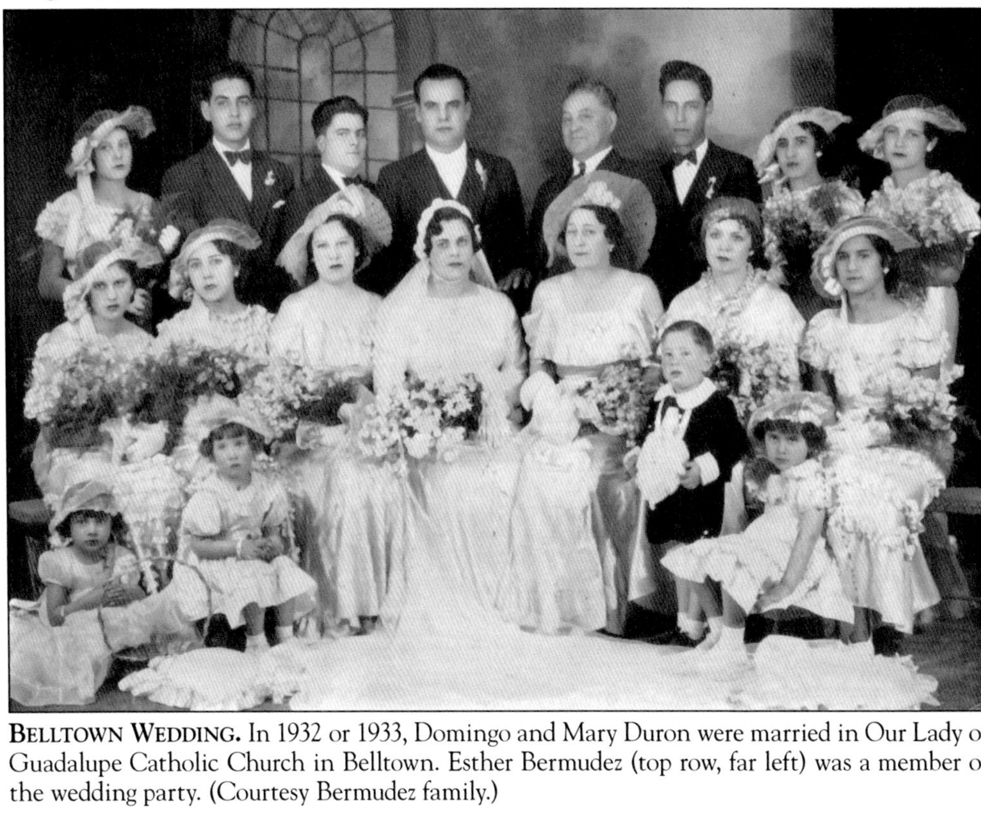

BELLTOWN WEDDING. In 1932 or 1933, Domingo and Mary Duron were married in Our Lady of Guadalupe Catholic Church in Belltown. Esther Bermudez (top row, far left) was a member of the wedding party. (Courtesy Bermudez family.)

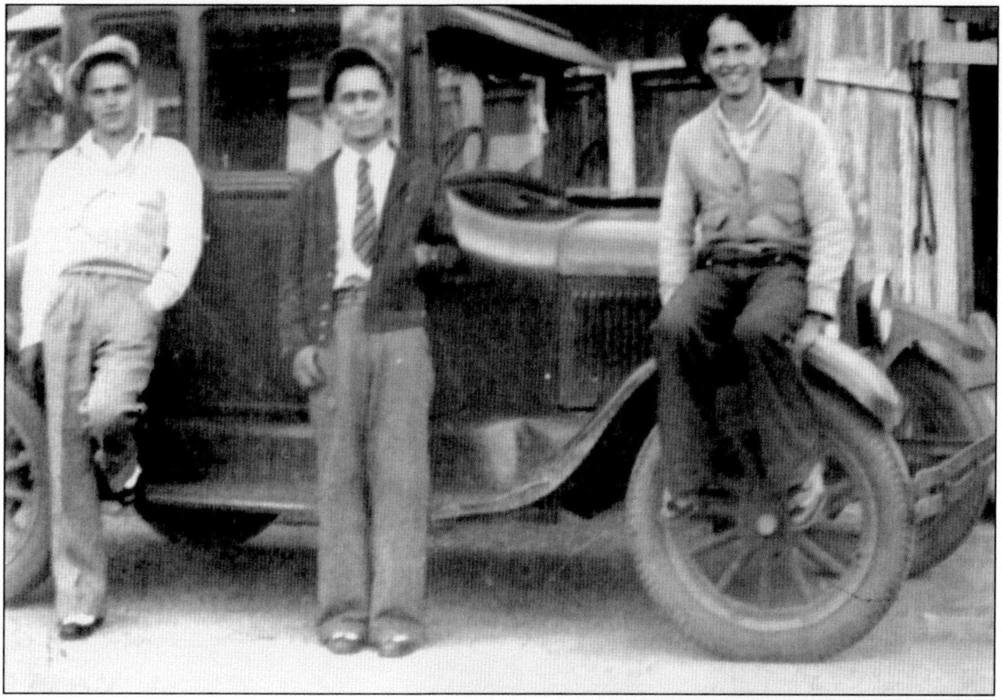

Bermudez Brothers. In 1933, Joseph, Henry, and Louis Bermudez stand in front of their house in Belltown. Their parents emigrated from Mexico to Belltown in 1919. (Courtesy Bermudez family.)

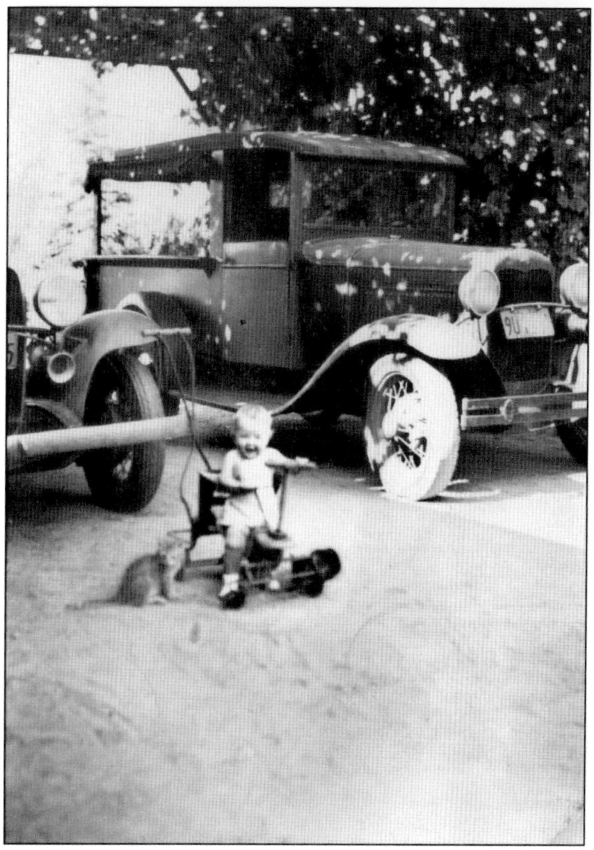

Zeitz Farm, Glen Avon. The Zeitz family owned property on the south side of Mission Boulevard at Lindsay Street in Glen Avon, where they raised turkeys. This photograph shows youngest daughter Clara with the farm trucks, *c.* 1935. (Courtesy Cates family.)

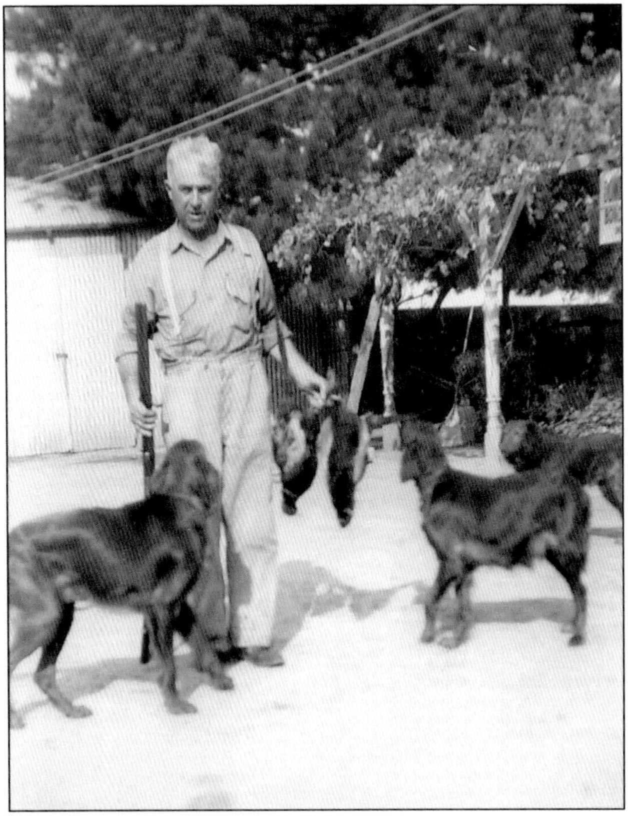

Dominico Galleano. This photograph, taken in 1934 or 1935, shows Dominico with his Parker shotgun and two pheasants he shot on his ranch in Wineville. Born in Italy in 1888, he immigrated to the United States in 1913. (Courtesy Galleano family.)

Galleano Family. Daughter Maddalena, father Domenico, and mother Lucia at the Galleano family home in 1938. Col. Esteban Cantu built the home in the 1890s. (Courtesy Galleano family.)

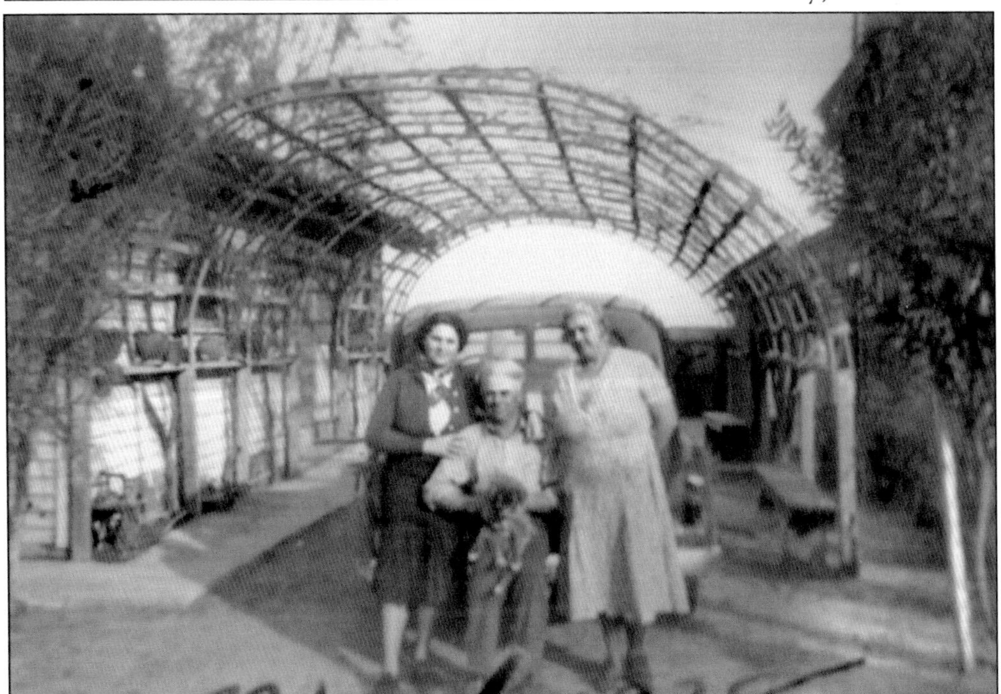

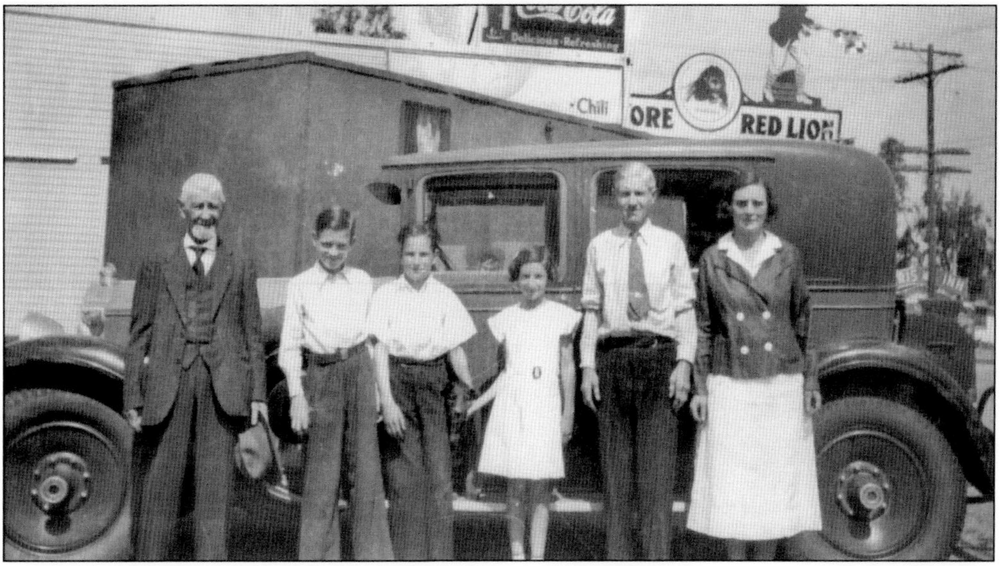

ST. MARIE FAMILY. The St. Marie family came to Riverside County from South Dakota and settled for one year in Glen Avon, where they ran the Gilmore Red Lion gas station as well as the grocery store and lunch counter in the same building. This shows the entire family in 1938 standing with their 1929 Packard sedan and homemade house trailer that they used on their journey to California. Pictured, from left to right, are grandfather Nathan St. Marie, Phillip, William, Caroline, Lawrence, and Marian St. Marie. William later became a Riverside police officer. (Courtesy Bill St. Marie.)

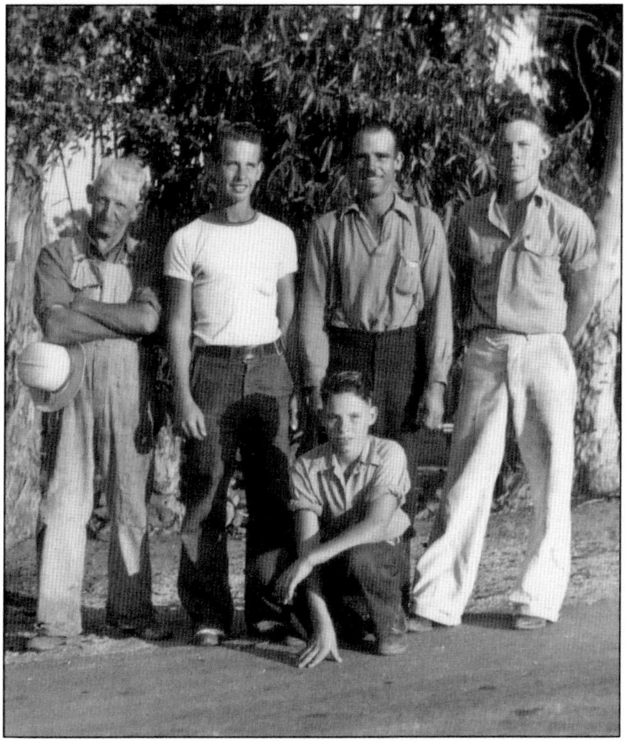

SANDELL FATHER AND SONS. On September 17, 1940, Edward Sandell and his sons Paul, Bill, George, and Bob stand at their home on the corner of Opal and Forty-fifth Streets. Forty-fifth Street was known at that time as Fourteenth Street. The Sandells were farmers and raised many different crops on their property, including alfalfa, oranges and grapes as well as keeping cows. Note the stand of eucalyptus trees in the background. Eucalyptus trees were often planted in Jurupa. Old stands of the trees can still be seen throughout the area. (Courtesy Janis Sandell McKee.)

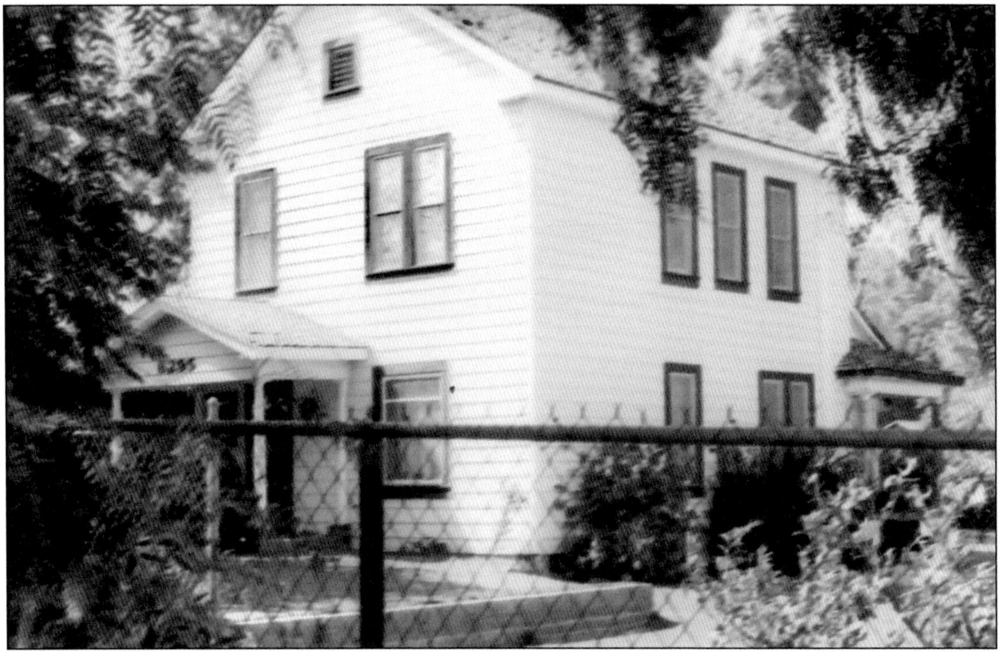

HOUSE AT OPAL AND FORTY-FIFTH STREETS. Although the Sandell family sold their home during World War II, this clapboard two-story home is still located at Opal and Forty-fifth Streets. This photograph of the house was taken in 1983. (Courtesy Riverside County Regional Park and Open-Space District.)

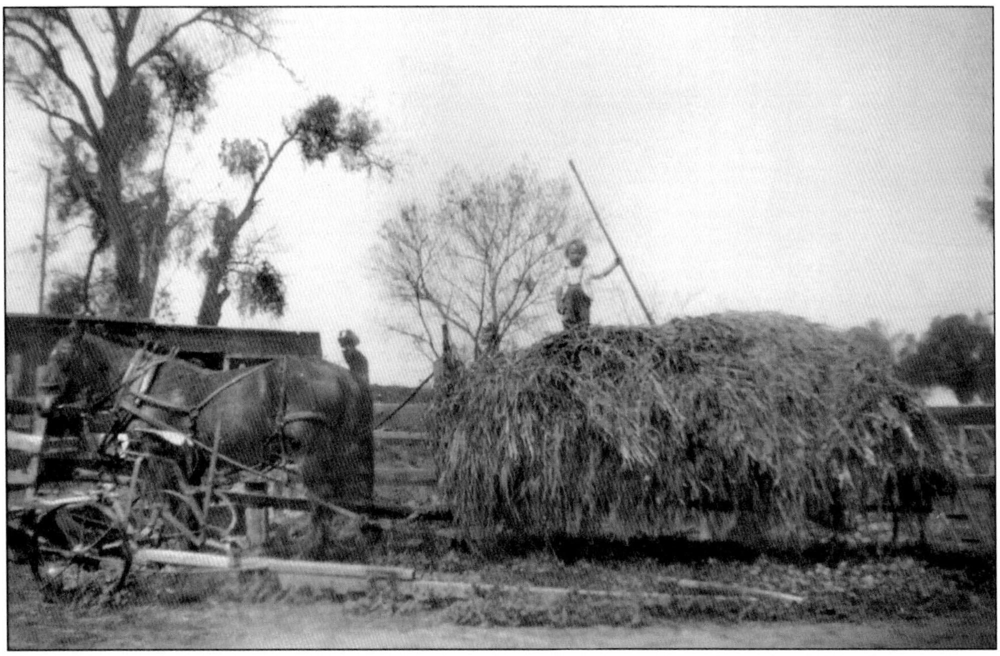

THORSON FAMILY FARM. Before the Mission Plaza Shopping Center was built on the corner of Mission Boulevard and Riverview Drive, it was the Thorson family's home and farm. This is Dorothy Thorson around 1941 standing on top of the hay wagon with the farm horse nearby. Dorothy was very unhappy when her father replaced the horse with a tractor. (Courtesy Dorothy Thorson Evans.)

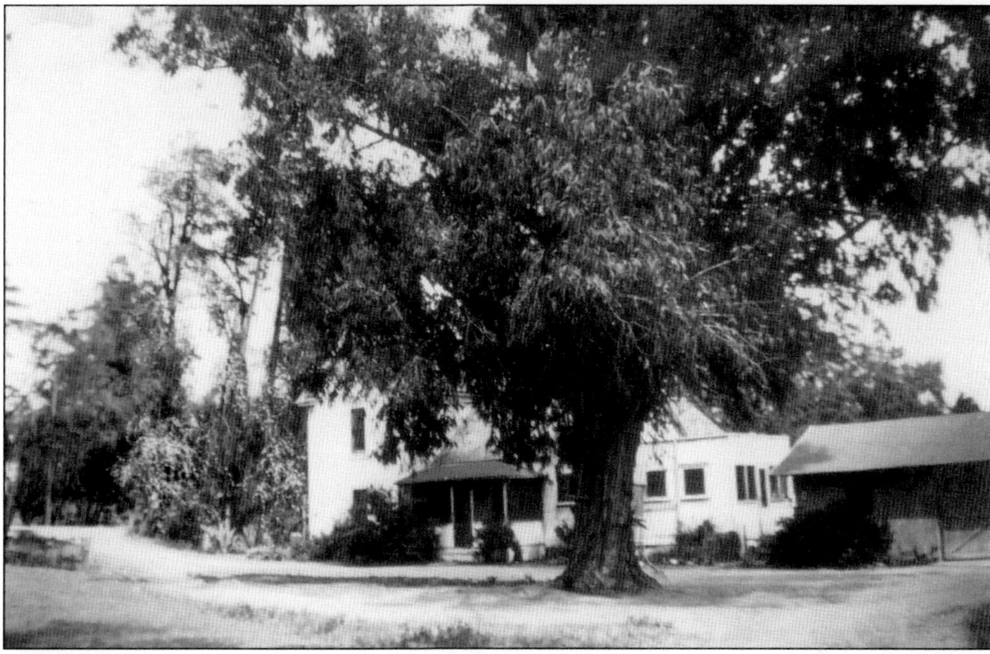

HOME AT MISSION AND RIVERVIEW. This is the Thorson family home at Mission and Riverview Drive. The Jurupa Ditch ran along the edge of the property on Riverview Drive, giving hours of fun to the children of the house. (Courtesy Dorothy Thorson Evans.)

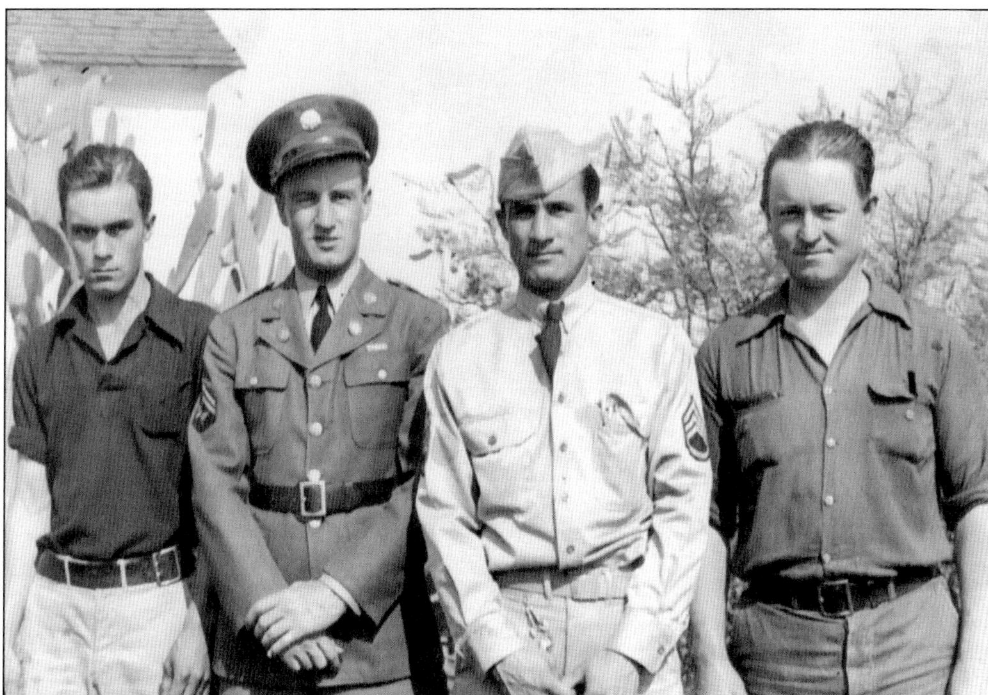

DIAS BOYS. The Dias boys grew up on Etiwanda Avenue in Mira Loma. This June 1942 photograph shows Paul, John "Ace," Louie, and Bob. All attended Union Joint School. (Courtesy Galleano family.)

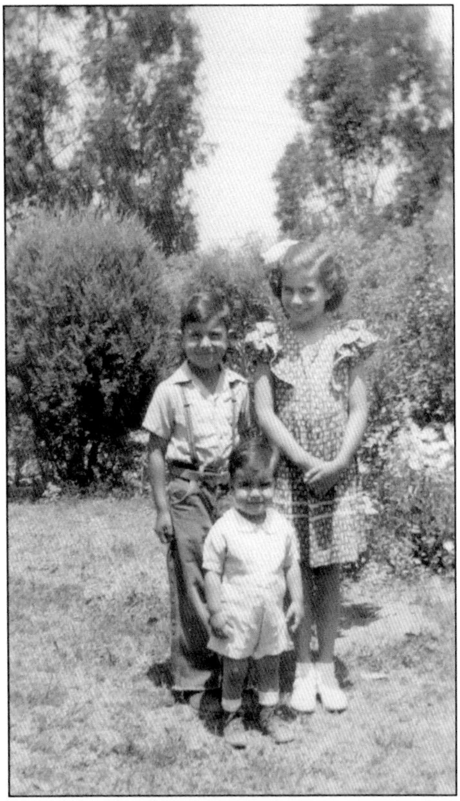

Parma Children. Around 1943, the Parma children are shown outside of their home on Troth Street in Mira Loma. They are Larry and Grace with Charles in the front. (Courtesy Grace Parma Sollecito.)

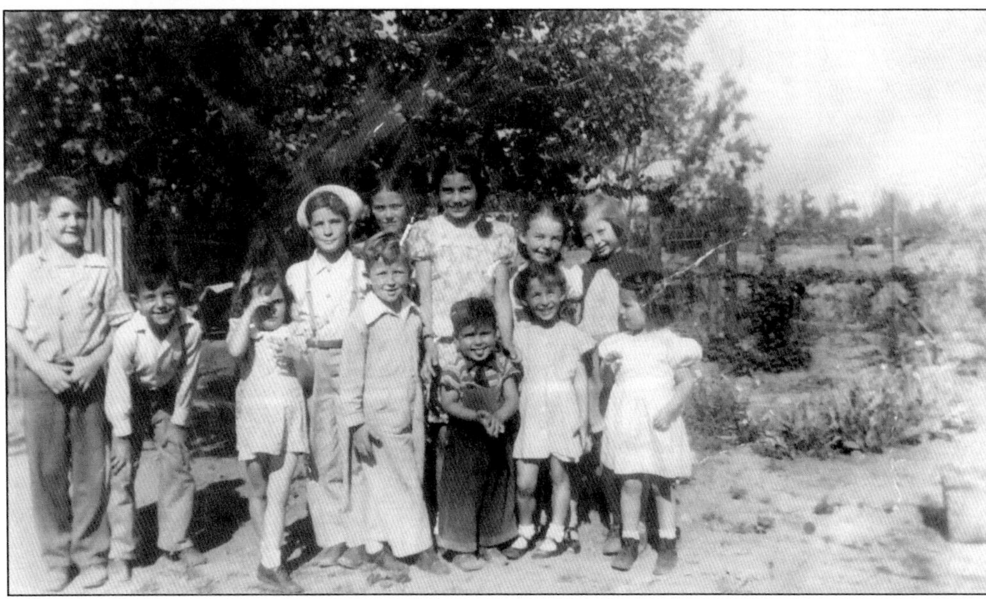

Mira Loma Birthday Party. Grace Parma celebrated her ninth birthday in 1945 in the yard of her home on Troth Street. Pictured, from left to right, are Charlie Tice, Larry Parma, unidentified, Wayne Brandon, Billy Brandon, Anna Tice (behind Billy), Grace Parma with her brother Charles in front of her, Joan Hostettler, Willa Todd, Claire Stitch, and Pauline Hostettler. (Courtesy Grace Parma Sollecito.)

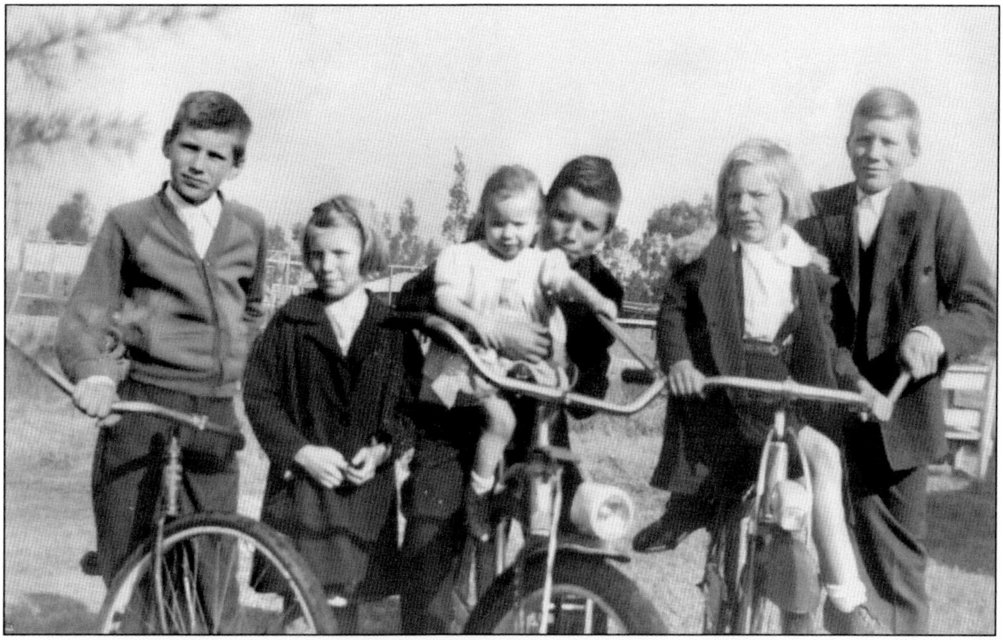

ABACHERLI CHILDREN. The Abacherli children pose *c.* 1945 with their bicycles at their Lorena Avenue home in Mira Loma. Pictured, from left to right, are Frank, Helen, Ben (holding Freda), Elsie, and Pius. (Courtesy Helen Abacherli Spencer.)

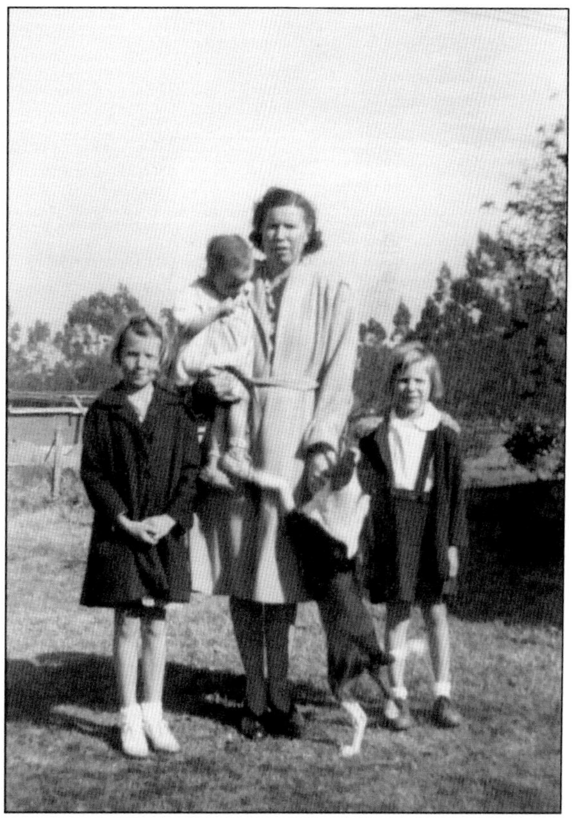

ABACHERLI MOTHER AND DAUGHTERS. Helen Abacherli is shown here with her daughters at the family home on Lorena Street in Mira Loma. Pictured here around 1945, from left to right, are daughter Helen, mother Helen holding Freda, and Elsie. (Courtesy Helen Abacherli Spencer.)

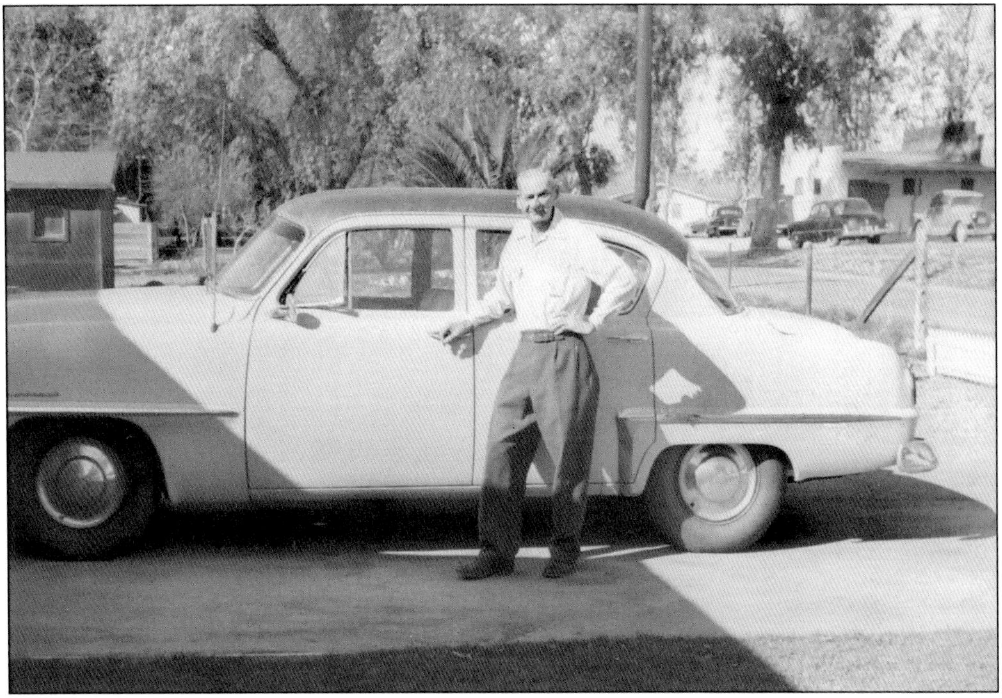

HOWEY HOME IN MIRA LOMA. In the 1940s, James Howey is pictured in front of his home on Martin Street in Mira Loma. Across the street to the right of the photograph is the old Mira Loma Post Office. (Courtesy Georgia Johnson Critchlow.)

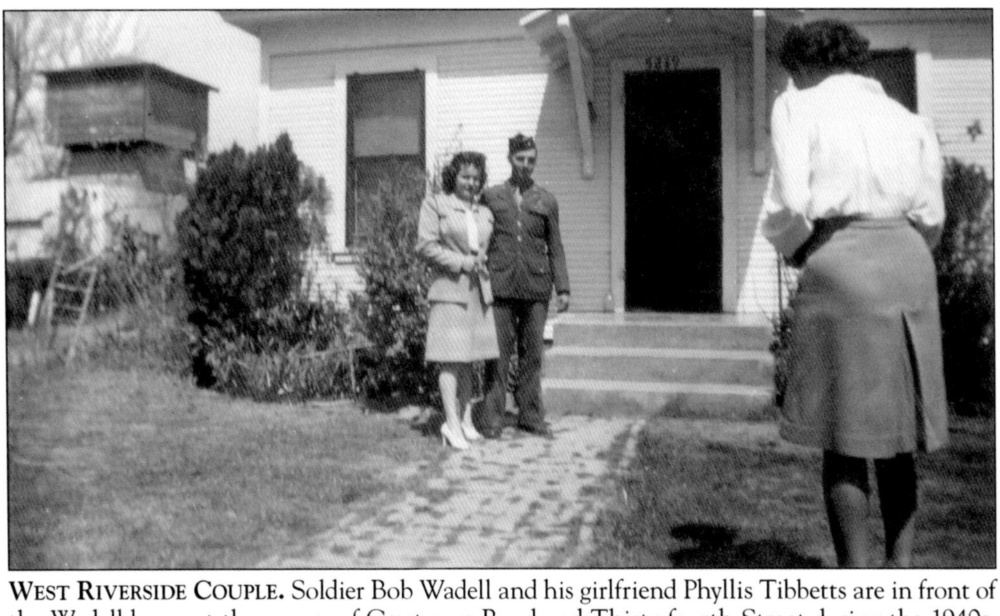

WEST RIVERSIDE COUPLE. Soldier Bob Wadell and his girlfriend Phyllis Tibbetts are in front of the Wadell home at the corner of Crestmore Road and Thirty-fourth Street during the 1940s. Bob's sister Mrs. Doss is taking the photograph. The tank house in the background is on the Greene's property on Thirty-fourth Street. (Courtesy Engelauf/Flowers families.)

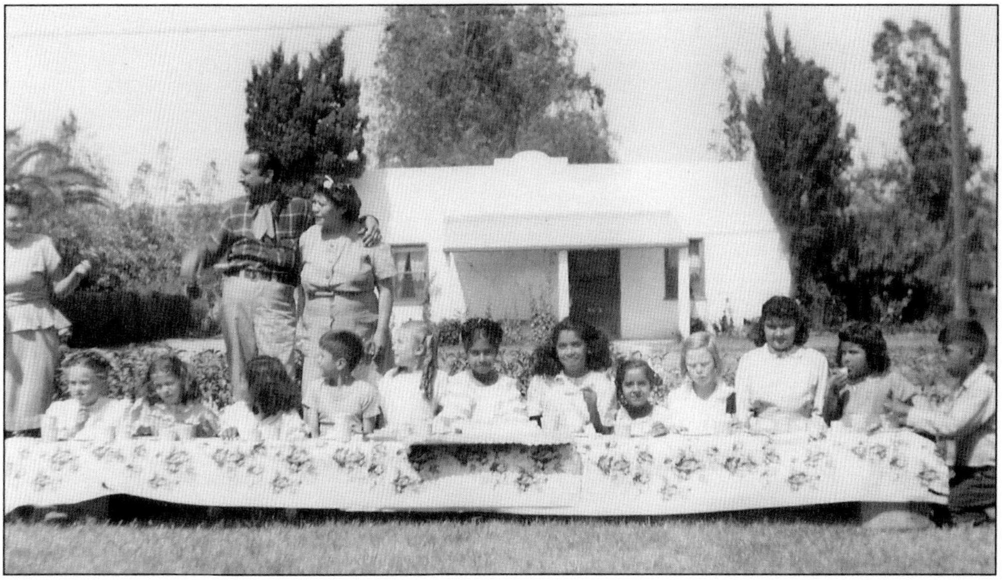

GLEN AVON BIRTHDAY PARTY. Ethel Chavez celebrated her birthday party in May 1947, in the front yard of her family's home on Mission Boulevard in Glen Avon. Adults in the rear are Phyllis Lopez, Frank Lopez, and Josephine Chavez. The children are Barbara Ergle, Rhea Diehl, Helen Lopez, David Lopez, Janet Starnes, Ethel Chavez, Rachel Ramirez, Betty Lopez, Gail Black, Sarah Marrufo, unidentified, and Alfred Ramirez. (Courtesy Ethel Chavez Sanborn.)

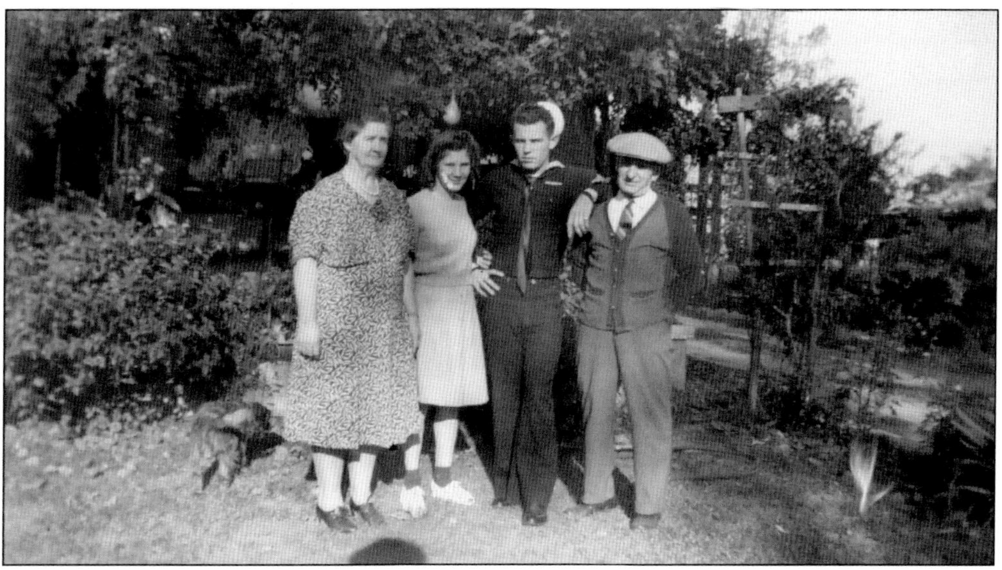

HOME ON LEAVE. Sailor George Engelauf is home on leave after having served in the Pacific theater in World War II. The Engelauf family members pictured here, from left to right, are Marcia, Eva, George, and William in the yard of their home on Thirty-fourth Street. (Courtesy Engelauf/Flowers families.)

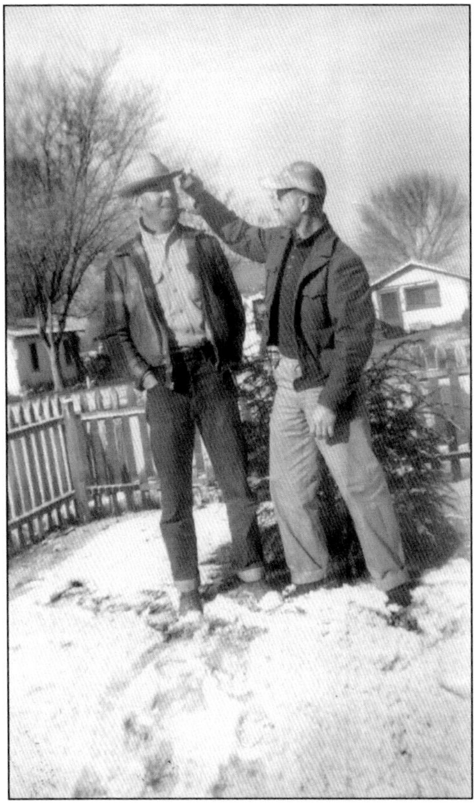

SNOW ON TWINNING STREET. In 1948, Paul Dickinson, left, and Jake McClure enjoy the snow on Twinning Street in Rubidoux. They were just two of the many men from Jurupa who served during World War II. (Courtesy Ruby Dickinson.)

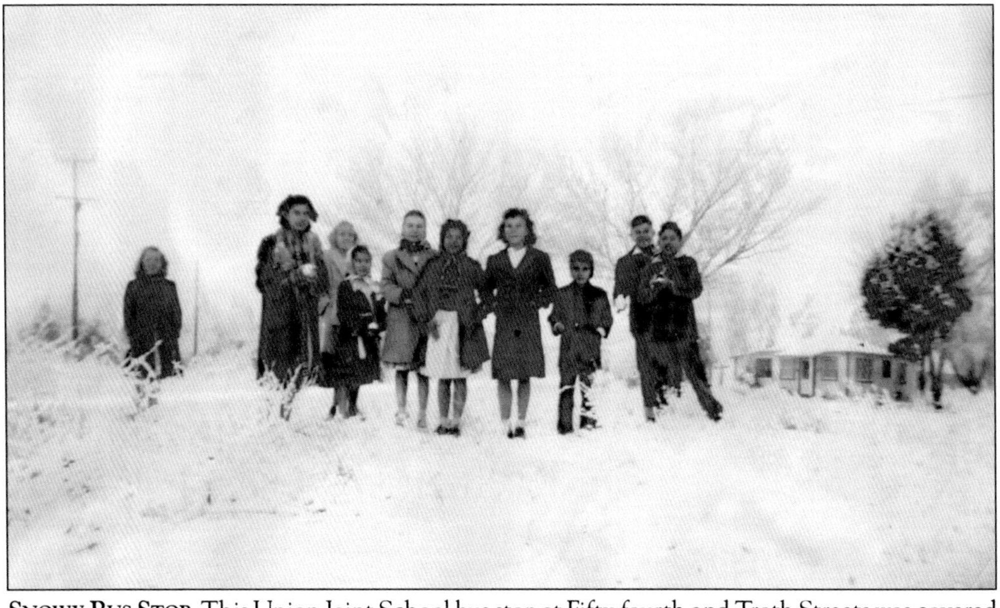

SNOWY BUS STOP. This Union Joint School bus stop at Fifty-fourth and Troth Streets was covered after an unusual snowstorm spread snow throughout Jurupa in 1948. The children, from left to right, are unidentified, Grace Parma, unidentified, Pauline Hostettler, Joan Hostettler, Betty Barrigan, Shirley Wells, Charles Parma, Larry Parma, and Leonard Barrigan. (Courtesy Grace Parma Sollecito.)

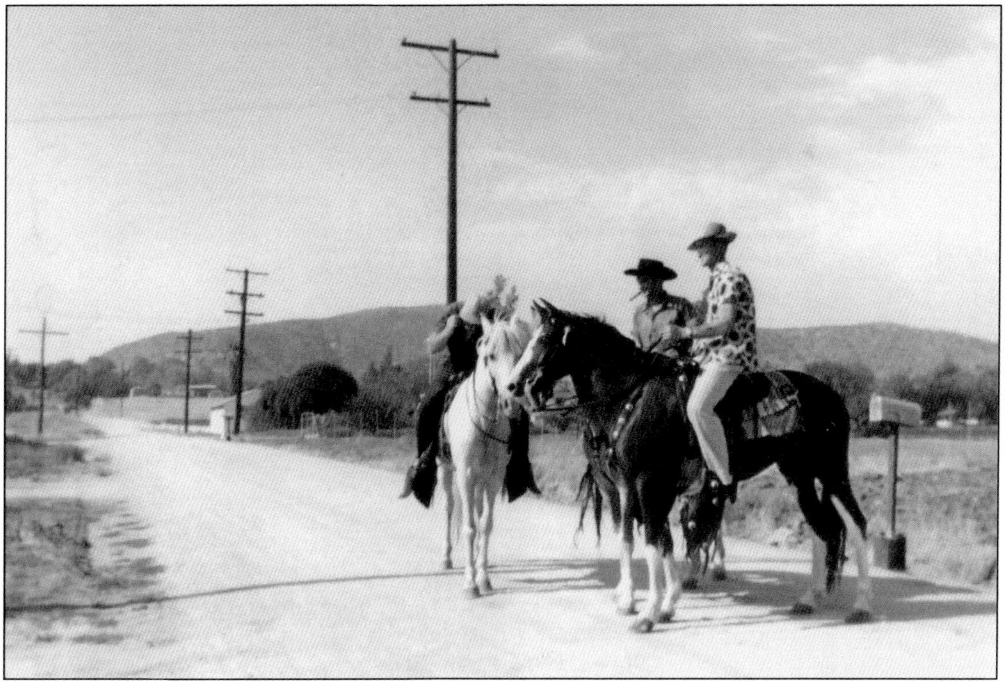

EUCALYPTUS STREET, PEDLEY. This 1954 photograph was taken on Eucalyptus Street in Pedley, looking north towards Limonite Avenue. On the horses, from left to right, are Del Coats, Virgil Coats, and unidentified. (Courtesy Julie and Del Coats.)

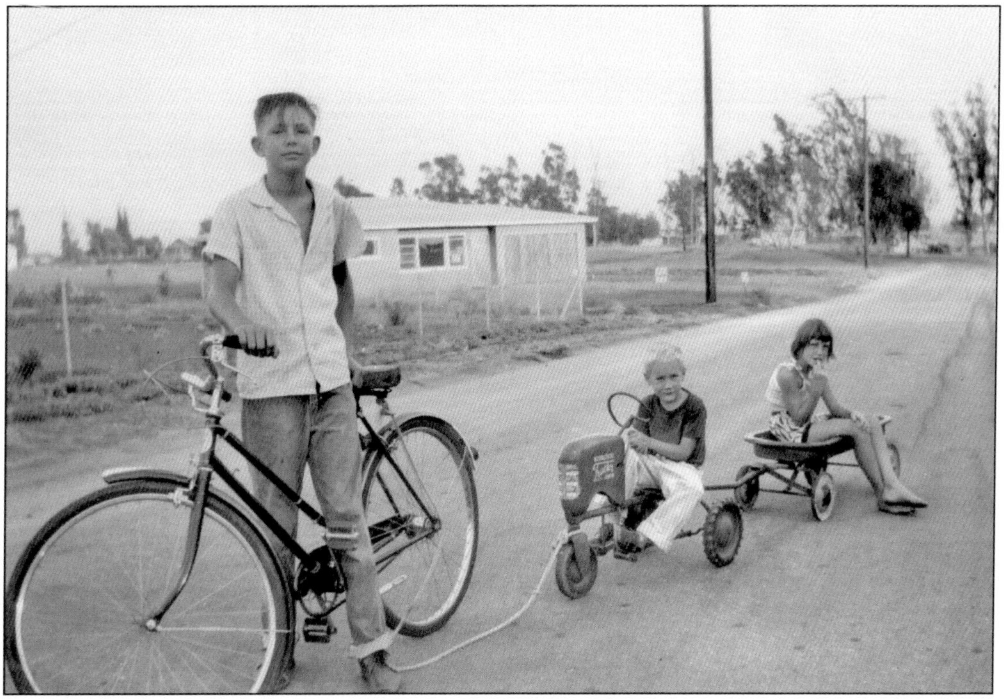

EUCALYPTUS STREET. Rick Coats, Kenny Blevins, and Judy Coats are making up their own fun on Eucalyptus Street in Pedley. This photograph looks southeast. (Courtesy Julie and Del Coats.)

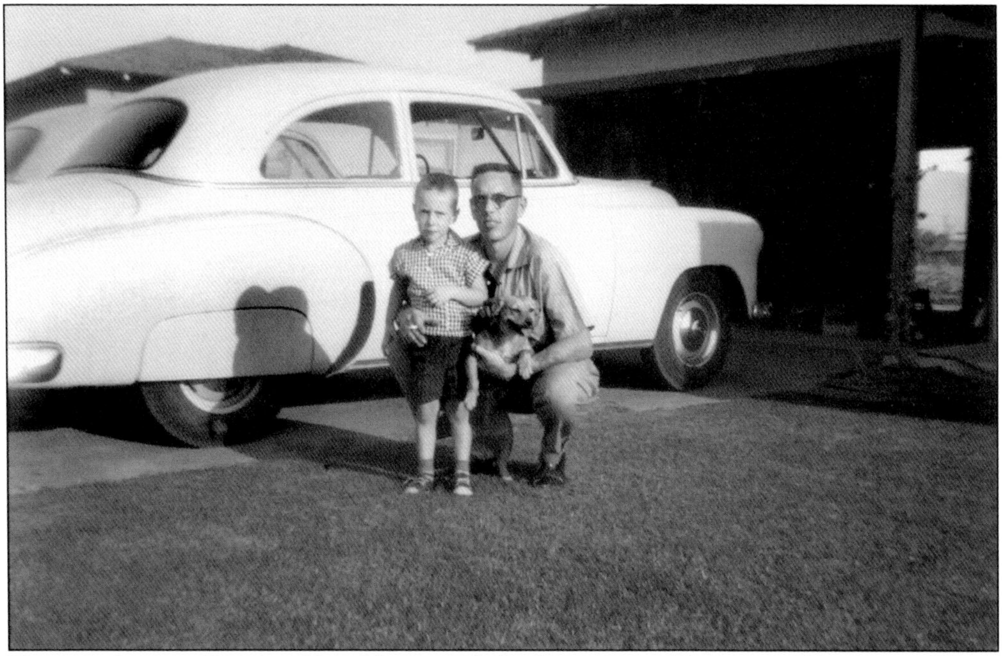

HUNTER STREET. Don Jarrell and his son Michael are pictured here in 1955 in front of Don's mother's house on Hunter Street in Glen Avon. (Courtesy author.)

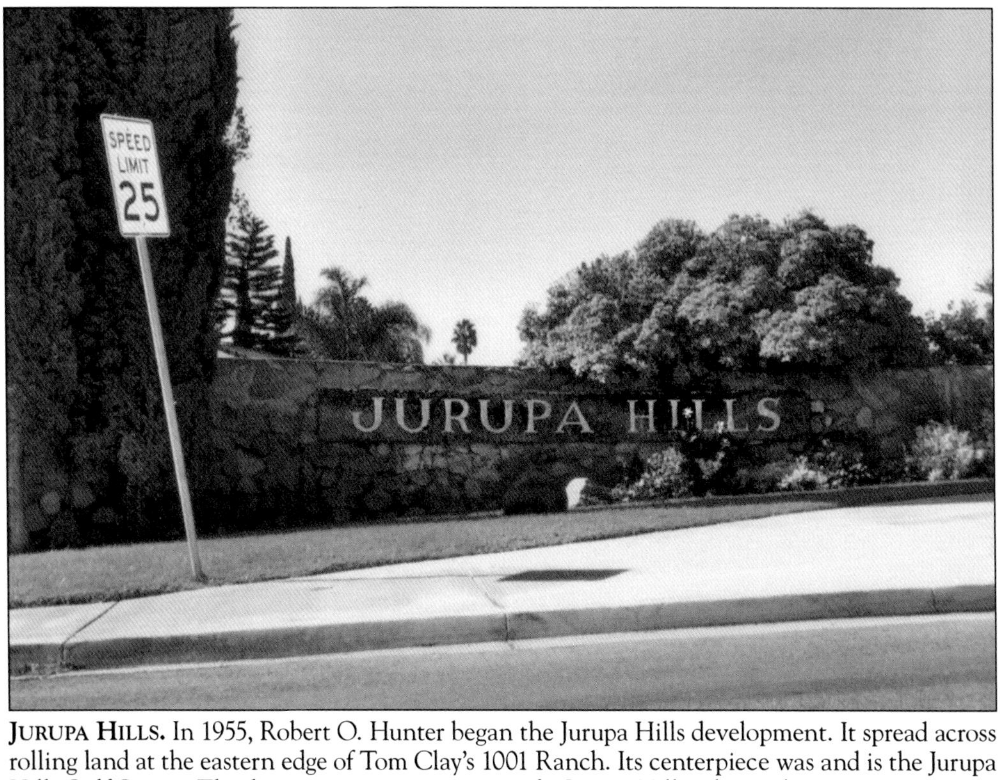

JURUPA HILLS. In 1955, Robert O. Hunter began the Jurupa Hills development. It spread across rolling land at the eastern edge of Tom Clay's 1001 Ranch. Its centerpiece was and is the Jurupa Hills Golf Course. The distinctive entry monument for Jurupa Hills is located at Limonite Avenue and Peralta Place. (Courtesy author.)

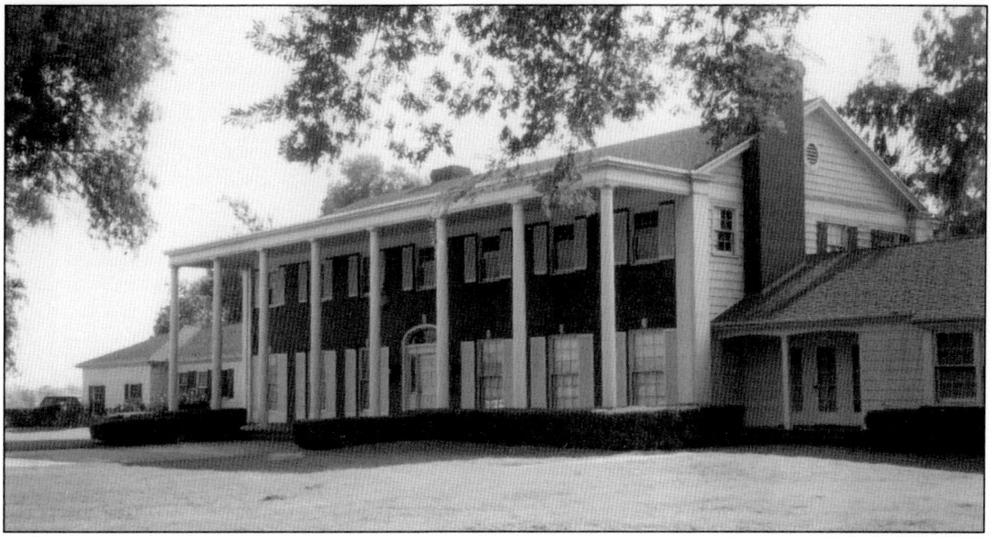

TINY NAYLOR HOUSE. Naylor was a well-known Los Angeles restaurant owner and thoroughbred-racing enthusiast. He bought land on Mission Boulevard next to the Santa Ana River for a thoroughbred farm. Around 1956, he built a southern-style mansion on the property. The house warming party is still remembered because of Naylor's famous guests, including bandleader Harry James and his wife, Betty Grable. Due to health reasons, Naylor himself never lived in the house. The house now has a Crestmore Road address and is headquarters for the Riverside County Regional Park and Open-Space District. (Courtesy Riverside County Regional Park and Open-Space District.)

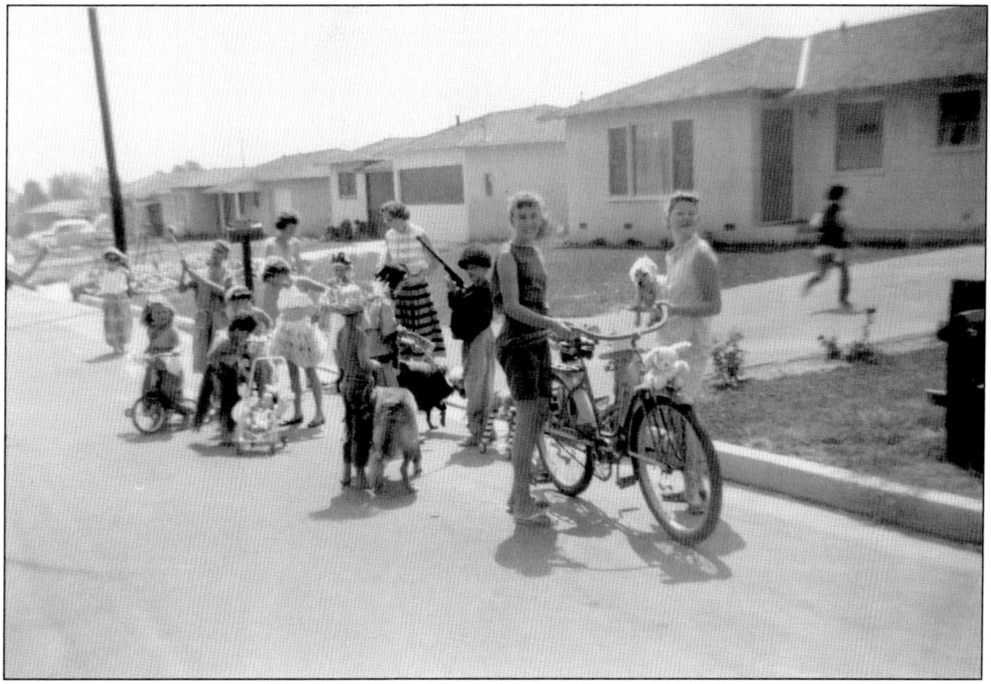

GORDON WAY PARADE. Gordon Way in Glen Avon was a new street in the early 1960s. In this March 1960 photograph, two moms, Nell Jarrell (by mailbox) and Emma Jane Kuma (in striped skirt), help organize a neighborhood parade. (Courtesy Cates family.)

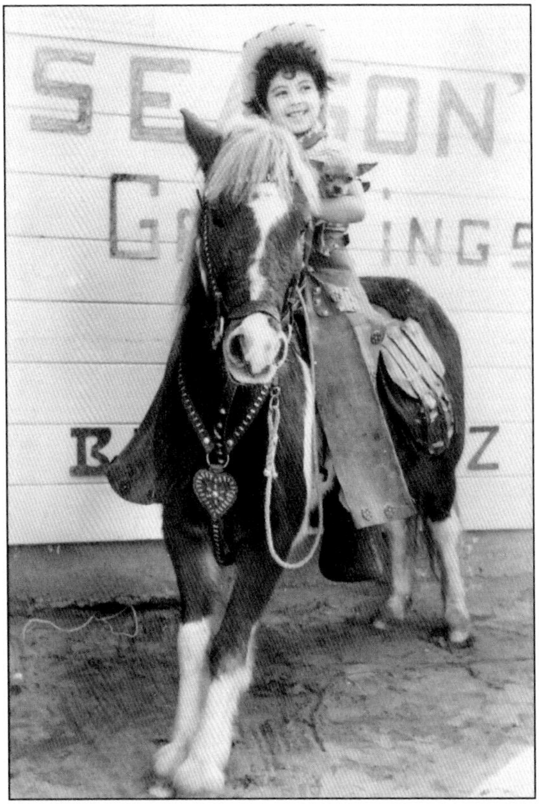

LYDIA BERMUDEZ, 1961. A man came through Belltown offering to take children's photographs on his pony. This photograph was taken in front of the Bermudez home at 2452 Hall Avenue. (Courtesy Bermudez family.)

HAY FIELD IN MIRA LOMA. Helen Spencer is shown here around 1972 sitting on a bale of hay in a field on Etiwanda Avenue, across from the Cow Girl Cafe. At that time, the property was part of the Vernola Ranch. It is now the Sky County housing development. (Courtesy Helen Abacherli Spencer.)

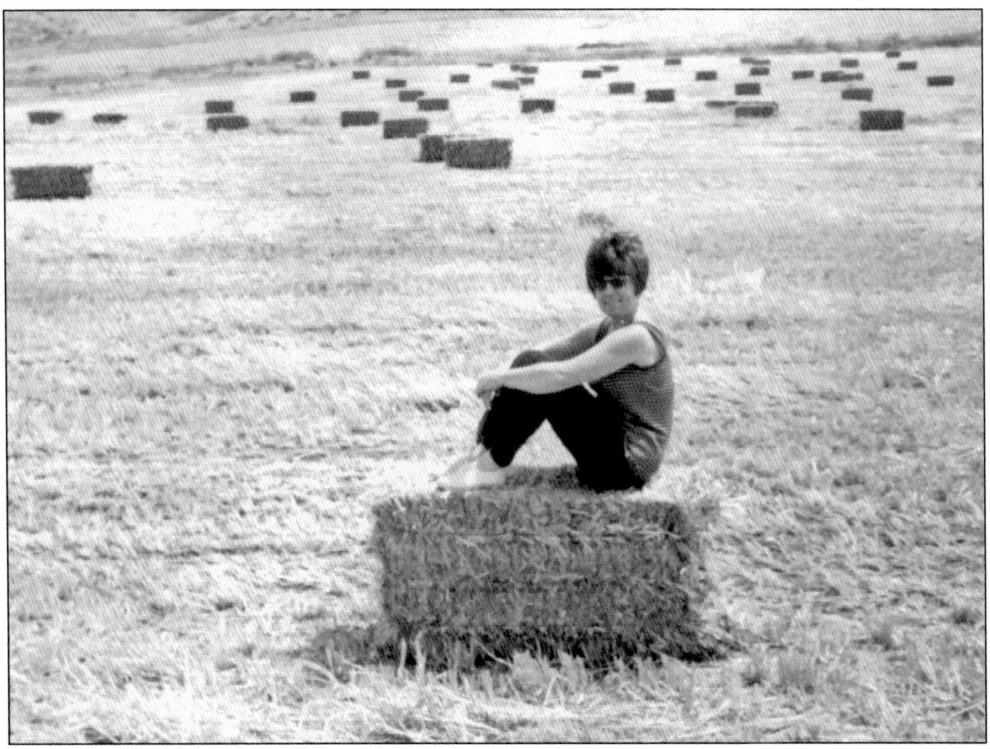

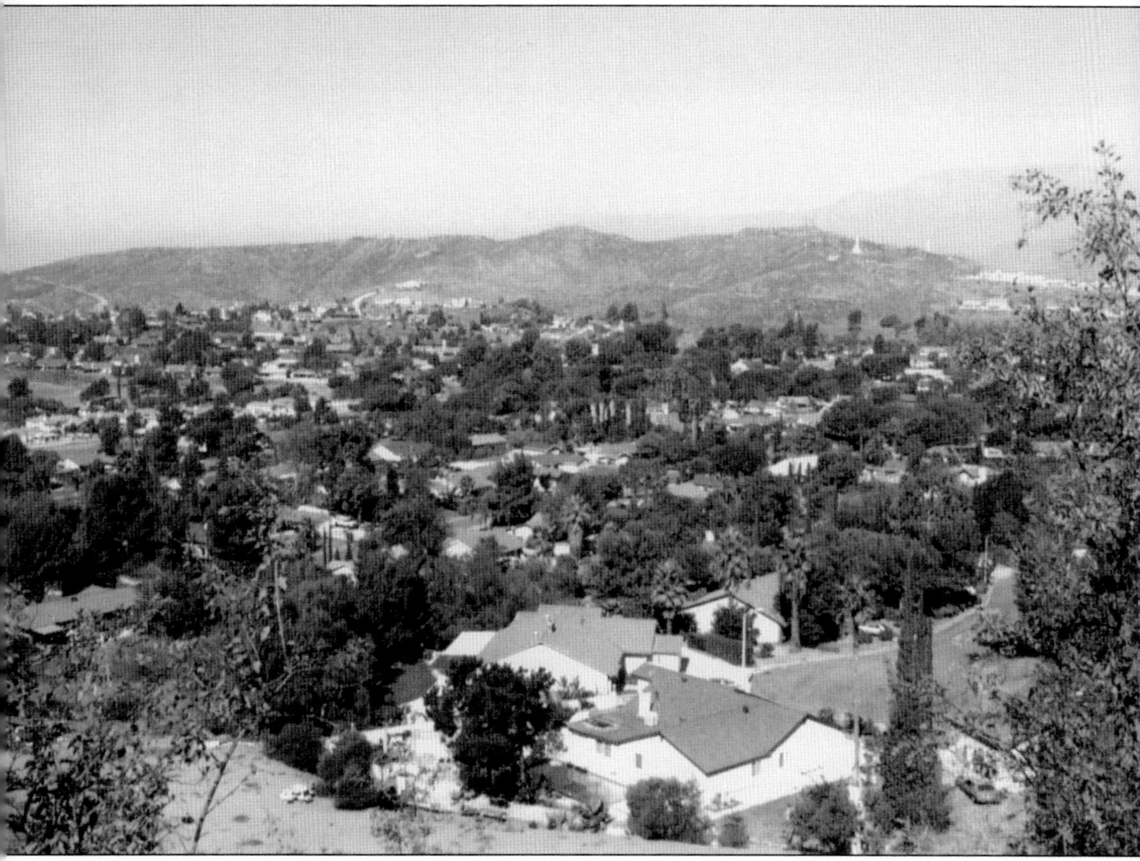

INDIAN HILLS. Begun in 1965 by Harold W. Heers as the 1001 Ranch Home and Country Club, the area at the intersection of Limonite Avenue and Camino Real later became known by its present name of Indian Hills. Chuck Cox and John West continued the development of the Indian Hills area. Now boasting shopping centers, schools, and a movie theater, it is one of the newer communities to add its name to Jurupa. This photograph looks northwest across the Indian Hills community. (Courtesy author.)

Bibliography

Condit, Ida Parks. *Jurupa Peace and Friendship*. Riverside, CA: 1984.

Galleano Winery. "The Historic Galleano Winery." Privately printed by the author, 2004.

Gunther, Jane Davies. *Riverside County, California, Place Names*. Riverside, CA: Jane Davies Gunther, 1984.

Kurz, Don. *Robidoux Rancho on the Jurupa*. Riverside CA: Don Kurz, 1972.

Kutch, Helen B. "An Historical Study of the Glen Avon School District." Master's Thesis, University of Southern California. Los Angeles, CA: July 1961.

Lech, Steve. *Along the Old Roads*. Riverside, CA: Steve Lech, 2004.